MARY

The Unauthorised Biography

MARY

The Unauthorised Biography

MICHAEL JORDAN

Weidenfeld and Nicolson
LONDON

First published in Great Britain in 2001 by
Weidenfeld & Nicolson

A CIP catalogue record for this book
is available from the British Library.

ISBN 0 297 84252 8

Set by Selwood Systems,
Midsomer Norton

Printed in Great Britain by
Butler & Tanner Ltd,
Frome and London

Weidenfeld & Nicolson

The Orion Publishing Group
Orion House
5 Upper Saint Martin's Lane
London WC2H 9EA

CONTENTS

ILLUSTRATIONS

The author and publishers would like to thank the following for their permission to reproduce pictures: National Gallery, London, 1, 2, 5, 6, 9, 10; Bridgeman Art Library, 3; Scala, 4; Sonia Halliday Photographs, 7; British Museum, 8.

One of the questions concerning the cult of Mary the Virgin that has long bothered me is why there has been so little serious investigation of the 'Marian phenomenon'. One has only to walk into a bookshop or library to discover volumes of material that is sycophantic towards the mother of Jesus Christ, mostly from the pens of staunch Roman Catholics. Few writers seem to have approached her biography in a spirit of open-minded journalistic curiosity. This book stems from more than two decades of exploration as a writer on the anthropology of religions, arising in part from unashamed conviction about the importance of the spiritual dimension to our temporal world but also from an intellectual curiosity born of journalistic training.

During the course of research, it became apparent that several recent analyses casting Christ in the role of a dying-and-rising god, akin to mythical figures well known from ancient Mesopotamia, largely miss the point. At most, Jesus of Nazareth seems to have been a man determined to champion much needed social reforms in Galilee while carrying a strong personal conviction concerning the divine restoration of Israel. Striking new evidence, however, indicates that he was far from being the architect of his destiny and that, from before his birth, this lay in the hands of a caucus of influential Jewish priests. Largely remaining anonymous, they believed passionately that the future welfare of the Jews lay in the restoration of the pagan cult and its deities. In Mary they possessed a sympathetic acolyte willing to be employed as the linchpin of aims which they subsequently carried forward into the early Christian movement.

My Marian odyssey began, inadvertently, in the British Museum in London during the 1980s while researching a history of mother goddess worship for an earlier book, *Gods of the Earth*. Behind the Hall of Egyptian Sculpture which attracts a daily throng of sightseers, is a less frequented gallery housing some striking carvings. Executed a little short of three thousand years ago and discovered during the nineteenth century among the ruins of the Mesopotamian city of Kalakh in the deserts of northern Iraq, some of them depict a sacred tree, thought to represent the symbolic presence of an Assyrian mother goddess. I remember being both captivated and perplexed by the composition of these carvings and they became one of the enduring catalysts for the research and, ultimately, the writing of *Mary: The Unauthorised Biography*.

On casual inspection, a link between fundamental aspects of Roman Catholic dogma and ritual associated with a pagan fertility *diva* unearthed from the ruins of a forgotten Assyrian city may seem highly implausible, and at first it did not strike me that such a connection existed. Yet disparate snippets of information began to emerge, strengthening this single tenuous strand into a remarkable web reaching across the gulf that appears to distance one from the other. A case gained credence that in Mary, the mother of Jesus, who stands as one of the most shadowy and improbable figures of the Bible, rests a fascinating and hitherto largely unrevealed facet of history.

Documentary evidence also began pointing to a disturbing catalogue of malpractice, deceit and self-interest on the part of the orthodox Christian establishment. The emerging scenario suggested that the image of the Blessed Virgin Mary, recognised today by hundreds of millions of believers worldwide, is a gross distortion, promoted and then sustained on pretexts that carry few Christian values.

Evidence will be presented that the Roman Catholic Church has fabricated Mary's portrait, although this accusation needs careful qualification. The misrepresentation lies not so much in the way in which the Church promotes the subject, though this often verges on the bizarre, but in what it has chosen to conceal and in the possible motives for that concealment. Has a myth been engineered because Mary never lived, other than in the minds of fanatical visionaries? Is she a heroine who is a pure figment of the imagination, or has her real biography been distorted because Roman Catholicism dares not reveal the truth?

Mary: The Unauthorised Biography is no flight of fancy. The documented evidence to be presented not only exists but is also accessible to those who choose to search for it.

Research into the pre-Christian background relies on primary sources as diverse as the early Mesopotamian Law Codes, Mesopotamian and Canaanite mythology, and the Jewish manual of religious practice known as the *Mishnah*, but also to no small extent on the books of the Old Testament. Ironically some of the strongest evidence about pagan deviation amongst Jews and early Christians can be found through a careful trawl of the orthodox biblical works. More revealing still are the apocryphal and pseudo-epigraphical texts of the Old and New Testaments, the scope of which was greatly enlarged following the discovery of the so-called Gnostic codices in Egypt in 1945. Useful secular sources include the works of Philo and Josephus, both writing their histories at or near the time of Christian origins. More modern sources include Ben-Sasson (*History of the Jewish People*) and the works of E. P. Sanders.

The early Christian era tends to present new problems of research. Because of the extensive destruction of pagan and non-orthodox writings, much of the evidence about lost works such as those of Celsus and the *Genna Marias* (that would, I believe, have provided some of the most conclusive evidence) can only be gleaned from the comments of their critics. Research has, therefore, involved lengthy examination of the books of the Christian fathers, including most notably Epiphanius, Origen, Irenaeus and Jerome. Eusebius' *History of the Church* is clearly biased and often inaccurate, but it also provides a valuable window on early Christian thinking.

Placed in isolation, much of the detail may appear innocuous and some is circumstantial. But when it is assembled and collated what emerges is far removed from the generally recognised traditions, which the Church asserts to be inalienable Christian history. To uncover the details does not demand a passport in hand and a permanently packed suitcase. It requires a prolonged and meticulous trawl, at times laborious, never less than fascinating, through ancient Near Eastern, Jewish and early Christian texts. Much of the evidence that might have been brought has been deliberately destroyed and some is now only accessed through the hostile writings of Christian polemicists. The Church has actively suppressed other material and discouraged the reading of still more.

Much of the groundwork for *Mary* was already to hand in the form of extensive research notes from *Gods of the Earth* and I owe retrospective thanks to the many academics and specialists whose advice and co-operation is acknowledged more fully under that title. I am also deeply indebted to the Director of Library Services at King's College, London, and to the staff of the British Library, for their help in locating source material during the more immediate years of preparation.

I owe a strong debt of gratitude to my agent, Mandy Little, for her generous support and constructive criticism during the research and writing of this book, including much reading, rereading and correcting of early drafts of the text. In the original concept the style of the book was that of a fairly gentle and personal quest for truth concerning a suspect side to Christian dogma. I must credit my chief editor, Toby Mundy, with having persuaded me to refine the work into one of more assertive advocacy. He has devoted considerable time and effort to collaboration on the greater part of the final version. In this context, I must also thank Alice Hunt who provided valuable advice on the typescript throughout the editing process and who worked exclusively on refining the final chapters. These acknowledgements would not be complete without special thanks to Ben Buchan, who took over the project in its closing stages and who has overseen the arduous route to publication, and to Jane Birkett who took responsibility for the final edit and for detailing the extensive reference sources.

Michael Jordan
June 2001

ONE

Introduction

Although many have been subjugated to error by means of torture, our fathers, by the hand of god, have endured and spoken valiantly, and this blessed city hath never been defiled with the error of Nazareth. And we are the heirs, and transmitters to our heirs, of heathenism, which is honoured gloriously in this world.

Abu al-Hasan Tabith of Varrhae-Harran (d. 901 CE)

Many who hold the faith of the son only build temples in the name of the mother.

Leonardo da Vinci (1452–1519)

Among the countless thousands of portraits of the mother of Jesus Christ, the *Immaculate Conception* by the seventeenth-century Spanish painter Diego Velásquez stands as one of the most memorable and masterly. In the austere style of the Counter-Reformation Velásquez painted Mary as a child-woman clothed in a plain dark dress, at once provocative and serenely beautiful. He has drawn her alone and supreme in the cosmos, her feet resting upon the globe of the naked and primeval earth emerging from a dark ocean. The twelve stars of the apocalypse frame her face and the fiery clouds of creation swirl chaotically about her. Beneath, barely visible, a ship sails the tranquil waters and the fount of life surges upward from its own wellspring. Here is captured the paradoxical quintessence of Mary – human, divine, innocent, knowing, and almost wholly the stuff of legend.

Velásquez is not interested in the flesh-and-blood reality of this obscure Galilean sheep-farmer's daughter. Into the imagery with which he surrounds her, he has woven an exquisite contradiction. In his painting, she is the Ever-Virgin child united with God, the barely pubescent and immaculate mother-to-be of the Christ, yet he has framed Mary with the symbolism of an older and more arcane belief which has little to do with the dogmas of Christianity. The stars, which float about her head, have been associated with celestial queens, anathema to Jews and Christians alike, from the very dawn of history. They have been attendant on Ishtar of Babylon, Astarte of Phoenicia and Ashtoreth of the Philistines. According to the interpretation of art critics, the ship floating on its timeless sea is the barque of Isis, the paramount goddess of Egypt whom the Greeks and Romans called *Stella Maris*, Star of the Sea. The primeval water of life surges from a fount of belief that was venerable long before Mary and Joseph walked the earth.

These things could be accounted for if they were merely evidence of an artistic dependence on age-old traditions. Less easy to explain is the fact that the principles for which they stand are not merely alien but in direct conflict with the Christian faith. Velásquez's portrait may epitomise the icon into which Mary has evolved for millions of her followers but it also conforms, in many respects, to the image of a pagan mother goddess – a prima donna at, or close to, the summit of the godly hierarchy, a sexually charged Queen of Heaven, bearer of deities, intercessor between the heavens and humankind, mediator of love and war. The attributes with which Mary is decked are indistinguishable in purpose and style from those of the great goddesses of the ancient world. Closer to her own time, much of the imagery with which Velásquez has surrounded Mary equates with that of Demeter, the mother goddess of the Greeks, and Kybele, the fertility *diva* of the Phrygians who was carried to Rome and adored as the *Magna mater*, the 'Great Mother'. There is just one fundamental difference in the image of Mary: the matter of her alleged lack of sexuality. Tradition has come to paint her as the antithesis of Eve, the eternally condemned first woman. While Eve stands as one who brought sin and death to the world through an awakening to the pleasures of the flesh, Mary, her *alter ego*, is the redemptrix. Through an absolute denial of sexuality she can save mortal womanhood from the perils brought by the original 'fall'.

Claims of Mary's authenticity would never stand up in a court of law because, apart from what is written in the Bible, there is little evidence of the existence of either Mary or Jesus Christ. Historians such as Josephus, Tacitus, Suetonius and Pliny the Younger who are near-contemporaries of Mary and Jesus, are largely silent on the subject. The only supporting comment about Jesus' existence (and if he lived he must, of course, have had a mother) comes from Josephus, who was born in Jerusalem in 37 CE ('Current Era', comparable with AD or 'Anno Domini'). Jesus is mentioned in his *Jewish Antiquities*, in a section concerning the early Christian community in Jerusalem and the rule of Pontius Pilate, the procurator of Judaea and Samaria from 26 to 36 CE.

> About this time there lived Jesus, a wise man, if indeed one ought to call him a man. For he was one who wrought surprising feats and was a teacher of such people as accept the truth gladly. He won over many Jews and many of the Greeks. He was the Messiah.
>
> [*Antiq.* XVIII.63]

These comments have been the subject of considerable controversy among historians, many of whom hold the view that they were added to Josephus' text by early Christian editors, precisely in order to substantiate Jesus' existence. In its favour, the passage is found in all the early manuscript copies of Josephus' work, while against its genuine nature, it is pointed out that the historian was a loyal Pharisaic Jew of high political standing and, therefore, could not have written that Jesus was the *messiah* (mah-shee'agh, meaning 'anointed one').

The Roman writers Tacitus and Suetonius were probably the first to mention Christians as a fringe sect, although neither identified Jesus as its inspiration. Suetonius, the historian of the imperial court at the turn of the first century CE, touched on the subject of Christians and his contemporary, Tacitus, named them as possible instigators of the Great Fire of Rome that had taken place some fifty years earlier. This he did, apparently, in order to divert blame from the thoroughly unpopular Emperor Nero [*Annals* XIV.44]. These references are minimal and the brevity adopted by both writers, who tended to report in detail on home and colonial life, indicates that, at the time, Christians were seen to be of little consequence. The private letters of Pliny the Younger (*c.* 61–113 CE), who became a Roman consul under the Emperor Trajan, constitute an intimate unofficial history of his time. In correspondence with Trajan in about 112 CE, Pliny was of the opinion that Christianity was based on nothing more than crude superstition.

I believe, however, that we should accept that Mary and her son were real people, as we do Herod, Pontius Pilate and other figures from the Bible. Truly mythical figures tend to live in a once-upon-a-time age governed by a dearth of verifiable information, whereas the scant biblical accounts of Mary and Jesus are lent authenticity by detailed reference to places, happenings and personalities that can be supported in history. The Gospel of Luke reports that Mary and Joseph were obliged to comply with a census under Caesar Augustus when Cyrenius was governor of Syria. It is clear that a census did indeed take place (though not precisely as Luke describes it). The writings of the evangelist Paul, whose missionary work is extensively reported, have been authenticated by scholars, so that we can place him fairly accurately in history as living from *c.* 3 CE to 64 CE. The mention of Jesus in Josephus' *Antiquities* is probably authentic although it may have been embellished with the contentious term *messiah* by a subsequent Christian redactor.

The case against Mary, as she is presented to us today, is that it is almost wholly a pretence that hides the real woman. One immediate certainty is that answers about her do not lie within the pages of the Holy Bible. The gospels, the Acts of the Apostles and the letters of St Paul include an amount of biographical detail so sparse that it could be contained on the back of an envelope. The gospel accounts of her life, claimed to represent an accredited contemporary source of information about the Mary of history, also lack serious credibility. The biblical writers infer, as will be explained, that she was born into a priestly family in the Roman province of Greater Judaea in Syrio-Palestine about two thousand years ago. They assert that she had a son, Jesus, who would be hailed as the Christian *messiah*. It is implied that she did not have sexual relations with a man at least until after the birth of Jesus, and that possibly she was a lifelong virgin. After a pregnancy brought about through Immaculate Conception, she gave birth in a stable near Bethlehem, raised her child with Joseph of Nazareth, and had very little contact with Jesus during his adult ministry, although she possibly attended his crucifixion. Certain apocryphal records suggest that she spent her childhood in the care of the Jewish Temple and, after the violent death of her son, passed her declining years with one of his favoured disciples, John the Divine, either in Jerusalem or in Ephesus.

So what is wrong with the limited biblical accounts we are encouraged to believe? The fact that various apocryphal authors place Mary in the care of priests in a temple from early childhood until puberty, the age when many Jewish girls of the time were expected to marry and bear children, raises important questions. It has been explained that Mary's parents dedicated her to the service of God in thanks for divine intervention after years of childlessness, yet the explanation does not hold water, as this book will demonstrate.

The Nativity story, as it has come down to us, is equally questionable and two of the gospel writers, Mark and John, evidently considered it too flimsy to be worth including in their narratives. Matthew and Luke claimed that Mary was an immaculate virgin chosen above all other women, through the spiritual power of a solitary universal god, to bear a uniquely divine son, the Saviour of the world. In doing so, according to the Matthew account, she was fulfilling the terms of a prophecy in Isaiah that predicted the miraculous events in Bethlehem.

Now all this was done, that it might be fulfilled which was spoken of the Lord by the prophet, saying, Behold, a virgin shall be with child, and shall bring forth a son, and they shall call his name Emmanuel, which being interpreted is 'God with us.'

[Matt. 1.22,23]

In Mary's day the myth of human parthenogenesis through superhuman intervention was not new, nor was it limited to the Jews. It had been woven into the fabric of Near Eastern folklore for thousands of years. Not only, of course, is virgin birth biologically impossible but this investigation will show that the translation from the Hebrew, in which the Isaiah prophecy was first written, into the Greek from which most modern versions of the Bible are derived, is inaccurate.

We also discover that in about the eighth or ninth Christian century the bare gospel versions of the Nativity which, for example, contain no reference to domestic animals, were padded out in order to make the story fit better with another prophecy from Isaiah.

The ox knoweth his owner, and the ass his master's crib.

[Isaiah 1.3]

St Francis of Assisi made the imagery of a rustic thatched barn popular in the thirteenth century, to appeal to sentimental European ideas about what kind of stable would be a suitable setting for the Nativity. In this context, I will present evidence that a particularly contentious aspect of the story of the birthplace has been suppressed and, possibly, removed from the biblical texts that have come down to us.

The anomalies contained in the biblical accounts are noteworthy but pale into insignificance beside the fabrications that arose after Mary's death. The personality which the Roman Catholic Church embroidered on the threadbare fabric contained in the gospels bears even less relation to reality. It is deliberately misleading, a disguise created artificially by people who never knew the real woman, and was part of a compromise reached through an acrimonious and at times violent doctrinal argument which took place within the early Christian movement. Over the course of time, the wrangling over Mary translated into an official dogma that was to become accepted as 'absolute truth'. Today, apologists argue that this dogma needs to be treated 'figuratively'. It is, more simply, a lie that has been put in place by a Church unable to reveal the true facts without destroying part of the very bedrock of its canon. From about the beginning of the second Christian century, Mary's cult followers set about embellishing the few details contained in the gospels and the apocryphal texts without the slightest regard for historicity. One of the more extra-ordinary aspects of what took place is that, although at first the embellishment amounted to popular folklore, it became incorp-orated into Mary's 'official' biography and laid the foundations for the reverence in which she is held today.

In the fourth century, the romance of the Immaculate Con-ception and the rejection of fleshly desires was beginning to blossom. For many of the leaders of the early Church it was beyond question that Mary remained anything other than a lifelong virgin. In her alleged rejection of sexual experience in favour of spiritual love she was a role model for successive generations of monks and nuns. By 411 CE St Augustine was proclaiming energetically that Mary was 'A Virgin conceiving, a Virgin bearing, a Virgin preg-nant, a Virgin bringing forth, a Virgin Perpetual' [*Sermons* 186.1] and this view encouraged extremism among more hard-bitten misogynists. Such men as the ascetic fourth-century Patriarch of Constantinople, John Chrysostom, argued against sexual activities in any shape or form involving women. So effective was he that the attitude of 'sex inside marriage if you must, but otherwise never' still pervades much of the Roman Catholic establishment. There is, of course, far more to the Marian cult than sexual abstinence. Mary has become an almost cartoon-like character who is all things to all people: beautiful virgin bride, grieving mother, heavenly queen, compassionate intercessor, leader of armies, mistress of the world. During the Cold War nearly two thousand years later, these attributes of a spiritual superwoman led thousands of fundamentalist Americans to the committed belief that Mary would save her followers in the moments before Armageddon.

An unfortunate problem with a large part of the 'official Marian biography' is that it is neither Jewish nor Christian but pagan, a contradictory situation reflected succinctly in Velásquez' portrait. The attributes with which she is now clothed have been diligently disguised and made to appear as if they stem from Jewish and Christian roots. Yet they are wholly at odds with the staunchly patriarchal doctrines of Judaism and Christianity, subscribing to the concept of a universal male deity without so much as a single *diva* in sight. The defence of Mariolatry put forward by the Roman Catholic Church is that the 'fundamental truth' of the biblical narratives became embellished with trappings which, if they seem to be pagan, are actually nothing more than artistic and poetic licence for the purpose of extolling Mary's majesty and tran-scendence.

Roman Catholicism dressed Mary in clothes that were more suited to its motives than true to her cultural roots and, in its inventiveness, it seems to have lost all sense of proportion. Liturgy and ritual are focused upon Mary to the extent that, in some parts of the Catholic world, she has become the main figure of adoration, which again flies in the face of Christian principles about worship of a single deity. On 24 March 1984 Pope John Paul II took advantage of the medium of television to reach a worldwide audi-ence of many millions when he knelt before the figure of Our Lady of Fatima in St Peter's Square and enhanced Mary's position still further by dedicating the entire planet to her Immaculate Heart. He confirmed that her motherly embrace encircles the world 'irrespective of religion and division'. It was a consecration which, he claimed, 'lasts for all time and embraces all individuals, peoples and nations'.

This defence simply will not do. Much as it requires something more than the protest movement of a liberal Jesus to explain Christianity, so does it demand a better explanation than miracles emanating from a Jewish country girl to account for the cult of Marianism. Indeed, there is a case for a more provocative version of events.

The advocacy for the real Mary draws on the fact that religion among the Palestinian Jews of the first century was far removed from the pure Yahwism of Moses. Christianity did not begin as radical innovation forged in a pure spiritual crucible. This book will produce evidence that the Christian movement evolved as a hybrid in which, for a considerable part of its formative period, old pagan beliefs went hand-in-glove with fresh ideas. Yet this fundamental detail has rarely been articulated; in fact, there is a case to be made that it has been consciously suppressed.

In failing to preserve the facts about the pagan influence on the origins of Christianity, and in particular on the portrayal of Mary, history has let us down. Within a hundred years of Mary's death, which probably occurred some time between 40 CE and 50 CE, the early Christian Church in Rome introduced censorship, in the name of religion, on a scale that the world had hardly witnessed. Backed by imperial power from the fourth century onwards, it bears an irrevocable responsibility for obliterating, often through force, generations of human record and for condemning to extinction the legacies of excellent minds.

The persecution of Christians by pagan Romans is easy to imagine. This was indeed the state of affairs during the first three hundred years after the Crucifixion, but it was a spasmodic pursuit and many of the Roman emperors actually exercised considerable tolerance towards Christians. Trajan, who ruled from 98 to 117 CE, issued a famous edict to Pliny, 'The Christians are not to be hunted down.' After the conversion of Constantine in 312 CE, however, the tables were turned and Christians took on the role of persecutors. Secular and ecclesiastical authorities together set about methodically destroying not only pagan culture *per se*, and all evidence of its acceptance by numbers of the Christian movement, but also Christian belief which 'did not comply' with the orthodox line. In common currency this became known as *heresy* (from the Greek *hairesis* meaning a school of thought), a term which, in the Christian sense, was unknown to the pagan world. Christians began to harass Christians as each faction claimed that it had the authority of 'absolute truth' on its side.

According to Eusebius, the Roman historian Hegesippus summed up the situation when he wrote, 'But when the sacred band of apostles had in various ways reached the end of their life, and the generation of those privileged to listen with their own ears to the divine wisdom had passed on, then godless error began to take shape, through the deceit of false teachers who, now that none of the apostles was left, threw off the mask and attempted to counter the preaching of the truth' [Eus., *Hist.* 32.4]. Truth, however, represented different things to different people.

In a fanatical campaign to cleanse the growing Christian world of undesirable cultural stains, both pagan and non-orthodox, newly converted emperors used troops to demolish pagan temples, many of which were regularly visited by Christian worshippers. In Alexandria there was once a famous sanctuary of the Romano-Egyptian god Sarapis in which stood a colossal statue of the deity. The Sarapis Temple became highly popular with pagan and Christian worshippers alike and survived until the end of the fourth century. Theophilus, the Christian Patriarch of Alexandria, took an axe to the cult statue in 391 CE and ordered the torching of the temple. Even Jewish places of worship did not escape, despite being protected for freedom of worship. For a limited period, in 388 CE, Christian zealots turned to burning synagogues. There is a record of restitution to the Jews, ordered by the Emperor Theodosius, for one such building demolished in Rome. When another was burned down at Callinicum on the River Euphrates, the local bishop refused to make the repairs.

Long before the conversion of Constantine in 312 CE, a different kind of demolition had been well advertised by the great bonfires in town squares in which non-Christian writings were consumed in the flames of ecclesiastical pedantry. The fate of the works of the pagan writer, Celsus, who circulated pamphlets critical of Christianity in the later part of the second century, was typical. After his death, his books and papers underwent meticulous destruction at the hands of the controversial Greek Christian theologian, Origen (184–254 CE), who was implacably opposed to the very existence of pagan literature. Writings from Christian pens that did not subscribe to the 'official line' suffered a similar fate and copyists were discouraged from replacing these works under threat of having their hands cut off. Virtually all the writings of the Gnostic teachers, including Marcion and Valentinus (both of whom lived in the turbulent second century), were destroyed and their ideas survive only in the attacks of their opponents.

Fanatical champions of orthodoxy included spokesmen such as Irenaeus, Tertullian and Epiphanius, the bishops of Lyons, Carthage and Salamis respectively. The intention of these men, who gained effective control of Christian policy-making between the second and fifth centuries, was brutally simple. It was to ensure that no trace of pagan belief and practice survived, in or out of the Christian movement, except perhaps what might be gleaned from the hostile scratching of Christian pens. As time went on, the clampdown against free religious expression became more draconian. Under the aegis of the dominant Christian bishops and, in the age of Constantine, that of imperial Rome, Christians took it upon themselves to follow, literally, the demands made of them in the Old Testament writings.

> If thy brother, the son of thy mother, or thy son, or thy daughter, or the wife of thy bosom, or thy friend which is as thine own soul, entice thee secretly, saying, Let us go and serve other gods ... thou shalt surely kill him. [Deut. 13.6–9]

The term 'serve other gods' was applied to anyone who did not subscribe to the official line of the apostolic bishops. Those who

failed to recant were either excommunicated or killed by crucifixion or dismemberment, their limbs suspended from gibbets
along the main streets of towns. Among those who suffered repeatedly were the Manichaeans, a Gnostic Christian sect founded
in the early 240s by a Syriac-speaking preacher named Mani.
Although he was executed by a Persian king in 276 CE, the Christianised Roman emperors maintained the death penalty for Mani's
followers. Rank was no obstacle. In 381 CE, a suspected heretic of
the sect named Priscillian, who had achieved the position of Bishop
of Avila in Spain, was executed on the orders of a special synod of
fellow bishops sitting in Bordeaux.

From the beginning of the fifth century pagans of all shades,
many of whom were also members of Christian sects, were being
hounded to the death by Christians. One of the well-recorded
incidents was the lynching of a woman in Alexandria in 415 CE
because she was a pagan teacher. Very little of the thoughts and
activities of such people, or the extent of their influence, has
survived. The Christian Church created its own version of history
in a process of containment which it almost – but not quite –
managed to complete.

The real Mary was destined to fall victim to this rewriting of
early Church history as various squabbling factions laid claim to
the truth about her and fought a battle royal over her identity.
In what Christian censorship has allowed to remain, to offer a
convenient analogy, it is as if we have been presented with a
portrait that has been worked and reworked, successive layers of
paint changing the original art work virtually out of recognition.
We are left to gaze at the image of a person whose features now
present a thoroughly distorted impression of who and what she
really was. The Roman Catholic Church demands that we stop at
this point and accept superficial appearances, curious as we may
be because all is not as it seems. If, however, we begin to dissolve
the outer brushwork, unexpected shapes, tones and textures start
to emerge. A new and altogether different layer of paint becomes
exposed to view. As we remove the layers, one by one, we finally

discover the portrait worked by the original artist. The true face of Mary that is revealed beneath the layers of biblical narrative and Church propaganda is infinitely more compelling than the fabrication.

This kind of critical examination is a taboo subject among Roman Catholics. The Vatican continues to guard Mary's contrived, fantasy image with great tenacity. Its object of devotion has been romanticised at the expense of reality, yet the same Catholic authority is ready to denigrate faiths such as Hinduism where the personalities of gods and goddesses are idealised into similar comic-strip proportions.

Mary's has to be a thoroughly complex and convoluted story yet there is a complete absence of depth in the biblical texts. Not only in Mary, but also in Joseph, and in Mary's parents Anna and Joachim, we seem to be looking at cardboard figures moving across a featureless and almost timeless stage. It is a sense of remoteness and unreality that affected even the earliest Christian commentators for whom these momentous events must have felt comparatively fresh. In his book *Paganism in the Roman Empire*, the American author Ramsay MacMullen makes a succinct observation about men like St Jerome (a passionate advocate of the Marian cause who was born in about 347 CE and lived most of his life in Rome, promoting the Christian message and campaigning against heretics): 'History is spread out before their eyes, but they see only events and persons floating in a timeless past, without caused links between them – a gallery of isolated portraits and anecdotes made classical by remoteness.' From a thin, two-dimensional melting-pot, however, Mary became the improbable star of an apocryphal 'mystery play', a legendary character who transcended reality. Nothing in our own time can illustrate such a metamorphosis more sharply than Diana, Princess of Wales, whose death engendered the same mixture of reality and myth.

It is easy to imagine that Mary has always been held in high esteem yet, once again, surprises are in store. Nine hundred million devotees worldwide follow Mary, literally to the death, but while theirs is claimed to be a devotion free from stain or taint, Mariolatry is, and has been, a divisive and contentious issue among Christians as a whole. The cult of Mary was instrumental in the early schism between the Greek Church in the East and the Latin faith in the West. It wrenched European Christendom apart with fearsome violence at the time of the Reformation when, in 1529, German princes rebelled against Roman Catholicism. They protested that the authority of the Bible must be restored over what they saw to be the errors of Rome. The Protestant spokesmen who took up the cry – Luther, and Calvin and the English bishops serving Henry VIII – believed Rome to be indulging in deeply suspect excesses, at times verging on the heretical. Protestants had become particularly concerned about the credentials of beliefs and practices associated with the 'packaging' of Mary. Since her cult has no basis in the writings of the New Testament it has not endeared itself to the Protestant Church. Not least among the causes of friction has been the apparent love-affair with principles that seem barely to distinguish Roman Catholicism from paganism. Yet, paradoxically, the miraculous nature of Jesus' birth is for millions of Christians one of the main defences of the argument that he is the Son of God. Even Protestants are willing, each Sunday, to recite the words of the *Credo* of St Athanasius that includes the declaration,

I believe in God the Father Almighty,
Maker of heaven and earth;
And in Jesus Christ, his only Son our Lord,
Who was conceived by the Holy Ghost,
Born of the Virgin Mary ...

In the quest for the real woman, it has been fundamental to keep in mind a number of criteria. The biography of Mary is inseparable from, and dependent upon, that of Jesus Christ; one is the mutually exclusive key to the other. The temptation exists to imagine Mary as a Christian woman, living in a Christian society and enjoying a good Catholic upbringing. But she was none of these things. On the contrary, she was a Jewish girl of questionable religious training and belief, living in an autonomous region of the Roman Empire and the rural surroundings of Galilee, a province that had once been part of the northern kingdom of Israel.

To uncover evidence of who, and what, Mary really was, has called for a close examination of small, often inconspicuous details from many sources and on many levels. It has necessitated gathering in and assembling a number of diverse elements, some gleaned from archaeology, others from historical documentation; yet others from contemporary accounts of political, social and economic conditions; and, of course, from legend itself.

The time-scale is daunting because the roots of legend often lie among traditions that thread back hundreds, and sometimes thousands, of years from the point in time at which the story achieved its recognised shape. The search has involved sifting material from a trail that leads back through the Israelite record into the misty realm of prehistory.

The argument of this book is that Mary was born into a family which did not subscribe to orthodox Judaism, the religion of Moses. Evidence will be presented to show that her upbringing took place in an environment with strongly pagan leanings and that she probably held lifelong religious beliefs which encompassed Jewish and pagan ideology. Jesus Christ was the product of a sexual rite honouring a pagan mother goddess in whose service Mary had been initiated as a special category of priestess.

This charge will be shrugged off by the Roman Catholic Church in the manner in which that organisation usually defends its dogmatic position. But for those of more open persuasion, disinclined to accept cant over fact, the evidence will reveal that the Marian cult not only lacks historical substance but also amounts to a carefully contrived falsification. The official dogma about the Blessed Virgin, part of which has been extended into Protestant Christendom, is a conscious corruption of history that has been promoted, and then enforced, by the Roman Catholic Church to suit its own needs. In doing so, it has sidestepped the founding principles of Christianity and encouraged two thousand years of division and conflict. Today its Marian ideology also continues, callously, to condemn millions of women to second-class citizenship.

For nearly two millennia, Madonna Maria Virgine has presented two conflicting personalities summed up in the striking paradox of Velásquez' *Immaculate Conception*. At stake in exposing the true biography of the Mother of Christ are some of the most cherished of all Christian beliefs.

TWO

Falling from Grace

In the case against Mary, the figure of biblical romance, the first and most important issue to clarify is that she did not grow up in a vacuum, nor did she live as a Christian. Mary was a Jewess in the turbulence of first-century Galilee, the northern frontier province of Palestine which had only lately joined the post-Exilic state of 'Greater Judaea'. For convenience, I am calling the 'first century' the period of fifty years either side of the birth of Jesus of Nazareth.

The culture to which Mary belonged followed traditions that had been built up over more than a thousand years. It is these age-old customs and beliefs that hold the key if we are to establish, with any conviction, how Mary's character and way of life, her family and friends were influenced. This chapter and the next will expose traditions (some of them peculiar to Galilee) which form the basis of a spirituality that is strongly at odds with the image conveyed through popular Jewish and Christian sentiment and help to establish what dictated the style and texture of the original, and as yet hidden, portrait.

Putting aside the matter of virgin birth, defenders of the glossy Christianised image of Mary, such as the distinguished ecumenical theologian, George H. Tavard, claim that she was a normal Jewish mother, faithful to the Torah and to the customs of her time. There is barely a shred of biblical evidence in support of this argument. On the contrary, the circumstances of Mary's early life suggest that she was not an ordinary mother, nor necessarily dedicated to Jewish customs established through the laws of Moses. Evidence points much more strongly in the direction of loyalty to a fusion of Mosaic and pagan principles, or *syncretism*. The loyalty had resulted, in part spontaneously and in part consciously, from intercultural contact over a long period of Jewish settlement in Palestine.

Too much contradicts the picture we are given by Jewish and Christian theologians like George Tavard, not only of Mary's fidelity to the religion of Yahweh but also of the entire Jewish people. The question arises: What were the pagan principles involved and where did they come from? The answers lie deep in Jewish history and in order to expose them we need to dig down to the very bedrock of the culture.

Before doing so, it is worth clarifying some terms that may be confusing. The ancestors of the Israelites were the 'Patriarchs' whose lives spanned the uncertain period of time from Abraham to Moses. They were also 'Hebrew', a word that in its ancient Aramaic form *'ebrai* means, literally, 'from the other side' and was possibly coined by the indigenous people old Canaan for migrants from beyond the Euphrates. The word also links with *'apiru*, an ethnic mix of disenfranchised Bronze Age nomads and, according to the Table of Nations (the genealogical account, found in Genesis 10 and 1 Chronicles 1, of the relationship between ancient peoples with whom Israel had dealings), with Eber, the eponymous ancestor of the twelve tribes. The Hebrews migrated from Mesopotamia soon after 2000 BCE and some settled in the land of the Canaanites. Other *'ebrai* continued their migration south-west into Egypt where they stayed until about 1250 BCE. On their return to Canaan, they joined the earlier immigrants and formed a tribal confederacy, briefly united as a single kingdom under David (1010–970 BCE), but then split acrimoniously into two self-governing monarchies, Judah in the south and Israel in the north. The modern state of Israel, founded in 1948, covers approximately the area of these two ancient kingdoms.

The term 'Jewish' as distinct from 'Israelite' refers to the post-Exilic temple state formed in 539 BCE after the return of exiles from Babylon where the upper echelons of Israelite society had been forcibly held since 587 BCE. 'Judaism' properly describes the religion of the Jewish people after the destruction of the Second Temple by the Romans in 70 CE. It became focused on the synagogue (though synagogue worship began during the Exile) and the home rather than the Temple with its sacrificial cult. The latter can conveniently be described as 'Yahwism', reverence to the Israelite god, Yahweh.

It is important also to identify what is meant by 'pagan', which I tend to use anachronistically. The word originated as a derogatory term, *pagani*, coined by Christians of the fourth century and it implied ignorant country people who had not enlisted as 'soldiers of Christ' through baptism. Pagan can also be taken to mean a doctrinal system, and although some modern historians will argue that paganism is essentially a matter of cult acts, without creed or teaching, their definition is too narrow. Pagans recognised a pantheon of gods and goddesses but were not committed to *revealed* beliefs in the Christian sense, nor did they recognise the concept of heresy. To suggest, however, that being pagan excluded recognition of a doctrine in the sense of a religious belief, is unfounded.

'Palestine', the name of a geographical region, does not occur in the Bible but is roughly synonymous with the expanded kingdom of David, slightly larger than the old Canaan. It was first coined by the Greek writer Herodotus (about 484–425 BCE) as *Palaistine*, a corruption of the name of the 'sea peoples', the Philistines, who overran the eastern Mediterranean in the twelfth century BCE. In biblical times Palestine included the narrow strip of land bounded to the west by the Mediterranean and inland by the Arabian desert. To the south-west, separated by Sinai, lay Egypt and to the north was the western extension of Syria.

Turning back to 1250 BCE, we find the tribes escaping from forced labour camps in Egypt and crossing the wastes of Sinai in search of their Promised Land. At face value, Jewish and Christian fiction has given us a glamorous picture of the Patriarchs waving the flag of their omnipotent god and marching in harmony into their new kingdom, but even the Old Testament texts conceded that matters were rather different.

From the outset, the course of Israelite religious history is coloured by *apostasy*, the abandoning of Mosaic religious principles and 'backsliding' into paganism. Reaching a clear view of the nature and extent of this is never straightforward, however, because the men who compiled the historical books of Old Testament texts were of Yahwist persuasion. As staunch supporters of the religion of Moses, it was hardly in their best interests to admit that paganism, or any other form of corruption, was rife in their midst.

There is an added twist in respect of the apostasy that took place in the northern kingdom of Israel. The surviving details come to us from the pens of southern-based scribes. No material remains from writers loyal to the north, which suggests that much of the record from the Israel kingdom was destroyed. What has been preserved as Jewish history tends to be slanted politically in favour of Jerusalem and the tribes of Judah and Benjamin, rather than the northern state of Israel including the regions of Samaria and Galilee and dominated by the half-tribe of Manasseh.

The Bible is not explicit as to whether Mary was born in the north but she evidently lived there for an accountable part of her life, certainly from the age of twelve when Joseph brought her to Nazareth, possibly from early childhood if she was raised in a northern religious sanctuary. At the time of her birth a general culture of condescension towards northerners by Judahites had prevailed for hundreds of years and the attitude of many, in particular towards Galileans, was one of barely disguised contempt. It reaches back to the period of the Kings, which spanned the centuries from the reign of David at the turn of the first millennium until Judah was forcibly subjugated as a Babylonian province in 588 BCE, and included the highest levels of society. The southern monarchy was claimed to be both dynastic and 'ordained by God', its rulers Yahwist to the letter. On the other hand the Israelite kings in the north were mere pretenders, appointees of prophets bending to foreign gods. Typical of the rhetoric is an alleged edict of Yahweh against Israel after the death of its rebel founder, Jereboam.

> I will bring evil upon the house of Jereboam, and will cut off from Jereboam him that pisseth against the wall, and him that is shut up and left in Israel, and will take away the remnant of the house of Jereboam, as a man taketh away dung, till it be all gone.
>
> [1 Kings 14.10]

The attitude of the Judahites had developed, in part, because the Galileans and their Samarian neighbours were a hybrid culture, born of intermarriage. This originated with foreigners who had been brought to the region during the eighth century BCE under a policy of 'ethnic cleansing'. Between 733 and 732 BCE the Assyrian despot, Tiglathpileser III, annexed Galilee, turning it into the Assyrian province of Magiddu with the city of Megiddo as its centre. Part of Tiglathpileser's strategy was one of mass deportation and resettlement and a fragment of Assyrian tablet of the time mentions that 13,150 people from the northern kingdom of Israel were forcibly exiled to Mesopotamia. Their replacements, Aramean and Chaldean tribes from Babylonia, mixed with the remaining Israelites. Galileans of the first century were descendants of these foreigners (essentially pagan immigrants) who had married into the peasant classes of Jewish society after the intellectual élite had been bundled off into Babylonian exile during the sixth century BCE. This background explains why the prophet Ezra, writing in the fifth century BCE, described the northerners in anonymous and rather derogatory fashion as the 'people of the land' rather than by their tribal names.

Ezra had some other terse comments to make. He called the Galileans who approached the civic elders on their return from the later Babylonian Exile, and offered assistance with the building of the new Jerusalem Temple, 'adversaries of Judah'. They were sent away with a 'flea in their ear' and the admonition, 'Ye have nothing to do with us to build an house unto our God'. This prompted an adverse reaction and we are then told by Ezra that the northerners 'weakened the hands of the people of Judah' by arguing *against* the rebuilding of Jerusalem [Ezra 4.1ff.]. Ezra's observations may be supported by a passing comment from the priestly writer Zechariah. His work is largely prophetic, a conversation with an angel focusing on the restoration of Jerusalem. Zechariah talks of the 'spirits of the heavens' in the form of four chariots going out to reunite the new Judaea. 'Behold, those that go toward the north country have quieted my spirit in the north country.' [Zech. 6.8] Some observers believe that this negative comment refers to the failure of Judaean envoys to complete satisfactory negotiations with the northerners.

Attitudes did not change. The Gospel of John contains a sharp reminder of the prevailing sentiment towards Galileans as late as the early Christian era, in the cynical remark attributed to the otherwise unidentified Nathanael of Cana, a friend of the disciples: 'Can there any good thing come out of Nazareth?' [John 1.46]

Unquestionably it was in the north that pagan practice was at its most persistent and tenacious. Jereboam of Ephraim, the first king of the breakaway state in about 922 BCE, was an unashamed pagan and the first Book of Kings refers openly to 'the sins of Jereboam', telling how he 'placed in Bethel the priests of the high places he had made'. 'High places' is the usual biblical term for pagan sanctuaries. It is used repeatedly throughout the Old Testament.

> And the children of Israel did secretly those things that were not right against the Lord their God, and they built them high places in all their cities, from the tower of the watchmen to the fenced city. And they set them up images and groves in every high hill, and under every green tree.   [2 Kings 17.9]

Apologists have come up with the popular explanation that, when Jereboam cast two golden bull calf statues, one for Bethel, the other for Dan, he was not commissioning blatantly pagan images proclaiming the Canaanite bull cult. Innocent beasts, they were akin to the cherubim guarding the Jerusalem Temple, under the protective gaze of whom the God of Israel would reign secure. But this excuse runs squarely in the face of archaeological evidence that the bull calf was the symbol of the Canaanite god Baal and of the Old Testament record, which shows that Jereboam was strongly sympathetic to the Baal cult.

> And he made an house of high places, and made priests of the lowest of the people, which were not the sons of Levi.
>
> [1 Kings 12.31]

Much of the defamation of the north amounted to southern propaganda emanating from Jerusalem, and the real story is suppressed. While Judah adopted a snobbish view about the Judahite royalty and Yahwist ideology, pagan interest gripped the whole Israelite population and considerably more of the Judahite kings and their predecessors practised apostasy than their paid scribes were allowed to admit. It took place with steady regularity from about 1500 BCE when the immigrants were under Moses' leadership.

> And Israel abode in Shittim [the last stopping place east of the Jordan in the land of Moab], and the people began to commit whoredom with the daughters of Moab ... And Israel joined itself unto Baal-peor [a pagan deity].
>
> [Num. 25.1ff.]

It went on through the era of the Judges until the death of Saul in the middle or late eleventh century BCE.

> Thus saith the whole congregation of the Lord, What trespass is this that ye have committed against the God of Israel, to turn away this day from following the Lord, in that ye have builded you an altar, that ye might rebel this day against the Lord? [Josh. 22.16]

It barely diminished during the period of the Kings from David to the Babylonian Exile in the sixth century BCE and it continued, as we shall see, after the return from Babylon up to and beyond the time of Mary's birth. Modern Jewish commentators set out to minimise past national weakness for pagan wiles but the evidence in the Old Testament speaks for itself. The Psalms of the Old Testament sum up the situation succinctly.

> They soon forgat his [Moses'] works; they waited not for his counsel: But lusted exceedingly in the wilderness, and tempted God in the desert ... They joined themselves also unto Baal-peor and ate the sacrifices of the dead ... Yea, they sacrificed their sons and daughters unto devils, And shed innocent blood ... Thus were they defiled with their own works, and went a whoring with their own inventions. [Ps. 106.13ff.]

The prophet Jeremiah expressed a similar sentiment and conceded that pagan apostasy penetrated even the bedrock of Yahwism, the prophets.

> And I have seen folly in the prophets of Samaria; they prophesied in Baal, and caused my people Israel to err. I have seen also in the prophets of Jerusalem an horrible thing: they commit adultery and walk in lies; they strengthen also the hands of evildoers, that none doth return from his wickedness. [Jer. 23.13]

Seductive advances first by Egyptians, then by Canaanites, Assyrians and Babylonians, over a long period, took their inevitable toll on the religion of Moses and apostasy is claimed to have led to the downfall of the Israelites. One of the later prophets, Micah, never one to shy away from doom and gloom, warned of ongoing retribution.

> Thus saith the Lord; Behold, against this family do I devise an evil, from which ye shall not remove your necks; neither shall ye go haughtily: for this time is evil.' [Mic. 2.3]

The Old Testament writers stressed that the reprobates always earned their just deserts, pointing out that transgression brings divine retribution, and Yahweh was not the broadly popular deity for whom the Israelite elders might have wished. The tribes quickly discovered positive advantages in the blending of their own austere religion with imported and more seductive devotions. After receiving the Covenant on Mount Sinai, Moses instructed the Israelites to worship a universal presence enigmatically called Yahweh, 'I am who I am'. Old Testament writers drew a character study that, although eloquent, was too sketchy to avoid liberal interpretation. Some Christian theologians, including Pope John Paul II, claim that Yahweh is of ambivalent sexuality but this is due to a vogue for social and political correctness in a modern climate where women voice increasing antagonism towards the Church's patriarchal image. The biblical Yahweh is identified as being the 'Lord' or *adon*, an indisputably masculine word. In the Book of Genesis the deity who decides, 'Let us make man in our image, after our likeness' [Gen. 1.26] is described as God. But when the creation of a man is actually carried out, the same deity becomes Lord.

And the Lord God formed man of the dust of the ground, and breathed into his nostril the breath of life.   [Gen. 2.7]

If Yahweh is male he is, however, also markedly different in nature from most gods in the ancient world who eat, drink, sleep, go to the lavatory, possess wives and generally demonstrate a prodigious appetite for sex both in and out of marriage. These deities, in other words, behave much as people do on earth. Yahweh, by contrast, is transcendent, without sensual needs and demanding no satisfaction. This places him apart from other deities and, crucially, no female consort joins him in the celestial bedchamber. Yahweh's permanent celibacy among the human flock means that lusty impregnation of virgins on altars becomes pointless since 'ritual romps' do not encourage this somewhat untypical God into energetic bouts of procreation.

The official ban on the Israelites performing sexual rites was in stark contrast with what was allowed among the nations that encircled them. The Canaanites, Assyrians, Babylonians, Hittites and Egyptians were all polytheistic and their pantheons of gods and goddesses not only enjoyed full matrimonial partnerships but found little problem in extramarital liaisons. The hosts of the pagan heaven spent a considerable amount of time engaged in sexual activity, and regular and tireless intercourse was the key to the health and vigour of nature and the nation. According to texts excavated from the vast library of cuneiform tablets at Ugarit, the ancient Canaanite city on the north Syrian coast at Ras Shamra, mother goddesses made love 'by the thousand' and their male consorts managed to sustain inexhaustible reservoirs of libido. The people of such nations needed no prompting to provide their deities, responsible for prosperity and fruitfulness in the material world, with encouragement.

Many ordinary Israelites must have felt that they were 'missing out' on the attractions of a religious calendar which emphasised the strongest and most powerful of human urges – sex. The Hebrews were strongly polygamous and Hebraism did not resist sexual activity *per se* but objected to the ban placed by the religious leaders on *cultic* sex. It was obvious that most of the states sub-scribing to sexually charged rites on behalf of their deities – Egyptians, Canaanites, Hittites, Assyrians and Babylonians – were eminently successful both politically and militarily. It is hardly surprising, therefore, that the Hebrews started to tire of their ascetic and sex-free religious programme in favour of more lib-erated forms of worship.

In any case, that which Moses demanded, his injunctions against adultery and worship of other gods, was fundamentally alien to the Hebrew nature. The Patriarchs had come originally from Mespotamia and their heritage was strictly pagan. Their ancestors were the nomadic Indo-European peoples who had colonised the fertile valley between the Tigris and the Euphrates thousands of years before Moses led his flock into their Promised Land. The religious orientation of the Patriarchs is not difficult to discover. Genesis actually describes some of them as being polytheistic. Laban, the father of Rachel and Leah, kept statues of household gods, which doubtless included fertility deities. They were of such importance to him that when Rachel removed them surreptitiously from his tent, Laban's unwitting nephew, Jacob, demanded extreme punishment for the thief.

> With whomsoever thou findest thy gods, let him not live: before
> our brethren discern thou what is thine with me, and take it to
> thee. For Jacob knew not that Rachel had stolen them [the images].
>
> [Gen. 31.32]

During the enforced stay of those groups that travelled to Egypt, Moses was probably influenced by the unusual monotheism of the Pharaoh Akhenaten who opted to merge the vast pantheon of Egyptian deities into one super-being, Aten. But even during incarceration, the Hebrews under Moses' leadership seem to have been more at home with local polytheistic idolatry. This was neither forgotten nor apparently forgiven and many centuries later the animosity of the prophets could still be directed against Egypt.

> Then said I unto them, Cast ye away every man the abominations
> of his eyes, and defile not yourselves with the idols of Egypt: I am
> the Lord your God. But they rebelled against me, and would not
> hearken unto me; they did not every man cast away the abom-
> inations of their eyes, neither did they forsake the idols of Egypt.
>
> [Ezek. 20.7]

Not surprisingly, by the time that Moses led the tribes out of captivity and entered into a pact with the austere and unfamiliar Yahweh, large numbers of his flock were 'a-whoring after other gods' [Judg. 2.17, 8.33]. They did this in preference to abstemious worship of a deity who, other than eventually permitting them freedom from Egyptian tyranny, had done them few favours and was said to disapprove of fornication and revelry. The ideological war between hard-liners dedicated to Yahwism and the more liberally inclined rank and file comes to light repeatedly in the Old Testament writings.

> And the children of Israel dwelt among the Canaanites, Hittites, and Amorites, and Perizzites and Hivites and Jebusites: And they took their daughters to be their wives, and gave their daughters to their sons, and served their gods. And the children of Israel did evil in the sight of the Lord, and forgat the Lord their God, and served Baalim and the groves.   [Judg. 3.5–7]

During the time of the Judges, and in the first centuries of the Kingship that followed from about 1000 BCE, the strongest outside pressure on the Israelites switched from Egypt to Canaan, a country that reached its cultural high spot somewhere between 1600 and 1200 BCE. The Canaanite national god Baal, a powerful fertility deity and also a god who died and rose annually in sympathy with the changing agricultural seasons, was attracting the newcomers almost as soon as they entered the region. His incestuous partner was the mother goddess Asherah, listed in documents found at Ugarit as one of many wives of the creator god Il, and as the mother of at least seventy children including Baal. The cult of Baal and Asherah often attracted women among its Israelite followers and these were people for whom Moses had little sympathy.

> And Moses said unto them, Have ye saved all the women alive? Behold, these caused the children of Israel, through the counsel of Balaam, to commit trespass against the Lord in the matter of [Baal] Peor, and there was a plague among the congregation of the Lord. Now therefore kill every male among the little ones, and kill every

woman that hath known man by lying with him.   [Num. 31.15–17]

'Peor' was one of Baal's more familiar epithets. The Book of Exodus conveys the idea that the Canaanite cult involved a regular round of orgiastic rites and sexually explicit rituals.

> Take heed to thyself, lest thou make a covenant with the inhabitants of the land ... and they go a whoring after their gods, and do sacrifice unto their gods ... And thou take of their daughters unto thy sons, and their daughters go a whoring after their gods, and make thy sons go a whoring after their gods.   [Exod. 34.12 ff.]

Written evidence from Ugarit suggests, however, that the interpretation may be largely unwarranted and that Canaanite religion did not automatically add up to a licence for excess.

Israelite interest in Baal became focused quickly in the north. Long before the formation of the breakaway kingdom of Israel, the Book of Joshua tells how the tribes of Reuben, Gad and the half-tribe of Manasseh were instructed by Moses to emigrate north into the Transjordan region of Gilead. There they elected to build a great altar described as a 'trespass against the God of Israel' and as 'the iniquity of [Baal] Peor' [Josh. 22.16,17]. It was, therefore, clearly the centre point of a sanctuary dedicated to Baal. When word of the sanctuary spread it triggered a vicious squabble between the Israelites at Shiloh, the major Yahwist religious centre before the division of the tribes, and those at Gilead, where the renegade elements were confronted and accused of pagan apostasy. The rebel tribes eventually agreed an apology to Yahweh but the adulteration of the Mosaic religion was already unstoppable.

The Israelite followers of the Baal cult frequently marked his sanctuaries with an epithet. A brief trawl of the Old Testament reveals shrines at Baal-berith, Baal-hamon, Baal-meon, Baal-peor and several others. It is likely that, in practice, worship of Yahweh went on side by side with fertility rites performed in Baal's honour and all that the Yahwist elders could do was to rage helplessly against the extent of idolatry.

> And I will destroy your high places and cut down your images and cast your carcases upon the carcases of your idols, and my soul shall abhor you. [Lev. 26.30]

> Thus saith the whole congregation of the Lord, What trespass is this that ye have committed against the God of Israel, to turn away this day from following the Lord, in that ye have builded you an altar, that ye might rebel this day against the Lord? Is the iniquity of [Baal] Peor too little for us, from which we are not cleansed until this day, although there was a plague in the congregation of the Lord, But that ye must turn away this day from following the Lord? ... Rebel not against the Lord, nor rebel against us, in building you an altar beside the altar of the Lord our God. [Josh. 22.16]

They also warned of furious retribution by God, which they claimed had already been witnessed when various indigenous Baal-worshipping tribes were slaughtered during the Israelite invasion of Canaan.

> Your eyes have seen what the Lord did because of Baal-peor: for all the men that followed Baal-peor, the Lord thy God hath destroyed them from among you. [Deut. 4.3]

For a while, in about 1200 BCE after the death of the hard-line Yahwist judge, Gideon, the Israelites turned formally to the worship of Baal under the title Baal-berith and Gideon's son, Abimelech, was sworn into office under a pagan covenant.

> And it came to pass, as soon as Gideon was dead, that the children of Israel turned again, and went a whoring after Baalim and made Baal-berith their god. [Judg. 8.33]

> And they gave him [Abimelech] threescore and ten pieces of silver

out of the house of Baal-berith, wherewith Abimelech hired vain
and light persons, which followed him.   [Judg. 9.4]

Worship of Baal took place in sanctuaries, across the length and
breadth of Palestine, known as 'high places' or *bamahs*. These
open-air temples were subject to a constant stream of biblical
invective, indicating their popularity among the mass of ordinary
people. The anglicised description does not mean that *bamahs* were
always positioned on the tops of hills. The term once described the
back of an animal and it was merely an area that was raised higher
than its surroundings. It could be a hilltop but it could equally
well be a man-made dais of stones, such as the ancient pagan altar
at Megiddo.

> For when I had brought them into the land, for the which I lifted
> up mine hand to give it to them, then they saw every high hill and
> all the thick trees, and they offered there their sacrifices ... Then
> I said unto them, What is the high place whereunto ye go? And
> the name thereof is called Bamah unto this day. Whereof say unto
> the house of Israel, Thus saith the Lord God; Are ye polluted after
> the manner of your fathers? and commit ye whoredom after their
> abominations?   [Ezek. 20.28ff.]

The *bamah* could even be part of a building. Many amounted to
domestic or family shrines and, in the towns and cities, they were
positioned on urban rooftops.

> And the children of Israel did secretly those things that were not
> right against the Lord their God, and they built them high places
> in all their cities, from the tower of the watchmen to the fenced
> city. And they set them up images and groves in every high hill,
> and under every green tree.   [Kings 17.9]

The early historical books of the Old Testament are not alone
in shedding light on pagan practice. Even the Psalms occasionally

endorse the chorus of complaint against the level of 'backsliding' towards Baal worship.

> They soon forgat his works; they waited not for his counsel: But lusted exceedingly in the wilderness, and tempted God in the desert ... They made a calf in Horeb, and worshipped the molten image. Thus they changed their glory into the similitude of an ox that eateth grass ... They joined themselves also unto Baal-peor and ate the sacrifices of the dead ... Yea, they sacrificed their sons and their daughters unto devils, And shed innocent blood, even the blood of their sons and of their daughters, whom they sacrificed unto the idols of Canaan: and the land was polluted with blood. Thus were they defiled with their own works, and went a whoring with their own inventions.   [Ps. 106.13ff.]

The tribes may occasionally have believed in divine retribution, such as the deadly outbreak of plague that struck soon after the building of the pagan altar in Gilead. But such 'warnings' were soon forgotten and the worship of pagan deities went on apace far beyond the era of the Patriarchs and the Judges.

Following the reign of David, which came about after Saul's rebellion against theocratic authority, his successor Solomon began an unapologetic drive towards apostasy that was to set a precedent for the rest of the centuries of Kingship. Tradition has it that Solomon's paganism incurred the wrath of God sufficiently for part of his kingdom to be taken away and given to Jereboam, effectively splitting the Israelite tribes into two irreconcilable kingdoms. But Solomon's pagan sanctuaries remained in active use for at least three hundred years, until they were torn down early in the seventh century BCE by one of the few truly Yahwist reformers, Josiah.

> And the high places that were before Jerusalem, which were on the right hand of the mount of corruption, which Solomon the king of Israel had built for Ashtoreth the abomination of the Zidonians,

and for Chemosh the abomination of the Moabites, and for Milcom
the abomination of the children of Ammon, did the king defile.
And he brake in pieces the images, and cut down the groves, and
filled their places with the bones of men. Moreover the altar that
was at Bethel, and the high place which Jereboam the son of Nebat,
who made Israel to sin, had made, both that altar and the high
place he brake down, and stamped it small to powder, and burned
the grove.   [2 Kings 23.13–15]

When the schism of the tribes came early in the tenth century
BCE, paganism became even more firmly identified with the north.
It was strongly supported from the reign of Ahab onwards and it
was he who officially introduced the Baal cult under pressure from
his pagan priestess wife, Jezebel, in the mid-ninth century.

He [Ahab] took to wife Jezebel the daughter of Ethbaal king of the
Zidonians and went and served Baal and worshipped him. And he
reared up an altar for Baal, which he had built in Samaria. And
Ahab made a grove: and Ahab did more to provoke the Lord God
of Israel to anger than all the kings of Israel that went before him.
                                                    [1 Kings 16.31–32]

As if to emphasise the point, the first Book of Kings also includes
a neat cameo on the occasion when Elijah counted four hundred
and fifty prophets of Baal-Asherah enjoying a feast at Jezebel's
table. If there was any lessening of northern apostasy it came only
during the ninth-century reigns of Jehoram and Jehu who, while
not always wholly loyal to the Mosaic covenant, none the less
opposed the Baal cult. These, however, were notable exceptions
in an otherwise unremitting love-affair with paganism.

THREE

Goddesses and Whores

The Baal cult, followed earnestly by many of the rank-and-file Hebrews, involved an intimate relationship with the Canaanite mother goddess, Asherah, and although Baal is often linked sexually with his sister Anat, the roles of the two goddesses appear interchangeable. Asherah gave her name to a strange object that was to arouse persistent vitriol among the Old Testament writers. The *asherah* was a sacred symbol representing the presence of the fertility goddess and although there are implications that it was sometimes modelled as a likeness of the deity, old votive inscriptions suggest that it was more in the form of a tree. It probably originated in antiquity as a living tree but evolved into a wooden stylised image or totem, and its name, *asheh-rah*, אשרה (*asheroth* – plural), has been translated euphemistically in the King James Version of the Old Testament as *grove*. The dedication of a Phoenician from Kition is directed to 'his lady the mother of the *asherah*' and at Ma'zub near Ptolemais a temple portico was built for 'Ashtoreth in the *asherah*'.

'Grove' is a confusing term because it is also used in contexts which have no apparent religious significance, when translating the Hebrew word for a living tree, *eh-shel*, אשל. The ambiguity is increased because, while the Jerusalem Bible makes distinctions between the Hebrew *peh-sel*, פסל, a graven or carved idol, and *mas-seh-chah*, מסכה, a more abstract symbol cast from molten metal, the King James translation invariably is that of *grove*.

The Old Testament writers railed against the *asherah* throughout much of the Israelite history, beginning with the Canaanite cult. When the powerful Mesopotamian kingdom of Assyria started exercising military muscle over Palestine in the ninth century BCE, and the Mesopotamian counterparts of Baal and Asherah stole the limelight, the Assyrian style of the *asherah* probably replaced that of Canaan under diplomatic pressure. The Assyrian goddess Ishtar does not appear by name in the Old Testament but her consort, Tammuz, is mentioned by Ezekiel. Other goddesses, such as Ashtoreth and Ashtaroth, who intrude into the biblical texts from time to time, reflect only regional variations on the name. Such was the devotion to the fertility goddess that her *asherah* stood for centuries in the Temple of Jerusalem beside the altar of Yahweh. Under the later domination of the Babylonians and Greeks it was still a matter for grave concern and it remained so into the early part of the Roman era.

We can gain a fair idea of what the *asherah* looked like from various sources. During the reign of Jehoiakim (609–598 BCE), a ruler who was strongly influenced by Babylonian and Assyrian cults, the prophet Jeremiah provided a remarkably candid observation of a wooden pole or trunk that was decorated with precious metals. It was hung with woven cloth and was sometimes carried about in procession rather than being anchored permanently in one place. Jeremiah probably described an *asherah* that stood in the Temple of Jerusalem. Because, however, he refers to 'uncircumcised nations' and his Old Testament book includes a long discourse about the worship of the Queen of Heaven 'amongst Jews which dwell in the land of Egypt', some biblical scholars have argued that he learned the details of the *asherah* when a refugee in Egypt. He had written the main bulk of his work in Jerusalem in about 627 BCE, and his experiences covered the last five reigns in Judah, but in 586 BCE he was forced to flee Palestine where he had lived during much of the Babylonian Exile. We cannot say for certain that his description is a direct observation of the *asherah* in the Jerusalem Temple. The argument of the 'Egyptian connection' is very speculative and has probably been promoted to minimise the extent of Judahite paganism.

For the customs of the people are vain: for one cutteth a tree out of the forest, the work of the hands of the workman, with the axe. They deck it with silver and with gold; they fasten it with nails and with gold, that it move not. They are upright as the palm tree, but speak not: they must needs be borne, because they cannot go. Be not afraid of them; for they cannot do evil, neither also is it in them to do good. Forasmuch as there is none like unto thee, O Lord ... But they are altogether brutish and foolish: the stock is a doctrine of vanities. Silver spread into plates is brought from Tarshish, and gold from Uphaz, the work of the workman, and of the hands of the founder; blue and purple is their clothing: they are all the work of cunning men.   [Jer. 10.3ff]

Jeremiah's description can be linked to the evidence of stone carvings found in the ancient Assyrian city of Kalakh, Calah of Genesis, the royal seat of the tyrannical King Ashurnasirpal II whose reign began in 884 BCE. The scenes depict Ashurnasirpal and his priestly attendant worshipping an *asherah* believed to represent their national goddess Ishtar. It is a caricature of a tree, a strange cat's-cradle of branches clothed in bands of metal or some other substance and ending in stylised seven-lobed leaf designs known as *palmettes*. Often the reliefs involve the king and a creature that seems to anticipate the winged guardian cherubim of biblical tradition. The king holds a bucket and a pine cone that is directed at the tree. The best guess is that the *palmettes* represent the seven lobes of which once the human uterus was believed to be constructed. The cone, phallic in appearance and having been dipped into the bucket containing holy oil or water, the semen of the gods, symbolises the fertilisation of the goddess. The semen analogy is drawn vividly in a Mesopotamian hymn from late in the third millennium BCE.

After Father Enki has lifted his eye over the Euphrates
He stands up proudly like a rampant bull.
He lifts his penis, ejaculates,

Fills the Tigris with sparkling water.
[Kramer, 1969]

The tree worship of Ashurnasirpal II was no isolated piece of devotion in Assyria. Three centuries after his reign, during the death throes of the empire, it was still fashionable with Ashurbanipal, the scholarly king who built the fabled city of Nineveh and had the *asherah* imagery incorporated into his artwork.

Jeremiah ·described the *asherah* 'beside every luxuriant tree' implying an association with wooded areas, although one of the strongest perennial complaints from Yahwists was over the erection of the *asherah* near, or inside, the Temple.

> Thou shalt not plant thee a grove of any trees near unto the altar of the Lord thy God, which thou shalt make thee. Neither shalt thou set thee up any image; which the Lord thy God hateth.
>
> [Deut. 16.21]

The most popular position, as in other parts of the ancient Near East, was probably on hilltops in rural shrines. This is confirmed in various descriptions scattered throughout the Old Testament and 'groves' must have been a common sight all over the Holy Land.

> Ye shall utterly destroy all the places wherein the nations which ye shall possess served their gods, upon the high mountains, and upon the hills, and under every green tree: And ye shall overthrow their altars, and break their pillars, and burn their groves with fire; and ye shall hew down the graven images of their gods, and destroy the names of them out of that place.   [Deut. 12.2–3]

According to the Book of Kings, there was a spate of pagan shrine-building during the reign of the Judahite king Reheboam, the successor to Solomon.

And Judah did evil in the sight of the Lord ... For they also built them high places, and images, and groves, on every high hill and under every green tree.   [1 Kings 14.22,23]

The books covering the time of Moses and the Judges are strewn with dire warnings against worship of the *asherah* and the sheer frequency of condemnation can probably be read as a measure of the goddess's popularity.

And the children of Israel did evil in the sight of the Lord, and served Baalim: And they forsook the Lord God of their fathers ... and followed other gods, of the gods of the people that were round about them, and bowed themselves unto them, and provoked the Lord to anger. And they forsook the Lord, and served Baal and Ashtaroth ... Nevertheless the Lord raised up judges, which delivered them out of the hand of those that spoiled them ... And it came to pass, when the judge [collective term] was dead, that they returned, and corrupted themselves more than their fathers, in following other gods to serve them, and to bow down unto them; they ceased not from their own doings, nor from their stubborn way.   [Judg. 2.11ff.]

Take heed to thyself, lest thou make a covenant with the inhabitants of the land whither thou goest, lest it be for a snare in the midst of thee: But ye shall destroy their altars, break their images, and cut down their groves.   [Exod. 34.12,13]

But thus shall ye deal with them [other nations]; ye shall destroy their altars, and break down their images, and cut down their groves, and burn their graven images with fire.   [Deut. 7.5]

A second object, a metal or stone pillar known as a *massebah* or *matz-tzeh-vah*, מצבה, usually stood side by side with the *asherah*. It symbolised the presence of Baal and it probably bore a strongly phallic appearance. In the days of the Patriarchs the *massebah* had simply been a pile of stones or a large single stone erected as a

commemorative monument. So, in English versions of the Pentateuch, the five books of the Old Testament covering early history –
Genesis, Exodus, Leviticus, Numbers and Deuteronomy – *massebah* is translated as 'pillar'. In the later books it is usually read as
'image'.

The Deuteronomist – the name given to one of the anonymous
Pentateuch authors – urged loyal Yahwists to go against the pagan
idolaters, 'overthrowing their altars and breaking their pillars', but
eventually the *massebah* found its way into the ritual trappings of
both north and south. The frequency with which the word crops
up in the Bible indicates a degree of popularity which continued
at least until the time of the so-called 'writing prophets' who lived
fairly late in the period of the monarchy.

The paganism of the Israelites gained considerable support
from outside when the northern kingdom underwent a cata-
strophic change of fortunes in the eighth century BCE. In 722 BCE,
having seen much of its élite expelled under Assyrian domination
during the reign of Tiglathpileser III, the last ill-fated ruler of
Israel, Hoshea, rebelled and Israel ceased to exist as a political
state. Galilee was already an Assyrian province and during the
reign of the Assyrian king, Shalmaneser V, it was the turn of
Samaria to be invaded by force. Shalmaneser's successor, Sargon
II, ordered further wholesale deportations of Israelites to Mesopotamia, using them as slave labour and replacing them with other
captive peoples. From that traumatic moment we have very sparse
records about what went on in the north and almost all our
information relates to the southern kingdom of Judah.

Assyria had undoubtedly been a strong influence on culture and
religious traditions in Palestine for some time before the actual
take-over of the north, and the Canaanite *asherah* was probably
changed to an Assyrian style as early as the ninth century BCE
when Assyria had become the dominant political and military
force in western Asia.

The last mention of *asherah* and *massebah* in the same context
comes in the Book of Micah. The minor prophet Micah, who

lived from about 740 to 697 BCE, was particularly hostile towards the *asherah* worshippers, and keen on the idea of divine retribution.

> Thy graven images also will I cut off, and thy standing images out of the midst of thee; and thou shalt no more worship the work of thine hands. And I will pluck up thy groves out of the midst of thee: so will I destroy thy cities. And I will execute vengeance and fury upon the heathen, such as they have not heard.   [Mic. 5.13]

A few more snippets of relevant information about the *asherah* can be gleaned from non-Jewish sources. In the Hittite legend of the missing fertility god, Telepinu, an evergreen *asherah* was set up before him and decked with gifts and this idea of decorating the object seems to have been the convention in much of the Near East. It is intriguing to discover that the practice was also copied in Jerusalem. At the time of Josiah's reforms, the Old Testament writer draws a graphic picture of female votaries of the cult who sat by the gates of the Temple weaving coloured decorations for the *asherah*.

> And he [Josiah] brake down the houses of the sodomites, that were by the house of the Lord, where the women wove hangings for the grove.   [2 Kings 23.7]

The pagan ritual associated with the *asherah* and *massebah* is never clearly detailed in the Old Testament but these were symbols of fertility and, as will be explained in more detail, the rites of Canaanites, Assyrians and Babylonians involved sexual activity. A key feature of complaint against foreign-imported cults, usually glossed over in euphemism or vague generality, is ritualised sex. The vagueness behind which the writers retreated is best summed up in the comments of two prophets, Ezekiel and Hosea.

> There were two women, the daughters of one mother: And . . . they committed whoredoms in their youth: there were their breasts

pressed, and there they bruised the teats of their virginity. And the names of them were Aholah the elder, and Aholibah her sister: and they were mine, and they bore sons and daughters. Thus were their names; Samaria is Aholah, and Jerusalem Aholibah. And Aholah played the harlot when she was mine; and she doted on her lovers, on the Assyrians her neighbours.   [Ezek. 23.2–5]

They sacrifice upon the tops of the mountains, and burn incense upon the hills, under oaks and poplars and elms, because the shadow thereof is good: therefore your daughters shall commit whoredom and your spouses shall commit adultery.   [Hos. 4.13]

The prophet Jeremiah was more specific in his accusation, referring to 'adultery with stones and with stocks'. In a cultic context 'stone' can only be the *massebah*, the representation of the fertility god. 'Stock' is used in two ways in the Old Testament: to describe a restraining device for a criminal or, as it is applied in this case, for a stump of wood, in other words a euphemism for the *asherah* of the goddess. Jeremiah therefore complains of sexual intercourse in association with the *massebah* and *asherah* of the 'high places'.

And I saw, when for all the causes whereby backsliding Israel committed adultery I had put her away, and given her a bill of divorce; yet her treacherous sister Judah feared not, but went and played the harlot also. And it came to pass through the lightness of her whoredom, that she defiled the land, and committed adultery with stones and with stocks.   [Jer. 3.8,9]

The fertility rites of the Assyrians, to whom Ezekiel refers, involved priestesses who served as sacred prostitutes and a detailed description of these rites (to be investigated shortly) comes from Mesopotamian literary sources. They compare closely with ceremonies described in Canaanite records and it is logical to assume, from the biblical emphasis on Israelites 'going after' the traditions of the pagan countries around them, that the same rites were copied by the Israelites, in which case they involved ritual prostitution.

Prostitution in Jewish society during biblical times was not as it may appear from a casual reading of the Old Testament texts. It does, however, form a crucial part of the investigation of Mary. In Mosaic law an indistinct line was drawn between two areas of sexual misconduct, adultery and prostitution, and circumstances were apt to cause confusion. The law prohibited harlotry and the children of a commercial prostitute were deprived of normal rights of inheritance. As the second-century Jewish historian Philo put it,

> According to the injunctions of the sacred scriptures the constitution of the law does not recognise a harlot; as being a person alienated from good order, and modesty and chastity.
>
> [Philo, *De Specialibus Legibus* III, 51].

None the less professional prostitutes were actually treated with greater respect than they are today. Ordinary commercial whoring was widespread and generally condoned among the Jewish rank and file. In the polygamous Israelite society, the more powerful members of the establishment frequently possessed several marital partners, and many records exist of men taking prostitutes as wives or concubines. A daughter could also be exploited as a prostitute to ease her father's poverty, and this opened the way to easy commercial enterprise. A barren wife could readily give a maid, effectively a concubine, to her husband for the purpose of bearing children. On this understanding Rachel gave Bilhah to Jacob [Gen. 30.3–4] and Leah presented him with Zilpah [Gen. 30.9]. The concubine relinquished all rights in the offspring of such a union who became, in the eyes of the law, the legal child of the foster mother.

Problems arose when a wife, or even a bride-to-be, was suspected of sexual misconduct. A woman coming to her husband's bed on her wedding night was expected to prove her virginity through inspection of the sheets on the morning after, earning the accusation of adultery if she failed. Among the weaknesses in the patriarchal Hebrew legal system, a husband could have a relationship with an unmarried woman without censure but a married woman committing the same act was considered guilty of a crime of such severity that it demanded an automatic death penalty.

> But if this thing be true, and the tokens of virginity be not found for the damsel: Then shall they bring out the damsel to the door of her father's house, and the men of her city shall stone her with stones that she die: because she hath wrought folly in Israel, to play the whore in her father's house. [Deut. 22.20,21]

The slender divide between adultery and prostitution is clear from the tangled relationship between Tamar and the Patriarch Judah, described in the Book of Genesis. Tamar, thought to have been a Canaanite woman, became the wife of Judah's first son, Er. When Er died prematurely having been 'wicked in the sight of the Lord', it was the responsibility of his younger brother, Onan, to father children with Tamar under a law known as Levirate, the obligation placed on a man to marry his childless brother's widow. For reasons not explained, Onan declined this duty and Tamar was required to 'remain a widow at her father's house'. She had no intention of leaving herself vulnerable as a childless woman so she came up with the plan of getting pregnant by Judah. Disguised as a prostitute, in Israelite convention veiled and therefore passingly anonymous, she took up position at a cross-roads, the traditional place for a courtesan to ply her trade.

> And she [Tamar] put off her widow's garments from her, and covered her with a vail, and wrapped herself, and sat in an open place which is by the way to Timnath … When Judah saw her, he thought her to be an harlot; because she had covered her face.
> [Gen. 38.14]

The liaison went without immediate risk but, understanding the legal implications if she was to bear a child, Tamar took insurance by obtaining certain of Judah's personal possessions including a signet ring, bracelets and his staff. This was a shrewd precaution because as soon as Tamar could no longer conceal her pregnancy Judah accused her of adultery and sentenced her to death. She was only reprieved after producing evidence to identify the father of the child.

The commercial whore was not, however, the only kind of prostitute in Israelite society. The translators of the King James Bible used the word 'harlot' indiscriminately and in doing so they sometimes distorted the sense of the original. The Tamar incident includes two distinct terms in the original Hebrew. When detailing how Tamar offered herself to Judah, the scribe used the word *zona*, meaning a professional woman who accepts payment for her sexual services, or perhaps a woman who has had sex before marriage. But the word which the scribe puts into the mouth of Judah's friend, Hiram the Adullamite, when searching for the mysterious woman with whom Judah liaised, is *qdesha*.

Qdesha occurs in the Old Testament texts in a limited number of instances while *zona* is more common, and the distinction between the two is drawn succinctly in the Book of Hosea.

I will not punish your daughters when they commit whoredom, nor your spouses when they commit adultery: for themselves are separated with whores [*zonim*], and they sacrifice with harlots [*qadesot*]   [Hos. 4.14]

The Old Testament writers were so reticent about the term *qdesha* that it is recorded in no more than a few instances. The word is applied to Tamar in Genesis 38. It is mentioned in connection with the prohibition against temple funding from the earnings of prostitutes in Deuteronomy 23. It introduces Hosea's wife, Gomer, in Hosea 1.

Qdesha is a borrowing from the Mesopotamian *qadistu* and it describes a temple priestess. One of the central aspects of the Mesopotamian cult was the honouring of the fertility goddess, Ishtar. Her temples were staffed by women devotees or votaries who served her daily needs and some of whom participated in her most sacred rite, the Marriage. The responsibilities undertaken by these women are detailed in the Mesopotamian Law Codes. In brief, they were called upon to represent the fertility *diva* in sexually charged dramas, which encouraged divine imitation in order to safeguard the prosperity and fecundity of the natural world.

The Old Testament writers may have avoided the term *qdesha* except by implication. A likely reference emerges towards the end of Exodus when the artisan Bezaleel is constructing the altar of Yahweh.

> And he made the laver of brass, and the foot of it of brass, of the looking-glasses of the women assembling, which assembled at the door of the tabernacle of the congregation.   [Exod. 38.8]

The description of women weaving hangings for the *asherah* in 2 Kings may also refer to votaries of the goddess. It infers that priestesses were a familiar sight in Jerusalem during at least some of the period of the Kingship.

In context, Judah, the Hebrew Patriarch, spoke of a commercial whore, since to consort with a sacred prostitute was inadmissible for him, but Hiram, a man of pagan Canaanite culture, referred to Tamar as a priestess. Hiram's term, as we shall shortly discover, was probably nearer to the truth and for this reason the incident of Judah and Tamar remains politically sensitive to Jews to this day. It is one of only four passages in the canon that the Mishnah directs must be read in Hebrew in the synagogue rather than in the more familiar Aramaic.

The Old Testament scribes had no word to describe a priestess because such a person did not officially exist under Mosaic law.

They needed to distinguish her from a *zona* but the word *qdesha* was problematic because it simply means 'holy woman', a loose term that may technically include devotees who have no association with prostitution. By and large, the writers seem to have used *qdesha* as a euphemism when they wanted to identify women initiated as sacred or temple prostitutes; the Revised Standard Version of the Bible in English translates *qdesha* more openly than the King James, as 'cult prostitute'. Distinction between commercial and religious prostitute becomes virtually impossible in the New Testament since the texts and their early copies were written in Greek, which recognised only the word *porne*, meaning women who engaged in extramarital sex for money.

The Mosaic legal position on sacred prostitutes differed markedly from that of Mesopotamia, the Law Code of Hammurabi on which a large part of Hebrew legislation was based. Throughout much of the ancient Near East religious prostitution was legally recognised, but under Jewish law it was anathema. Nevertheless, in the face of vigorous efforts at suppression and in spite of general denial, cult priestesses were recognised through long periods of Jewish history. It is equally clear from admonitions in the Psalms of Solomon – the first-century BCE works of a group of devout Jews responding to the capture of Jerusalem by the Romans – and the Mishnah that the vocation endured down to and beyond the first century.

In pre-Exilic times, prohibitions against the *qdesha* extended to the rejection of any monetary gain passed over as a temple offering.

There shall be no whore of the daughters of Israel, nor a sodomite of the sons of Israel. Thou shalt not bring the hire of a whore [*qdesha*], or the price of a dog [*keleb*], into the house of the Lord thy God for any vow: for even both these are abomination unto the Lord thy God. [Deut. 23.17–18]

Do not prostitute thy daughter, to cause her to be a whore; lest the land fall to whoredom, and the land become full of wickedness.

[Lev. 19.29]

In spite of official rejection, the *qdesha* received biblical acknow-
ledgement from as early as the time of Samuel when Eli, one of
the last of the minor Judges, was head priest of the sanctuary at
Shiloh.

> Now Eli was very old, and heard all that his sons did unto all Israel;
> and how they lay with the women that assembled at the door of
> the tabernacle of the congregation.   [1 Sam. 2.22]

Ritual prostitution in pre-Exilic Jerusalem involved both men
and women. The male votary described in Deuteronomy should
properly be termed a *qadesh* but the writer is sufficiently derogatory
to call him a *keleb* or dog. In the King James Bible *qadesh* becomes
'sodomite' while in the Revised Standard Version it is translated
as 'male cult prostitute'. Occasionally there is disagreement about
the meaning: in the Greek Septuagint translation of the Book of
Job [36.14], dating from the third century BCE, *qedeshim* (plural)
becomes 'angels' while Jerome, the author of the Latin Vulgate of
the late fourth century, refers to them as 'effeminates'.

The frequency of verbal attack on the fertility rites by Old
Testament writers counters any claim that they were fringe aberrations. We find strong criticism in the Pentateuch but accusations
are also raised in the books of Judges, Samuel and Kings as well
as in the later Chronicles. These are generally directed towards
Israelites indulging in sexual relations with their foreign neighbours and, because of old enmities, the Egyptians are often singled
out, occasionally with a hint of male envy.

> And Israel abode in Shittim, and the people began to commit
> whoredom with the daughters of Moab ... And Israel joined itself
> unto Baal-peor: and the anger of the Lord was kindled against
> Israel.   [Num. 25.1ff]

> And they transgressed against the God of their fathers, and went a

whoring after the gods of the people of the land, whom God
destroyed before them.   [1 Chron. 5.25]

Thou hast also committed fornication with the Egyptians thy
neighbours, great of flesh; and hast increased thy whoredoms, to
provoke me to anger.   [Ezek. 16.26]

Intermarriage with foreigners was seen by the elders of the
tribes to be an open door for 'bedroom paganism' and legislation
was introduced to discourage these matches but it fell short of a
comprehensive ban. The Book of Numbers [36.1–12] probably
reflects the position most accurately when it discriminates against
heiresses marrying outside their own tribes, but this limitation
was not widely advertised and the law may, at times, have been
interpreted over-zealously in order to discourage foreign marriages. Deuteronomy [7.3,4] specifically rejects all such contracts,
irrespective of whether the bride-to-be was an heiress or not.
Exodus [34.15,16] and Joshua [23.12,13], falling short of outright
condemnation, give gloomy warnings that Israelite sons marrying
foreign wives are at risk of being seduced into worship of foreign
gods. As late as the second century BCE the Palestinian Jewish
author of the Book of Jubilees, compiled as a retrospective account
of the instructions handed down by God to Moses, argued that
the Covenant demanded a more general prohibition.

And if there is any man in Israel who wishes to give his daughter
or his sister to any man who is from the seed of the Gentiles, let
him surely die, and let him be stoned because he has caused shame
in Israel. And also the woman will be burned with fire because she
has defiled the name of her father's house and so will be uprooted
from Israel.   [Jubilees 30.7]

In practice, ordinary Israelite fathers had no particular aversion
to their daughters becoming the wives of foreigners. This frequently brought the reward of marriage into affluent families and

it served to warm diplomatic relations. In any event, the Patriarchs had set a convenient precedent. Reuben had married a Canaanite named Ada, Simeon tied the knot with another Canaanite named Adiba'a, Levi wed an Aramite, Melka, and Judah took as his wife a Canaanite named Betasu'el. But intermarriage also oiled the wheels for allowing foreign religious practices to merge fairly easily with those of the Mosaic Covenant.

> And the children of Israel dwelt among the Canaanites, Hittites, and Amorites, and Perizzites, and Hivites, and Jebusites: And they took their daughters to be their wives, and gave their daughters to their sons, and served their gods. And the children of Israel did evil in the sight of the Lord, and forgat the Lord their God, and served Baalim and the groves. [Judg. 3.5–7]

By the time of the Assyrian conquest of Israel in 722 BCE, the sexual behaviour about which the elders made objection had ceased to involve only foreign women. Much of the importunity took place between fellow Israelites and, whether or not it crossed ethnic and cultural divides, it was believed to be a principal cause of Israel's downfall.

> Moreover the Lord saith, Because the daughters of Zion are haughty, and walk with stretched forth necks and wanton eyes, walking and mincing as they go, and making a tinkling with their feet: Therefore the Lord will smite with a scab the crown of the head of the daughters of Zion, and the Lord will discover [Heb. 'make naked'] their secret parts. [Isa. 3.16–17]

Micah, who was probably an eighth-century contemporary of Isaiah, was in no doubt that religious whoredom linked to apostasy, particularly in the north, was the main culprit.

> For the transgression of Jacob is all this, and for the sins of the house of Israel. What is the transgression of Jacob? is it not Samaria?

And what are the high places of Judah? Are they not Jerusalem? Therefore I will make Samaria as an heap of the field, and as plantings of a vineyard: and I will pour down the stones thereof into the valley, and I will discover the foundations thereof. And all the graven images thereof shall be beaten to pieces, and all the hires thereof shall be burned with the fire, and all the idols thereof will I lay desolate: for she gathered it of the hire of an harlot, and they shall return to the hire of an harlot.   [Mic. 1.5–7]

Hosea, another minor prophet, who lived in the reign of Jereboam II during the latter part of the eighth century BCE, shared similar views.

The Lord said to Hosea, Go, take unto thee a wife of whoredoms and children of whoredoms: for the land hath committed great whoredoms, departing from the Lord. So he [Hosea] went and took Gomer the daughter of Diblaim; which conceived, and bare him a son. And the Lord said unto him, Call his name Jezreel; for yet a little while, and I will avenge the blood of Jezreel upon the house of Jehu, and will cause to cease the kingdom of the house of Israel.   [Hos. 1.2–4]

Hosea had been instructed by God to redeem his wife Gomer from harlotry and it is likely that she was a *qdesha* because Hosea is one of the few writers in the Old Testament to use the word specifically. He makes repeated references to Gomer's devotion to Baal and the rewards gained in her service to the Canaanite cult of the god.

For she did not know that I gave her corn, and wine, and oil, and multiplied her silver and gold, which they prepared for Baal ... And I will visit upon her the days of Baalim, wherein she burned incense to them, and she decked herself with her earrings and her jewels, and she went after her lovers, and forgat me, saith the Lord.
           [Hos. 2.8,13]

Ritual prostitution provided vitriolic ammunition for the pens of several other Exilic and post-Exilic writers. Ezekiel, disparaging about the behaviour of both kingdoms, reserved his strongest criticism for religious prostitution in the north.

> There were two women, the daughters of one mother: And they committed whoredoms in Egypt; they committed whoredoms in their youth: there were their breasts pressed, and there they bruised the teats of their virginity. And the names of them were Aholah the elder, and Aholibah her sister: and they were mine, and they bare sons and daughters. Thus were their names; Samaria is Aholah, and Jerusalem Aholibah. And Aholah played the harlot when she was mine; and she doted on her lovers, on the Assyrians her neighbours.   [Ezek. 23.2–5]

Although the record of cult in the north ceased abruptly at the time of the Assyrian take-over in 722 BCE, evidence of apostasy and the prostitution with which it was associated continued in the state of Judah. There is repeated biblical evidence that the *asherah* was installed in the Jerusalem Temple for long periods between the accession of Solomon in about 970 BCE and the deportation of Zedekiah to Babylon in 598 BCE. Wherever the *asherah* was set up in the ancient Near East, its very nature as the embodiment of the fertility goddess would have required the presence of priestesses.

Among the most extreme pagan rulers of Judah was Manasseh, the successor to one of the reformist kings, Hezekiah.

> For he [Manasseh] built up again the high places which Hezekiah his father had destroyed; and he reared up altars for Baal, and made a grove, as did Ahab king of Israel; and worshipped all the host of heaven, and served them. And he built altars in the house of the Lord, of which the Lord said, In Jerusalem will I put my name. And he built altars for all the host of heaven in the two courts of the house of the Lord.   [2 Kings 21.3–5]

So controversial was Manasseh's reign that he did not escape disapproval in the books of Chronicles. These records, in comparison with Kings, are less severe in their criticism of pagan practice.

> For he [Manasseh] built again the high places which Hezekiah his father had broken down, and he reared up altars for Baalim, and made groves, and worshipped all the host of heaven, and served them. Also he built altars in the house of the Lord, whereof the Lord had said, In Jerusalem shall my name be for ever. And he built altars for all the host of heaven in the two courts of the house of the Lord. [2 Chron. 33.3-5]

The religious direction of Judah constantly veered one way, then the other. When, in 640 BCE, Josiah took over the Judahite throne from Manasseh's short-lived pagan successor, Amon, he attempted to reform the country, yet again, back to Yahwism.

> And the king commanded Hilkiah the high priest, and the priests of the second order, and the keepers of the door, to bring forth out of the temple of the Lord all the vessels that were made for Baal, and for the grove, and for all the host of heaven: ... And he put down the idolatrous priests, whom the kings of Judah had ordained to burn incense in the high places in the cities of Judah, and in the places round about Jerusalem. [Kings 23.4ff.]

But Josiah's changes proved as unpopular as those of Hezekiah. Judah found itself under increasing foreign pressure from Mesopotamia and by the time Zedekiah had ascended the throne, apostasy had effectively become chronic in the south, much as it had been in the north before loss of independence.

> Moreover all the chief of the priests, and the people, transgressed very much after all the abominations of the heathen; and polluted the house of the Lord which he had hallowed in Jerusalem ...

they mocked the messengers of God, and despised his words, and misused his prophets, until the wrath of the Lord arose against his people, till there was no remedy.   [2 Chron. 36.14ff.]

Such was the state of affairs as Assyrian influence waned and Judah became faced with tyranny from a new power-brokering neighbour, Babylon. Paganism, and in particular the fertility cult of the mother goddess, was set to continue embracing all levels of Jewish society.

FOUR

The Exile

The greatest influence on Israelites living in the centuries after the collapse of Assyrian power was to be that of the neo-Babylonians, the second Babylonian dynasty that was established in 614 BCE when Cyaxares the Mede marched into Assyria, followed by Nabopolassar, the Babylonian overlord. He and Cyaxares made a treaty that two years later saw the Assyrian capital of Nineveh reduced to rubble. If there is a single name that epitomises visions of ancient Near Eastern idolatry and pagan splendour it is surely Babylon, the Akkadian word meaning 'Gate of God'. In 586 BCE, after Zedekiah had rebelled against the new Babylonian strongman, Nebuchadnezzar II, Jerusalem was placed under siege. When the city fell, Nebuchadnezzar took the most senior members of the priesthood to a village named Riblah and executed them. Jerusalem was effectively demolished on his instructions, and the remaining Israelite élite, including what was left of the senior tier of clergy, the Sadoquites, was then bundled off to languish in Babylonia. Only the poorest Judahites were left as tenants of the 'Promised Land'.

What did ordinary Jews actually think about all these momentous and traumatic events? It is an important issue because their changing fortunes influenced their beliefs. Religion was not the abstract and pigeonholed style of worship that it has become in the modern world but a faith that encompassed an entire way of life, and we find that people reacted in quite different ways. Yahwist cant, promoted by religious leaders including Ezekiel and Jeremiah, put the troubles of the Jews down to their idolatrous transgressions in the past and, in particular, to Manasseh's forty-five years of paganism. Yahwist elders remained firmly of the opinion that the curse of subjugation had been brought upon them as a consequence of wholesale transgression against their god.

> Therefore will I cast you out of this land into a land that ye know not, neither ye nor your fathers; and there shall ye serve other gods day and night; where I will not shew you favour.   [Jer. 16.13]

> The sin of Judah is written with a pen of iron, and with the point of a diamond: it is graven upon the table of their heart, and upon the horns of your altars; Whilst their children remember their altars and their groves by the green trees upon the high hills.
>
> [Jer. 17.1–2]

Others, however, came to a different conclusion about the root causes of national success and failure. Since the two dominant forces in the region, the Assyrians and their Babylonian successors, took rejection of their deities by vassal states, including Judah and Israel, to be demonstrations of defiance, periods of repression and hardship in Judah had tended to coincide with the reforms against pagan idolatry. Hard-line Yahwism was seen in the Mesopotamian power bases to be little more than rebellion among people who had already achieved a long-term reputation for making a nuisance of themselves. It was dealt with severely. In about 704 BCE Sennacherib, the Assyrian despot, sent a chilling message to the reformist Judahite king, Hezekiah, after which he took forty-six cities in Judah.

> Let not thy God in whom thou trustest deceive thee, saying, Jerusalem shall not be delivered into the hands of the king of Assyria. Behold, thou hast heard what the kings of Assyria have done to all lands, by destroying them utterly.   [2 Kings 19.10–11]

Periods in which pagan shrines and pagan worship were actively welcomed by Judahite rulers, probably dictated as much out of political expediency as any purely religious conviction, were marked, in contrast, by comparative peace and prosperity. The reign of Jereboam, two centuries before that of Hezekiah, saw idolatry flourish in the northern kingdom. It was also a reign of economic growth and prosperity. Josiah, another staunch Yahwist, had inherited a measure of stability and economic prosperity from his pagan predecessor, Manasseh. The latter part of Josiah's reign, however, was marked by upheaval and change culminating in his death near Megiddo at the hands of the Egyptians, making one of their periodic aggressive sorties into Palestine. To an essentially superstitious people, already attracted by the lure of pagan cult and pagan ideals, the message of history was far from clear cut.

Even Jeremiah, swallowing what must have been a bitter personal pill, was forced to report the defiant attitude among ordinary people who believed precisely the *reverse* of the argument that Yahwism was the route to salvation.

> We will certainly ... burn incense unto the queen of heaven ... as we have done, we, and our fathers, our kings, and our princes, in the cities of Judah, and in the streets of Jerusalem: for then had we plenty of victuals, and were well, and saw no evil. But since we left off to burn incense to the queen of heaven, and to pour out drink offerings unto her, we have wanted all things, and have been consumed by the sword and by the famine. And when we burned incense to the queen of heaven, and poured out drink offerings unto her, did we make her cakes to worship her, and pour out drink offerings unto her, without our men?' [Jer. 44.17–19]

Old Testament history reveals sobering and surprising details of the cultural legacy which came down to Mary's more recent ancestors and the extent to which paganism had appealed to Hebrews of all ranks.

A close inspection of the records detailed in 1 and 2 Kings and 1 and 2 Chronicles reveals the statistics of pagan leaning across the span of the monarchies in the two kingdoms of Judah and Israel, from the reign of David. In the north, although national identity and integrity was comparatively short-lived, the break-away state of Israel was never clearly and unequivocally Yahwist but opted for syncretism from its foundation under Jereboam until its conquest by Assyria. The Ishtar cult then became obligatory, with an influence that came to bear increasingly on the south from the ninth century BCE onwards.

The Kingship in the southern state of Judah lasted through twenty-three reigns, from Saul in the middle or late eleventh century BCE to Zedekiah. Of the Judaean rulers a mere six, we are informed by the Old Testament chroniclers, were committed Yahwists – David, Asa, Jehoshaphat, Hezekiah, Josiah and Jehoahaz – representing little more than a third of the overall span of Judaean Kingship. With the arguable exception of Saul, others including Solomon, Reheboam, Abijah, Joash, Amaziah, Uzziah and Jotham were ambivalent, either openly permitting pagan practice in Jerusalem or converting to paganism during their reigns. The remaining nine kings, including Jehoram, Ahaziah, Athaliah (the mother of Ahaziah who became regent), Ahaz, Manasseh, Amon, Jehoiakim, Jehoiachin and Zedekiah, were thoroughly idolatrous. Paganism therefore prevailed in Jerusalem, at an official level, during a minimum of 256 out of roughly 425 years of the rule of kings.

With the exile to Babylon our sources change. The books of the Old Testament can be separated into three main sections. The first, including the Pentateuch – Genesis, Exodus, Leviticus, Numbers and Deuteronomy – and a few other related works including Joshua and Judges, effectively covers the 'romantic age' of Israelite history until the demise of Saul. The more realistically documented political record from the accession of David to the Babylonian Exile is contained largely in the books of Kings and Chronicles. From the Exile onwards, however, the situation is more dependent on the rhetoric of Exilic and post-Exilic prophets such as Ezekiel and Jeremiah and is therefore less well defined.

These later writings reveal that, aside from the lowest levels of society, one important group remained behind in Palestine, part of the priestly tribe of Levi, who kept up a semblance of Yahwist religious life. As for the remnant of the population, they must have continued their worship in the 'high places' that had been reopened after the failure of Josiah's reforms. The implication is made clear in the writings of Jeremiah. The uneasy blend of Yahwism and paganism was set to continue in what was left of Judah, much as it had in centuries past.

Meanwhile the main body of Judahites was forcibly settled on the Chebar river near the city of Nippur where it remained for forty-seven years until, in 539 BCE, the Persian armies of Cyrus the Great marched in and put an end to the Babylonian hegemony. During that half-a-century, however, bonds grew between the exiles in their newly formed synagogues and the pagan Babylonians. As a consequence, many ex-patriots probably came to see the destruction of the Jerusalem Temple and subsequent loss of independence less in terms of Yahwist retribution and more as proof of the superiority of Babylon's heavenly ranks.

Internal differences between Jewish religious orders also built up during the years of incarceration. Long before the Exile, lines had been drawn between the Levites, who had been the first appointed religious leaders under Aaron, and the powerful Sadoquite family, which now dominated the priesthood. Sadoquites administered the sacrifice while the Levites had largely been relegated to menial tasks, not least because of memories, centuries old, of a *faux pas* which had been committed at Sinai. Bored with waiting for Moses to descend from his mountain rendezvous with God, the Israelites had fallen into the most blatant form of apostasy by encouraging Aaron to cast a bull calf idol of gold which would parade before them *en route* to the Promised Land. Aaron had been neither forgiven nor forgotten by the newer priesthood.

Paganism was set to continue in the post-Exilic state of Judaea. When the Hebrews were eventually liberated, having become known as Jews, Cyrus allowed them home to Jerusalem to begin what has been called the Second Temple or restoration period under his sponsorship. At first they seemed to have been determined not to return to pagan ways. But if we look carefully at the comments of some of the post-Exilic writers, we discover tell-tale traces that all was not as the hard-line Yahwists might have wished. Because many decided to remain in their adopted country as part of the first Jewish *diaspora*, those returning were only a minority of the Jewish Babylonian deportees. The restoration group included very few Levites, perhaps discouraged from going home because of discrimination in favour of the priests. On the other hand, the westward-bound caravans included the four Sadoquite families who would form the core of the reconstruction government in Jerusalem. These families, in company with other members of the displaced élite, had been familiar for several decades with the traditions of Babylonia going on around them. The traditions included rule by god-kings, time-honoured Mesopotamian festivals of death and renewal that took place in the spring of each year, and Sacred Marriages that constituted the high point of the fertility cult, designed to ensure the continuing fecundity of the land, its livestock and its people. It is inevitable that at least some individuals had not escaped falling in love with Babylonian religion.

One aspect of the Babylonian cult with which the exiles would have come into first-hand contact was the sacred prostitute, the priestess of the fertility cult. Since the Hebrew *qdesha* can only have been copied from a Canaanite or Mesopotamian model, the function and position of the Babylonian priestess in society provides a vital window on the cultural background of Mary.

The Mesopotamian legal system gave sacred prostitutes much greater credibility and although large parts of the Semitic world chose gradually to suppress the activity of such women, Babylonian legal documents indicate that their profession continued at least into the early Christian era.

Even ordinary prostitutes received fairer consideration in Mesopotamia than elsewhere. Under early Sumerian legislation [SC II

$ 18 in Langdon, 1920], a man who fathered children on a pros-
titute when his wife was childless had to provide for her and her
children became his heirs. In Babylonia a prostitute could marry
a free man and earn the rights of the first or legal wife, while in
Assyria under a law known as the *Mare Estrata* [MAL 41, 1.II, in
Pritchard, 1950] the children gained rights of inheritance when
the father had none by his proper wife.

The highest rank among the sacred prostitutes was the *entum*,
which describes simply 'a mistress' or 'a lady' although in its
Sumerian form, *lukur*, it can mean 'bride' or 'sister of the god'.
Many were princesses, either children or sisters of the king, but
the *entum* was also the daughter of the gods and she lived in the
service of a number of deities. She was not only above any stain
or shame but was immensely respected in society. The goddess
herself was frequently addressed as the prostitute and she readily
admitted, 'A prostitute compassionate am I'. The *entum* was eulo-
gised as having 'loins suitable by their purity for the *en*-ship' and
any false imputation on her moral conduct was considered to be
in very poor taste. Until the moment of intercourse with her god-
king she remained a 'holy virgin', untouched and isolated.

The restrictions binding these priestesses to chastity did not
necessarily mean that they remained virgins or that they rejected
sex, but that they were protected from secular violation. Their
sexual role, while in office, was confined to the Temple and the
cult. Not only were they strenuously safeguarded from slander,
their material welfare was guaranteed. The first of the Mesopotamian Law Codes, the Lipit-Ishtar, gave security to the *entum*
throughout her life.

> If the father (is) living, his daughter whether she be a high priestess,
> a priestess or a hierodule [the temple servant of a deity] shall dwell
> in his house like an heir.   [Lipit-Ishtar 22, in Pritchard 1950]

The earliest information we have about an *entum* is inscribed
on a cup found during excavations at the ancient city of Ur, which

lay on the River Euphrates near the head of the Arabian Gulf and reached its zenith towards the end of the third millennium BCE. The inscription includes only the name and rank of the priestess, Ninmetabarri, the daughter of a king of the Sumerian city-state of Mari towards the end of the Early Dynastic period in the 24th century BCE. Among the best recorded high priestesses of later times was Enheduana, the daughter of Sargon the Great; other notable ones included those of Naram-Sin of Akkad, Ur-Bau of Lagash, Ur-Nammu and Shulgi. The last king of Babylon, Nabonidus (556–539 BCE), made his daughter, Bel-shalti-Nannar, the high priestess at Ur and this infers that the rite sometimes involved incest. The *entum* seems to have served in office for a fixed period before retirement in favour of a younger woman. Mesopotamian records show that a priestess called Enanedu took over as *entum* during the sixth year of the reign of Warad-Sin in 1816 BCE after the retirement of her predecessor, Enshakiag-Nanna, who had been installed in the twenty-third year of the reign of a preceding ruler, Sumu-Ilu. Enshakiag-Nanna would probably have been in her fifties when her term of office ended. A retired *entum* was permitted to marry but discouraged from bearing any further children and it was considered a bad omen if, under certain astronomical conjunctions, men had intercourse with a woman who had previously been an *entum*.

The *qdesha* may have equated with one or more categories of priestess. Beneath the illustrious rank of *entum* was a *naditum* who could also be in the harem of the god and who lived in a special protected cloister of women. Like the *entum*, she was highly respected in society and often enjoyed substantial personal means. Old Babylonian economic contracts from Sippar show that nearly 70 per cent of its business transactions involved at least one *naditum*. She could be married but not legally bear children since, obviously, she could not perform her duties as a votary if she also became a mother. According to some authors, she may even have been sterilised, in which case she was obliged to give her husband a slave girl for child-bearing. If a vow of chastity was required of her she was entitled, like the *entum*, to legal protection from slander.

A third class of priestess known as a *sugetum* is described in several places in the Code of Hammurabi [CH 137.144.145. 183.184, Pritchard, 1950] which superseded the Lipit-Ishtar Code. The *sugetum*, more of a lay priestess who could act as kind of concubine, did not enjoy the protection afforded to a legitimate wife and, even if she had children in a relationship, the man was entitled to leave her without penalty. Apparently she was of a lower status than the *entum* or *naditum*, both of whom were classed as *hierodules* or persons in official priestly service.

> If a man married a *hierodule* and she did not provide him with children and he has made up his mind to marry a *sugetum*, that man may marry the *sugetum*, thus bringing her into his house [but] with that *sugetum* ranking in no way with the *hierodule*.
>
> [Pritchard, 1950, CH 145]

It appears to have been the highest category, either Babylonian *entum* or Sumerian *lukur*, who took part in the Mesopotamian Sacred Marriage: the ecstatic intercourse of a divine ruler and his high priestess acting out the role of the fertility goddess and her incestuous consort, the dying-and-rising god. The Marriage was an essential rite of regenesis that took place in the first month of the New Year, Nisan, at the time of the harvest when the effects of drought could be at their most severe. Records of the Marriage between the fertility goddess Inana and her son Dumuzi in the city-states of Sumer, start from as early as the third millennium BCE. Hymns and legends indicate that its purpose was to invoke fresh germination of crops after the rise of the waters of the Tigris and Euphrates yet also to escape from the immensely destructive capacity of the two rivers when they flooded. This was a matter that lay largely in the capricious hands of Inana, whose womb the peasant farmer husbanded. The earth was her temporal self, as was all that grew from it, and unless famine and desolation were to rule, the womb had to be fertilised, in myth by Dumuzi but in reality by the seminal rain from the skies to bring new life to the fields and orchards.

This rite was no apology for a ritualised orgy and the priestess earned enormous respect. She and the god-king were enacting the celestial consummation asked of the goddess. An ecstatic love-song dedicated to Shu-Sin, ruler of the Third Dynasty at Ur in about 2221 BCE, reveals a touching tenderness and mutual affection.

O my [lord] who is . . . of word, my son of Shulgi!
Because I uttered it, because I uttered it, the lord gave me a gift,
because I uttered a cry of joy, the lord gave me a gift,
a pendant of gold, a seal of lapis lazuli, the lord gave me as a gift,
a ring of gold, a ring of silver, the lord gave me as a gift.
O lord, thy gift is brimful of . . ., [lift] thy face [unto me],
O Shu-Sin, thy gift is brimful of . . ., [lift] thy face unto me.

O my Shu-Sin who hast favoured me,
O my Shu-Sin who hast favoured me, who hast fondled me,
O my Shu-Sin who hast favoured me,
O my beloved of Enlil, my Shu-Sin,
O my king, the god of his land!

[Kramer, 1969]

In the ruins of the city of Uruk a necklace was found lying close to the Eanna sanctuary of Inana. An exquisite piece of jewellery, encrusted with semi-precious stones and lapis-lazuli, it is inscribed with the words, 'Kubatum, the *lukur*-priestess of Shu-Sin'. For her there may have been little thought of an ordeal because, in her eyes, she was to be deflowered by a god. Her partner in marriage, her king, was the living incarnation of the dying-and-rising god and on this night of passion and delight he was the incestuous *lover and son* of the fertility goddess.

In Babylonian times the rite took place within a special room which formed part of the *giparu*, the official residence of the priestess, perhaps decorated like a leafy bower under the green trees which may have provided the original setting. An inscription indicates that the *entum* Enanedu was the 'patroness who had the *giparu* built as its *entum* office on the sacred site' and she speaks of 'my abode the *entum*-ship'. Likewise Nabonidus, who rebuilt the *giparu* at Ur for his daughter, Bel-shalti-Nannar, recorded on its building bricks, 'For Sin, my Lord, I built the *giparu* temple, the house of the *entum* priestess'.

The origins of *giparu* may lie in the old threshing floors used to separate the grain at the time of harvest. At Uruk an inscription reads,

> At the lapis-lazuli door which stands in the *giparu* she [Inana] met the *enu*-priest; at the narrow door which stands in the [grain] storehouse of the Eanna she met Dumuzi [her son and lover].

Significantly it was on such a threshing floor that one of five notable biblical women, Ruth, seduced Boaz while he was winnowing barley.

The role of the *entum* is wreathed with mystique. According to the Greek writer Herodotus, legend had it that the temple of Zeus Belos, or Marduk, in Babylon had an eight-storey tower, at the top of which was a sanctuary containing a golden couch on which slept a lone woman. On an appointed day the god visited the sanctuary and rested his head on the bed to have intercourse with the woman.

According to detailed Babylonian records, on the eve of the New Year a bed made of cedar and rushes was prepared in the *giparu* house. It was spread with a specially made coverlet sprinkled with fragrant oils and, as the climax of the rite approached, the virgin priestess chosen to fill the part of the goddess was bathed and prepared. We can imagine that on a heady New Year's Eve, a young woman, probably of great beauty, became immortalised in history as she lay beside her king so that the parched and dead fields of her country might bloom again. A hymn celebrating the occasion bubbles with sexual imagery.

> *As for me, my vulva. For me the piled-high hillock,*
> *Me, the maid, who will plough it for me?*
> *My vulva, the watered ground – for me,*
> *Me, the Queen, who will station the ox there?*

A chorus of onlookers would raise their answer to the questions posed by the goddess queen.

> *O Lordly Lady, the king will plough it for you!*
> *Dumuzi the king will plough it for you!*
> [Kramer, 1969]

A royal hymn from the Isin-Larsa period in the late third millennium BCE describes in the most intimate detail how a ruler named Iddin-Dagan playing the part of Dumuzi celebrated the Marriage with his priestess.

The king joins Inana for the Sacred Marriage rite. In the palace, the house of counsel of the land, the lock of all countries ... for the 'Lady of the Palace' they have installed a dais, [and] the king that is the god dwells with her – so as to care for the life of all countries, to inspect the first right day, to perfect the *me* on the day of no moon, at the New Year, on the day of the ritual, they laid out the bed for my lady. They purified the bed-straw with cedar essence, and laid it down for her bed. Beside it they arranged her bedspread. When the bedspread had joyfully improved the bed, my lady bathed for the pure loins, she bathed for the loins of the king, she bathed for the loins of Iddin-Dagan. Holy Inana rubbed herself with soap, she sprinkled oil and cedar essence on the ground. The king went to the pure loins with head high, with head high he went to the loins of Inana. Ama-usum-gal-ana [a local name for Dumuzi] shares the bed with her, in her pure loins he is entertained.

[Romer, 1965, pp. 133–4, and Reisman, 1971, pp. 190–1]

There is archaeological evidence for the existence of the *giparu*. In the 1920s the archaeologist Sir Leonard Woolley found what he believed to be a Sacred Marriage chamber at Ur dating from the end of the Third Dynasty, about 2000 BCE. Nearly half of the room was taken up by a low platform on which, according to some inscriptions, a ceremonial bedstead may have stood. Mass-produced terracotta models of the bed, many of them probably left behind as temple offerings, have been discovered at various Sumerian sites, and metal plaques embossed with the same scene have been found in Assyrian excavations. A model bed in the British Museum, with two naked figures lying in an intimate embrace described in the legends of the Sacred Marriage, has an odd feature in that the legs are shorter at the foot, allowing the bed to tilt forward giving a clearer view to its audience.

The Babylonian high priestess taking the part of the fertility goddess, Ishtar, served as consort of the western Asiatic moon god, Sin, and the *entum* Enheduana called herself the 'wife of Nanna' (the moon god's old Sumerian name before it was changed to Sin). Ishtar was intimately involved with the demise and restoration of life reflecting the moon's cycle of waxing and waning, its resurrection causing its devotees to be born again, and most of her priestesses also served Sin. Here a possible link emerges with the Jewish pagan tradition because it is inferred that Aaron's sister, Miriam, may have been a votary of the moon god.

Then came the children of Israel, even the whole congregation, into the desert of Zin in the first month: and the people abode in Kadesh; and Miriam died there, and was buried there. [Num. 20.1]

The Book of Numbers implies that the 'wilderness of Zin' was in the extreme south of Palestine but Zin may be a corruption of Sin, which would make the place sacred to the moon god. The translators of the Greek Septuagint and the Latin Vulgate thought this was so because they used the same form for both names. The historian Josephus believed that Miriam had been buried on a mountain called Sin, possibly Mount Sinai, at the time of the new moon in the month Xanthicus which equates with the first day of Nisan, the beginning of the Mesopotamian year [*Antiq.* IV.78]. In due course evidence will be brought that in the Middle Ages Miriam's namesake, Mary the Virgin, also gained close symbolic links with the Moon.

Ishtar, as well as being the Queen of Heaven revered by pagans and pagan Jews alike and said to be the 'mother of men' and 'mother of gods', was also the consort of her son, the dying-and-rising god, Tammuz. Why Tammuz played this role is unclear since there are no surviving records or heroic myths in which he features strongly. But he became the immortal son and lover who impregnated the womb of the goddess with new life and, like Jesus Christ, he was commonly envisaged as 'the shepherd' of his people.

> *I cast my eye over all the people*
> *Called Dumuzi to the godship of the land.*
> *Dumuzi the beloved of Enlil*
> *My mother holds him ever dear*
> *My father exalts him.*

[Kramer, 1969]

The Marriage was practised in Mesopotamia over many hundreds of years. A temple festival record from the end of the fourth century BCE confirms that it was taking place officially in Babylon as late as the Hellenistic period, although not necessarily in the form of a physical act of sex. The festival 'round' included a ritual known as the *hasadu* which emulated the physical rite but perhaps in a more symbolic form with statues replacing living players. Whether or not an old-style consummation took place in Babylonia, records suggest that the ceremony was conducted amidst splendour and great excitement in the *bit giparu* house on the temple field.

> In month Kin-dinana-ulul the work of Ishtar ... the Mistress of gods purifies her body in the divine river. In Eternuna ... she gives directions to Sin and Ningal ... the completed (sanctuaries?) they oversee the purification rites of Anu and Ishtar ... of the statue, the likeness of Ishtar with the star of Anu ... its lighting up shows forth ... the king (?) in the kingship of heaven, he establishes a holy dwelling. A ha-da-su-du was arranged ... the lovers ... purification ... love making.   [McEwan, 1981, p. 177]

Until recently no proof had emerged from Mesopotamia that a *raison d'être* for the enactment of the Sacred Marriage was the conception of a Sacred King. Ostensibly the Marriage was intended as a plea to the mother goddess to restore the bounty of the living earth and its people after the dearth of winter. None the less sexual intercourse had natural consequences and in the heroic mythological age, the 'once-upon-a-time era', Dumuzi (the predecessor of Tammuz) is said to have been the product of a union between Lugalbanda, a great warrior-king of Sumer, and his goddess Inana. Dumuzi then became the incestuous lover of his mother in order to preserve the sexual equation between immortal 'ever-virgin' and mortal god-king.

The more verifiable 23rd-century-BCE king, Gudea of Lagash, announced that he had 'no mother and no father and was the son of the goddess of Lagash'. The god-king, Sargon the Great, left an inscription that his mother was 'of lowly birth' and that he 'knew not his father', the latter term being a frequently used euphemism for divine parentage. Sargon, as we have discovered, was among the first recorded rulers to have made one of his daughters a priestess of the cult and he may have introduced a tradition whereby only girls of high birth became Inana votaries. Before his reign, these special priestesses seem to have been drawn from the ranks of common people and the reference to 'lowly birth' can only suggest that Sargon's mother had been not an earthly royal but a temple votary taking the part of a heavenly queen.

The most direct evidence linking the Sacred Marriage with the birth of the Sacred King relates to Ur Nammu who reigned from 2113 BCE as the first king of the Third Dynasty at Ur. A recently deciphered text describes how the gods 'Rewarded Ur Nammu for his piety and ensured his royal line by giving him a son, born of the *entum* priestess of Nanna in Nippur.'

The impressions brought back by the exiles from Babylon did not fade readily as the years passed. The Jewish apocryphal author, Jeremy, writing in about 307 or 306 BCE, more than two hundred years after the end of the Exile, was still describing the richness and authority of the Babylonian idols and the priestesses of the fertility cult on whom the priests bestowed gifts of silver and gold.

> But now shall ye see in Babylon gods of silver and gold and of wood, borne upon shoulders which cause the nations to fear.
>
> [Jeremy 4]

> And taking gold, as it were for a virgin that loveth to go gay, they make crowns for the heads of their gods; and sometimes also the priests convey from their gods gold and silver, to bestow it upon themselves; and will even give thereof to the common harlots.
>
> [Jeremy 9]

In the centuries between the return from exile in Babylon in 539 BCE and the era of Roman occupation, during which Mary was born, the Jewish people in Palestine carried on a scarcely diminished love-affair with paganism and the fertility cult of Mesopotamia. It is a situation that has been stoutly denied by some Jewish historians. In his contribution to a comprehensive study, *A History of the Jewish Peoples*, Menahem Stern persists with the illusion of a people solidly behind Jewish orthodoxy and monotheism.

The outstanding characteristic of the Jewish religion during the Second Temple era [that constructed under the sponsorship of Cyrus the Great after the return from Babylonian Exile] was the exclusive predominance of its monotheistic belief in the same form that had developed in the preceding generations ... Palestinian Jewry remained unswervingly faithful to the Jewish religion throughout the generations after the Hasmonean Revolt. Even the most extreme accusers did not include idolatry among the sins for which the generation of the destruction of the Temple [by the Babylonians] was castigated.   [Ben-Sasson, 1976]

Stern's statement may make comfortable reading but it is not supported by known facts. The message of Yahwist solidarity that permeates the Jewish canon (under Christianity the Old Testament) is palpably inaccurate but the illusion became increasingly important through the periods of Greek and Roman domination. The Old Testament stood for something more than a chronicle of Jewish history and a book of social and moral law. It became a rallying focus for Jewish nationalism. Jewish identity was sustained through the very existence of the Bible. So the books of the Old Testament have to be read with one eye on the fact that they were also an exercise in political jingoism. Much as Karl Marx extolled the theoretical benefits of a classless society in *Das Kapital*, so the Old Testament writers gave us the ideals of Judaism, as wished for by the Yahwist establishment, but not necessarily the reality experienced by the common people.

In the era of the Patriarchs, and their more long-term interest in the pagan cults around them, the Hebrews were overtly polytheistic. The religion of pre-Exilic Israel was, at best, *henotheistic* (recognising the existence of a supreme but not unique god) and as the Book of Exodus reveals, even the most die-hard Yahwists did not reject the existence of other deities but believed that only their God was universal.

Thou shalt have no other gods before me ... Thou shalt not bow down thyself to them, nor serve them. [Exod. 20.3ff.]

Religious unity during and after the Babylonian Exile is also largely a myth. The prophet Jeremiah was one of those few intellectuals who remained in Jerusalem with the poorest section of the community before he was obliged to flee to Egypt in 586 BCE after the assassination of the reformist Babylonian governor of Judaea, Gedeliah. Jeremiah expressed concern about pagan leanings among the exiles.

Let not your prophets and your diviners, that be in the midst of you, deceive you, neither hearken to your dreams which ye cause to be dreamed. For they prophesy falsely unto you in my name: I have not sent them, saith the Lord ... Because ye have said, The Lord hath raised us up prophets in Babylon: Know that thus saith the Lord of the king that sitteth upon the throne of David, and of all the people that dwelleth in this city, and of your brethren that are not gone forth with you into captivity; Thus saith the Lord of hosts; Behold, I will send upon them the sword, the famine, and the pestilence, and will make them like vile figs, that cannot be eaten, they are so evil. [Jer. 29.8ff.]

Jeremiah was probably right to be concerned because the restoration community carried these 'evil fashions' back to Jerusalem. A late section of the Book of Isaiah, probably added in the second century BCE, leaves little doubt that pagan rites were being observed among the Jews who had returned to Judaea.

I have spread out my hands all the day unto a rebellious people, which walketh in a way that was not good, after their own thoughts; A people that provoketh me to anger continually to my face; that sacrificeth in gardens, and burneth incense upon altars of brick; ... Your iniquities, and the iniquities of your fathers together, saith the Lord, which have burned incense upon the mountains, and blasphemed me upon the hills: therefore will I measure their former work into their bosom. [Isa. 65.2ff.]

While it looks forward to the messianic coming, the Book of Daniel supports this suggestion. Probably written at the turn of the first century BCE by an unknown writer of the Maccabean period, it gives a similar picture of widespread pagan apostasy in Jewish society.

> And he [the Messiah] shall confirm the covenant with many for one week: and in the midst of the week he shall cause the sacrifice and the oblation to cease, and for the overspreading of abominations he shall make it desolate, even until the consummation, and that determined shall be poured upon the desolate. [Dan. 9.27]

In reality, the Holy Land remained plagued with political and religious turmoil. Palestine was, as it still is, a region ripe for plucking over which others watched with a greedy eye. It benefits from a long, strategically valuable coastline on the Mediterranean and it has enjoyed great natural resources including, in biblical times, valuable cedar forests which were notably lacking either in ancient Egypt or Mesopotamia. Judaea, as it became known after the return of the Jews from the Babylonian Exile, was potentially affluent. The countryside was lusher and more fertile than it is today and, with agriculture very much the mainstay of the economy, most of the Palestinian population were farmers. A contemporary, if glamorised, picture is drawn in the correspondence of an anonymous Alexandrian Jew, the so-called 'Letter of Aristeas', written some time between 180 and 145 BCE and reading like a tourist brochure:

> For great is the energy they expend on the tillage of the soil. The land is thickly planted with a multitude of olive trees, with crops of corn and pulse, with vines too, and there is an abundance of honey. Other kinds of fruit trees and date palms cannot be compared with these. There are cattle of all kinds in great quantity and

a rich pasturage for them.   [Ben-Sasson, 1969, p. 232]

Judaea had also become a land of artisans and craftsmen. In the Aristeas letter, Jerusalem was 'a city of many trades' and, because of its geographical position, Syrio-Palestine was now enjoying the benefits of booming international business. Trade routes to and from the Far East and the various Arab nations closer to home were bustling and the Italian markets were beginning to open up, looking towards Europe. When the coastal cities were taken over, Judaea also gained control of a lucrative glass manufacturing trade in Phoenicia.

Any material advantage, however, was offset by almost constant political and military strife. A weakening of national identity beset Judaea and this, above all, resulted from dilution of the Yahwist faith. The influence of earlier dominant powers in the region – Egypt, Assyria, Babylonia and Persia – had been to the detriment of Yahwism, but in the fourth century BCE a new and equally strong force, not particularly evident from a reading of the biblical texts, descended on the region. In 323 BCE, after an unsuccessful incursion by the Phoenicians, Alexander of Macedonia ousted the Persians who had controlled Palestine since the fall of Babylon and introduced Classical Greek culture under what has been termed 'Hellenisation'. Alexander the Great's premature death later that year opened the door briefly to one other military influence, the Ptolemies of Egypt, but the Macedonians came back in 200 BCE in the shape of the Seleucid dynasty and their influence remained dominant until Roman times.

Hellenisation amounted to accepting new secular ways, but it also led to the introduction of Greek religious and philosophical concepts – paganism with a fresh slant. At first Hellenism was a vogue of towns and cities where the Jewish upper classes, largely the priesthood, began to socialise freely with the settlers and many of the ancient Semitic communities took on distinctly Greek colours. In the rural backwaters change was less immediate and villages retained the old traditional ways, but these had already been deeply affected by earlier influence from Mesopotamia to the east and country folk showed less than wholehearted enthusiasm for Yahwism. Eventually Greek beliefs, including pantheons of gods and goddesses, sacred marriages, sacred kings and the rest, became added to what was already, in reality, a tortuous religious mishmash.

The Seleucid government heavily endorsed Hellenisation which, on the whole, amounted to a gentle introduction of European pagan culture. The infusion brought certain benefits because the Greek landlords employed more efficient methods of farming that produced higher crop yields but this was offset by stiff government levies. The local Jewish populace enjoyed few privileges and shouldered a punitive taxation system. The financial burden was partially relaxed for a time during the heyday of the Seleucids but when the dynasty began to suffer defeats, its leaders also demanded increased funding which resulted in more high taxation.

Hellenisation also brought idolatry to the forefront again. The second century Seleucid despot, Antiochus Epiphanes, encouraged the Jewish people to pursue pagan practices much as they had done in the past and, according to a staunchly partisan Jewish historian named Jason of Cyrene, the response amounted to widespread support and enthusiasm.

> And the king wrote unto his whole kingdom, that all should be one people, and that every one should give up his [religious] usages. And all the nation acquiesced in accordance with the command of the king. And many in Israel took delight in his [form of] worship and they began sacrificing to idols and profaned the sabbath. Furthermore the king sent letters ... that they should build high places and sacred groves and shrines for idols ... and many of the people joined themselves unto them, all those who had forsaken the law; these did evil in the land, and caused Israel to hide in all manner of hiding places.   [1 Macc. 1.41 ff.]

Jason draws contemporary and graphic cameos of Jewish

popular paganism. He relates, for example, how ordinary Jews offered sacrifice to the 'deities of the street', the images of Greek gods which stood in the porches of the houses [1 Macc. 1.55]. There exists, however, far more damning evidence. The second Book of Maccabees reports that during Antiochus Epiphanes' reign the temple was more or less given over to the pagan fertility rites of gentiles.

> Harsh and utterly grievous was the onslaught of evil. For the temple was filled with debauchery and revelling by the Gentiles who dallied with harlots and had intercourse with women within the sacred precincts, and besides brought in things for sacrifice that were unfit.
>
> [2 Macc. 6.3ff.]

The changes in religious practice were allegedly beyond Jewish control, yet in reality they gained tacit support not only from the rank and file but also from influential quarters inside the Jewish community. The first Book of Maccabees, probably completed by Jason of Cyrene during the last quarter of the second century BCE, is almost certainly true to history. He names the 'lawless men' who backed Antiochus Epiphanes as Tobiads, a non-priestly family of Judaean origin whose rise began in southern Gilead before the Babylonian Exile and who became influential as tax gatherers in Jerusalem in about the mid-third century BCE.

> In those days there came forth out of Israel lawless men and persuaded many, saying: 'Let us go and make a covenant with the nations that are round about us; for since we separated ourselves from them many evils have come upon us'. And the saying appeared good in their eyes; and as certain of the peoples were eager [to carry this out] they went to the king and he gave them authority to introduce the customs of the Gentiles. And they built them a gymnasium in Jerusalem according to the manner of the Gentiles. They also submitted themselves to uncircumcision, and repudiated the holy covenant; yea, they joined themselves to the Gentiles, and

sold themselves to do evil.'   [1 Macc. 1.11]

Suggestion that pagan interest was peculiar to Antiochus Epiphanes' administration can be discounted since the picture did not
change greatly after his departure.

> In the one hundred and fifty first [162–161 BCE] year Demetrius
> the son of Seleucus came forth from Rome ... and there came unto
> him all the lawless and ungodly men of Israel; and Alcimus led
> them desiring to be [high] priest. And Alcimus strove for the
> high priesthood. And there were gathered unto him all they that
> troubled their people, and they got the mastery of the land of Judah
> and did great hurt in Israel. And Judas saw all the mischief that
> Alcimus and his company had wrought among the children of
> Israel, worse than [that of] the Gentiles.   [1 Macc. 7.1,21ff.]

Not all of the changes were peaceful and, at its more draconian,
Hellenisation resulted in various 'abominations' that were less
than popular. The mood of many Jews began to darken when,
in 169 BCE, Antiochus Epiphanes pillaged the so-called Second
Temple which had been built over the ruins of Solomon's sanctuary
destroyed by the Babylonians. Antiochus turned an acquisitive
eye to the altar, the precious vessels and offerings, the veil, the
chandelier and other valuable objects, many of them either crafted
in solid gold or plated with gold. Two years later the worship of
the Greek high god, Zeus, was enforced in the sanctuary and
lawful Jewish sacrifice was disallowed, a state of affairs which
persisted for several years. Many Jews viewed the pillaging of the
Temple treasures as little less than rape and this act of blatant
piracy led to the first armed clashes with the Seleucids.

In the mid-second century the Hasmoneans, an influential
priestly family, raised an army and declared war, triggering a
backlash that was eventually to throw the Macedonian rulers out
of Palestine. It has been said by Menahem Stern that the eventual
outcome of the Hasmonean campaign was helped by 'the bound-

less loyalty of the Jewish masses to their religion' but this is modern propaganda at work. The revolt was far from solid and the militants who took up arms probably did so in a mood of nationalist fervour and in reaction to the indignities forced on them by the secular Seleucid rulers rather more than from a sense of pious dedication to the Torah.

The response of the Jewish people to perennial subjugation and enforced religious changes was a deepening frustration, a mood laid bare in one of their most poignant hymns, composed at about the time of the decisive Battle of Panium against the Seleucids in 200 BCE.

> Deliver me out of the mire, and let me not sink: let me be delivered from them that hate me, and out of the deep waters. Let not the waterflood overflow me, neither let the deep swallow me up, and let not the pit shut her mouth upon me. Hear me, O Lord; for thy lovingkindness is good: turn unto me according to the multitude of thy tender mercies. And hide not thy face from thy servant; for I am in trouble: hear me speedily. Draw nigh unto my soul, and redeem it: deliver me because of mine enemies. Thou hast known my reproach, and my shame, and my dishonour: mine adversaries are all before thee. Reproach hath broken my heart; and I am full of heaviness: and I looked for some to take pity, but there was none; and for comforters, but I found none. [Ps. 69.14–20]

According to the first Book of Maccabees, by no means all Jews followed this line. Many members of the intellectual classes, including the Tobiads, remained pro-Seleucid and other influential members of the community, such as the Judaean High Priest, Alcimus, who ostensibly supported the Hasmonean cause, still kept strong private sympathies with Hellenism, particularly while the Seleucid army remained a force to be reckoned with.

The Jewish war against the Seleucids was won in 164 BCE and the victorious Hasmonean general, Judas Maccabeus, restored the Temple and its trappings. The rich farmlands in Galilee and

Samaria, abandoned for centuries first to Asian then Greek migrant landlords, were returned to Jewish control and the name 'Greater Judaea' came to represent all of Palestine. New Jewish settlers took advantage of two valuable export commodities in the shape of the balsam groves of the Jordan valley and the thriving fishing industry around the Sea of Galilee.

By the turn of the first century Jerusalem had become the hub both of government and intellectual and religious life, but Galilee, separated from Jerusalem by Samaria, had kept a rustic character almost wholly committed to agriculture. In pre-Exilic times the Judahite rule in Jerusalem had largely neglected Galilee in political terms. A typical example had been the gift of twenty Galilean cities to Hiram of Phoenicia in exchange for supplies for the construction of Solomon's Temple [1 Kings 9.11ff.]. After the Exile the sophisticated Judaeans in the south appear to have viewed the north as a cultural 'disaster zone', heaving with superstitious peasants and dark goings-on and improved only by a few newly built Greek cities. The Galileans were traditionally labelled as hot-headed revolutionaries who had absorbed too much foreign culture, over too long a period, ever to be considered reliable Yahwists. Maccabees records how, in 164 BCE, Simon Maccabeus was obliged to retaliate against hostile pagans in Galilee [1 Macc. 5.9ff.] and Josephus describes its inhabitants as being 'inured to war from infancy'. He also details them rebelling against the rule of Herodians. E. P. Sanders suggests in his book *Jesus and Judaism* that many Galileans of Mary's generation were little more than forced recruits to Yahwism. Their interests were driven by expediency, and even if they were loyal Jews of long standing it is impossible to judge how strictly and thoroughly monotheistic they were.

The Galileans and Samaritans were not alone, however, in their religious ambivalence because the Hasmoneans brought little more consensus to Jewish religion in any other part of Judaea. While improving the political and economic position, they also effectively changed the entire structure of government. This in itself meant religious change. Until the Exile to Babylon, Yahwism had been under the supreme control of the king as the head of the Temple hierarchy and the clergy were his civil servants. The title of high priest, *hakkohen haggadol*, had not yet come into being and with limited exceptions, all noted in the second Book of Kings and believed to be late alterations of the text, the pre-Exilic biblical writings refer only to a 'chief priest', the *kohen harosh*. Allegedly descended from Sadoq, the first holder of priestly office in the reign of Solomon, it was the *kohen harosh* who supervised the Jerusalem Temple work force [Num. 25.10–13]. After the Exile the high priest, a government appointee, effectively stood in for the abolished monarchy, becoming the religious and civil head of the Jewish community complete with all the royal paraphernalia. Under the Hasmoneans this all-powerful cleric acted as king in both name and authority [Hag. 1.1,12,14; 2.2,4]. The *hakkohen haggadol* was strongly resented by those who considered the only legitimate claimant to the Judaean throne to be a descendant of David and so became a key factor in the way that attitudes developed.

The episode of Jewish history finally leading up to the birth of Mary was no less fraught nor did pagan interest wane. By the first century BCE sizeable sections of the clerical and lay population still followed a religion that amounted, at best, to a hotch-potch of Yahwist and pagan tradition. Uncovering the details of how this blend of culture was treated represents the next chapter in the search for the real Mary.

FIVE

The Promise

The last chapter in the background of Mary's life brings us to the period in time when it was prophesied that a *messiah* would be born to the Jewish nation. The prediction was not the famous utterance of Isaiah that begins 'A Virgin shall conceive' but one made many centuries earlier by the Patriarch Jacob.

> The sceptre shall not depart from Judah, nor a lawgiver from between his feet, until Shiloh come; and unto him shall the gathering of the people be. [Gen. 49.10]

On his deathbed in Egypt, Jacob had foretold that the coming of the *messiah* would take place when Israel was under the rule of a foreign king, one not of the tribe of Judah. In Jacob's obscure augury 'Shiloh' seems to be a corruption of *siloh*, an old Hebrew word with the same meaning as *messiah* or 'anointed one'. It is not thought to be related to the place-name Shiloh and it was perhaps to avoid confusion that, in the Greek Septuagint version of the Old Testament, the term was amended to *sello*, meaning 'the one to whom it belongs'. The expression 'a lawgiver from between his feet' means a ruler who is one of Judah's succession. It has been well established, from various biblical passages in which the expression also occurs, that 'between his feet' is a euphemism for male genitalia. This is made clear by Isaiah in a warning of retribution against the Israelites for their sins.

In the same day shall the Lord shave with a razor that is hired,

namely, by them beyond the river, by the king of Assyria, the head
and the hair of the feet.   [Isa. 7.20]

An apposite comment to this effect is also contained in Ezekiel.

Thou hast ... opened thy feet to every one that passed by, and
multiplied thy whoredoms.   [Ezek. 16.25]

The fifty-year period before Mary's birth saw the collapse of
the Hasmonean dynasty. Its leadership eventually fell out with the
strictly orthodox, scholarly class of Jews, the Pharisees, because of
increasing tyranny and, in Pharisaic opinion, a serious neglect of
the holy way of life. The ancient Jewish historian, Josephus, reveals
in *Antiquities* that under John Hyrcanus, the autocratic king of
Judaea from 135–104 BCE, the Hasmoneans were seen by the
Pharisees to have abused religious principles that had been laid
down in the Torah. The Hasmonean dynasty had also pushed for
still further integration between Jewish, Hellenistic and Babylonian families, strongly resented by many conservatives.

The Romans effectively ended Judaean independence. The
Consul Pompey laid siege to Jerusalem in 63 BCE in order to
quell an internal feud between two ruling Hasmonean brothers,
Hyrcanus and Aristobulus and, until his removal by Julius Caesar
in 48 BCE, held the reins of power in Syrio-Palestine. Caesar took
a more congenial attitude towards the Jews and the Hasmonean
dynasty clung to nominal power for a while, but the breathing
space was short-lived. The Hasmoneans were dragged into the
losing side of a civil war between his murderers and Mark Antony
following Caesar's assassination in 44 BCE. They were stripped of
authority in all but name when the Roman army marched back
into Palestine in 37 BCE to put down an invasion of the eastern
provinces of the Roman Empire by Parthians from a region south-
west of the Caspian Sea.

To the north and east, Syria became a Roman province. Judaea
was allowed to retain a degree of self-rule under the control of the

powerful new Herodian clan. Coming from the Idumean region in the south, these foreigners (in the sense of not being Jews) had ingratiated themselves as staunch supporters of Rome and in 40 BCE, some twenty years before the birth of Mary, the son of the first Palestinian governor, Herod Antipas, had been rewarded with the effective control of Palestine. Much against popular sentiment he was decorated with the title of 'King Herod the Great' and it was under his authority that the last of the Hasmonean leaders, Antigonus Mattathias (40–37 BCE), was thrown out of office.

Herod the Great, little more than a Roman lackey backed by the legions, soothed his personal fears of insurrection by quashing virtually all civil rights. He deprived the traditional Jewish government, the *sanhedrin*, of political power and set up a privy council of his own. He also continued to support Hellenism by backing a new and powerful élite made up of leading Jewish and Greek families, and ended the strongly linked roles of king and high priest, another fundamental principle of Judaic religion at the time. This resulted in virtual anarchy whereby no less than twenty-eight incumbents held the post of *hakkohen haggadol* in quick succession between Herod's coronation in 37 BCE and the fall of Jerusalem to the Roman army in 70 CE.

The Herodians were another unwelcome imposition on an already cynical Jewish populace which had been forced to accept them against the clear wish of the majority, but the effect went deeper. The Roman army backing the Herodians was pagan to a man and its invincibility reinforced the message that paganism equated with success. The Jews loathed foreign domination but, as we have seen in the writings of Jeremiah, many believed that the gods of their pagan masters were accountably more likely to offer protection and military victory than the unseen deity of Moses. Pagan practice thus continued apace among sections of the Jewish community. We do not always have clear details of what this practice involved because, like so much from the Jewish pagan perspective, records have been destroyed. What remains is the fulsome criticism of its more orthodox opponents.

Until the post-Exilic period, Jeremiah had been one of the few writers to be specific in his accusations linking the *massebah* and *asherah* (the symbolic images of the fertility goddess and her consort) in the 'high places' with sexual rites involving prostitution.

> For of old time I have broken thy yoke, and burst thy bands; and thou saidst, I will not transgress; when upon every high hill and under every green tree thou wanderest, playing the harlot.
>
> [Jer. 2.20]

After the capture of Jerusalem by Pompey in 63 BCE, however, an anonymous group of devout Jews compiled a collection of manuscripts, the Psalms of Solomon. Written originally in Hebrew, they were then copied into more accessible Greek and Syriac for public consumption. These manuscripts provide clear evidence that ritualised sex had penetrated the heart of Jewish society fifty years before Mary's birth. The priesthood was indulging in a catalogue of religious deviance and earning ridicule from the Roman authorities.

> They set up the sons of Jerusalem [the priests] for derision because of her prostitutes. Everyone passing by entered in broad daylight. They derided their lawless actions even in comparison to what they themselves were doing; before the sun they held up their unrighteousness to contempt. And the daughters of Jerusalem were available to all, according to your judgements, because they defiled themselves with improper intercourse. [Ps. Sol. 2.11ff.]

> Why are you sitting in the council of the devout [the priestly Sanhedrin] you profaner? ... excessive in words, excessive in appearance above everyone, he who is harsh in words in condemning sinners at judgement. And his hand is the first one against him as if in zeal, yet he himself is guilty of a variety of sins and intemperance. His eyes are on every woman indiscriminately, his

tongue lies when swearing a contract. At night and in hiding he
sins as if no one saw. With his eyes he speaks to every woman of
illicit affairs; he is quick to enter graciously every house as though
innocent. May God remove from the devout those who live in
hypócrisy.   [Ps. Sol. 4.1ff.]

The allegations made by the authors are severe and works like
the Psalms of Solomon would hardly have drawn attention to the
'profaners in the council of the devout' if backsliding priests did
not exist. The Psalms even include prayers intended to preserve
the authors from those 'honeytraps' into which others were falling.

Save me, O Lord, from the wicked, sinful woman and from every
woman who sets traps for the simple, and let not the beauty of a
wicked woman lead me astray.   [Ps. Sol. 16.7ff.]

The authors are thought by biblical scholars such as R. B. Wright
of Temple University, Philadelphia, not to have been from among
more hard-line groups like Pharisees or Essenes. They were probably pious moderates, their accusations directed against the last of
the Hasmonean priesthood which, they alleged, was corrupt and
lawless, sanctioning and co-operating in acts of prostitution within
the Temple precincts. It was effectively this same priestly caste
that operated in Herodian times, albeit overseen by civil servants
without strong sympathies for the Hasmoneans.

A later apocryphal work, the *Testament of Moses*, while hostile
on the record of the Hasmoneans, also attacks the Herodians. It
describes Herod the Great as 'a wanton king, rash and perverse,
who will judge them as they deserve'. Giving weight to critical
review by placing it in the mouth of an ancient sage, the *Testament*
finds Moses lecturing to his successor, Joshua, and it repeats the
accusation of sacred prostitution. From the safety of hindsight the
Testament of Moses predicted renewed apostasy in the post-Exilic
period. It also warned that, in the era of Roman rule, 'wives will
be given to the gods of the nations'. This refers to a traditional

Babylonian practice whereby, according to the writer Herodotus, it was the duty of every Babylonian woman to prostitute herself once in her life to a stranger within the precinct of the temple of the fertility goddess Ishtar. The dating of the *Testament of Moses* is significant. It was compiled in the late first or early second century CE, which means (assuming that its subject matter was topical) that ritual prostitutes existed in Jewish society during Mary's lifetime.

The specific religious centre in which the prostitution took place is not clear-cut. The Psalms of Solomon emphasises the Jerusalem Temple, probably because its authors were residents of the city, but other sacred places were also recognised by Jews, during the period of the monarchy and later. They included local shrines and several important sanctuaries. Information is hard to come by because those who supported the legitimacy of the state temple (and refused to acknowledge any other) drew up the records. But Israelite temples were built at Shechem, Bethel, Mambre, Beersheba and Gerizim in Samaria. Mambre was still a place of pilgrimage for Jews in Roman times. Josephus records that the Maccabean leader, John Hyrcanus, destroyed the Samaritan temple at Mount Gerizim in 129 BCE. The Gospel of John implies that it was rebuilt and was in use at least until the first century CE. A Samaritan woman who defended the religious authority of Gerizim challenged Jesus.

> Our fathers worshipped in this mountain; and ye say that in Jerusalem is the place where men ought to worship. Jesus saith unto her, Woman, believe me, the hour cometh, when ye shall neither in this mountain, nor yet at Jerusalem, worship the Father.
>
> [John 4.20,21]

The sanctuary at Bethel may have been more important. Bethel, which was located in the northern hill country of Ephraim, south of Shiloh, was the place where the Patriarch Abraham had built an altar and where Jereboam founded his cult of calf worship. During the reforms of Josiah it was partly destroyed but seems to have been spared further plunder after the fall of Jerusalem to the Babylonians. Zechariah implies that an important Jewish religious centre survived somewhere in the north when, in an obtuse comment, he refers to envoys from Jerusalem going north: 'Behold, these that go toward the north country have quieted my spirit in the north country.' [Zech. 6.8]. It is possible that he is describing the Bethel sanctuary whose priests may have stayed on as a dominant religious force in Palestine during the Exile. Zechariah goes on to note that in 518 BCE envoys were dispatched to 'the house of God ... to pray before the Lord, And to speak unto the priests which were in the house of the Lord of hosts' [Zech. 7.3]. This visit took place during the reign of the Persian King Darius the Great, but it was he who partly financed the rebuilding of the Jerusalem Temple and, at that time, it was still in ruins. So Zechariah must have referred to a different sanctuary at which the Sadoquites who returned from exile were obliged to negotiate with a rival priestly group. Zechariah's comment supports evidence already discussed, from the Book of Ezra, that when the northerners had their offer of help to rebuild the Jerusalem Temple rejected they started to make life politically difficult for the returning exiles.

Whichever temple or temples are implicated, we know from the Psalms of Solomon and from the Books of Kings that the Jerusalem Temple had frequently been associated with whores. The possibility exists, of course, that this institution, the seat of the judiciary and the focus of Jewish piety, had become open to ordinary commercial whoring – women from the streets practising freely among the senior ranks of the priesthood. But we also know from Kings, and the writing of Jeremiah, that the Jerusalem Temple housed the *asherah* of the fertility goddess, which means that it must have had its attendant priestesses. Babylonian records establish that the duties of the priestesses included looking after the day-to-day comfort of the goddess whose image stood in the Ishtar temples in Babylon, praying for the life of the king as the temporal symbol of the nation's prosperity and managing the estates belonging to the cloister of priestesses. It is more probable, therefore, that any prostitution taking place at the core of religious life and cult was centred round devotion to the *asherah* and the activities of sacred prostitutes.

Allegations of Jewish interest in pagan fertility rites during the first century are supported by evidence found in a source separate from the biblical and apocryphal texts, the Mishnah, one of the principal holy books of Judaism upon which the Palestinian and Babylonian Talmuds are drawn. The Mishnah purports to be a collection of sayings bearing the names of authorities who lived before the destruction of Jerusalem in 70 CE but, more accurately, it amounts to a code of descriptive rules compiled towards the end of the second century CE by Jewish intellectuals. Large sections are taken up with warnings against various kinds of improper conduct, many of which carry sexual overtones, and the extent of the caveats against such aberrations tends to provide a convenient rule of thumb to measure their significance.

The regulations include a prohibition of bathhouses devoted to the worship of the Greek goddess of sexual love, Aphrodite [*Abod. Zar.* 3.4.A], but among the more damning indictments a section called the *Abodah Zara* focuses on a long, perhaps obsessive examination of the *asherah* including practical tips on the identification of the cult object and a list of the prohibitions. Ostensibly it refers to paganism taking place in village communities, but nothing suggests that caution about the *asherah* was directed exclusively at outmoded 'backwater' remnants of pagan society and the compilers are unlikely to have emphasised their proscriptions if most Jews had been 'cured' of interest in paganism.

There are three kinds of *asherahs*:
> a tree which one planted to begin with for idolatry – lo, this is prohibited.
> [if] he chopped it and trimmed it for idolatry, and it sprouted afresh, he may remove that which sprouted afresh.

[if] he set up an idol under it and then annulled it, lo, this is permitted.

What is an *asherah*? Any tree under which is located an idol.

Any [tree] which people worship.

One should not sit in its [an *asherah*'s] shade, but if he sat in its shade he is unclean.

And he should not pass underneath it, but if he passed underneath it, he is unclean.

If one has taken pieces of wood from [an *asherah*], they are prohibited for benefit.

How does one desecrate [an *asherah*]? [If] one trimmed it or pruned it, took from it a branch or twig, even a leaf –

lo, this constitutes desecration.

[if] one has trimmed it for the good of the tree, it remains forbidden.

[if he trimmed it] not for the good of the tree, it is permitted.

The *Abodah Zara* confirms that the *asherah* was wooden, either a consecrated living tree or a man-made object, and a separate section, the *Orlah*, lists a miscellany of forbidden items associated with the *asherah* or likely to be misused in its construction.

Leaves, young sprouts, sap of vines and budding berries [of vines] are permitted [for use] under [the laws of] orlah ... but they are forbidden [for use] under [the prohibition of] the *asherah*.

[*Orlah* 1.7–8]

A stolen or dried up palm branch is invalid. And one deriving from an *asherah* or an apostate town is invalid ... A stolen or dried-up myrtle branch is invalid. And one deriving from an *asherah* or an apostate town is invalid ... A stolen or dried up citron is invalid. And one deriving from an *asherah* or from an apostate town is invalid.

[*Sukk* 3.1–3,5]

A nest which is up at the top of a tree which has been consecrated is not available for benefit, but is not subject to the law of sacrilege.

And that which is on an *asherah* tree one may flick it off with a
reed. [*Me'il* 3.8]

The *Abodah Zara* specifically forbids the sale to pagans of fir cones.
This ruling might have been made on grounds of protecting a
vital economic interest since, in biblical times, the products of
Palestine's extensive cedar forests were something of a rare commodity in the Near East. The emphasis on cones, however, suggests that it was to thwart rituals of anointing similar to those once
seen in Assyria. Had the prohibition been commercially driven it
would have been against the sale of seeds.

Mary's generation was familiar with all this and the mass of
evidence points to numbers of her Galilean contemporaries
engaging in pagan worship. It is unfair to suggest that all the
religious criticism levelled at Jewry in the first century, most from
within its own ranks, was focused on rejection of monotheism in
favour of paganism. Some of the aggravation concerned failure to
observe the instructions laid down in the Torah – anything from
improper conduct of sacrifice, purity, cleanliness, relaxation of laws
concerning consumption of unauthorised foods and the misuse of
Temple funds. Criticism was also fuelled by sectarian rivalries.
The dominant Pharisees demanded a way of life based on abstention, the Zealot extremists who supported them were prepared to
fight for political freedom, the Sadducees tended towards ostentation, and the penchant of the Essenes for severe asceticism and
isolation placed them at the other extreme.

None the less much of the complaint *was* about idolatry and
improper sexual conduct, with the finger of blame being pointed
not only at ordinary people but also at a significant section of the
priesthood. There is no clear record of when Jewish religious
leaders first became involved in apostasy but, according to some
influential first-century opinion, pagan backsliding at 'high level'
had been a long-term problem. The Greek writer, Strabo, who
lived from about 64 BCE until 21 CE, notes in his *Geography*:

> For some time his [Moses'] successors followed in his footsteps but then the priesthood fell into the hands of superstitious and, later, tyrannical elements.

Strabo's comments largely echo the view of even the more moderate Palestine-watchers from the second century BCE onwards, that the Judaic clergy had been, and continued to be, in a chronic state of spiritual degeneracy. Yet it was into the authority and care of this priesthood, supposedly cloistered in an exclusively male domain apart from a court that women could occasionally visit, that Mary and a sorority of other young virgin girls like her were committed for their moral and practical upbringing.

Within this climate of pagan interest the Jews yearned passionately for the rebirth of the kingdom of Israel with the restoration the Davidic throne. The thwarting of Israel's spiritual destiny was fuel to the fires of those members of the community who looked for retribution from on high to fall around the heads of Israel's oppressors. The agony of suppression would, they believed, be resolved through divine intervention with the *messiah* marching at the head of his triumphant army. In spite of the failings of God's chosen people he would deliver them up from the wrong levelled against them and restore their greatness through a massive, if selective, apocalypse against the nations that had brought them low.

The era of Herodian rule was not the first time that the Jews had sought deliverance. During the Assyrian oppression of the eighth century BCE, Isaiah had felt compelled to boost morale in the face of extreme hardship by offering the Israelites some splendidly jingoistic encouragement.

> For unto us a child is born, unto us a son is given; and the government shall be upon his shoulder; and his name shall be called Wonderful, Counsellor, the mighty God, The everlasting Father, the Prince of Peace. Of the increase of his government and peace there shall be no end, upon the throne of David, and upon his

kingdom, to order it and to establish it with judgement and with justice from henceforth even for ever.   [Isa. 9.6–7]

Yet the promised salvation had not come and Palestine had been fought over, ravaged and won by new waves of conquerors who considered it a jewel worth taking. The cream of the 'chosen people' had been dragged off into a second long period of enforced captivity in Mesopotamia, this time in Babylon. Now they demanded vengeance.

> *Glorify the Hand, and praise the Right Arm,*
> *Waken indignation and pour out wrath,*
> *Subdue the foe and expel the enemy,*
> *Gather all the tribes of Jacob*
> *That they may receive their inheritance as in days of old.*
> *Have mercy on the people that is called in Thy name,*
> *Israel whom Thou hast called Thy first-born.*
> *Give testimony to the first of Thy works*
> *And fulfil the vision proclaimed in Thy name.*
>   [*Wisdom of Ben Sira*, 36]

The Herodian administration gave the Jews strong reasons for believing that the arrival of a *messiah* was imminent. Herod the Great was no harsher than many previous overlords of Judaea, but the Herodians had opened up a unique political situation that fulfilled the terms of the deathbed prophecy made by Jacob. In the ancient world, oracular predictions were regarded very seriously. They were messages from a god, divine wisdom delivered through a human intermediary. Most Jews living in the first century would have known, as part of their folklore, Jacob's prediction that a *messiah* would come at a time when the Judaean king was no longer a man from among them (a lawgiver who was not from 'between Judah's feet').

Until the Babylonian Exile, Jews had been ruled from within their own house and even in the restoration period they maintained a priestly government of high-ranking families which, though hardly a monarchy, was drawn from within their ranks. When Herod was granted the title of 'king', centuries-old tradition changed dramatically. Herod's father's family was Idumean and, according to the Jewish historian, Josephus, his mother was an Arab. Not only were the positions of king and spiritual figurehead now split and beyond the control of the Jewish people, but their ruler was a foreigner. This is crucial in the search for the real Mary. It was not her alleged Immaculate Conception of Jesus that heralded the arrival of a *messiah*, but the appearance of the Herodians. They provided the conditions for Jacob's prophecy to come true and this allowed Christian Jews to cast Mary, retrospectively, as Jesus' immaculate mother.

The time-honoured belief in messianic deliverance was also rooted in the so-called Davidic Covenant, made when David inherited his Israelite kingdom from Saul in about 1010 BCE. David considered it to be his God-given largesse to found a dynasty that would safeguard Palestine, for all time, as the promised land of the Hebrews.

> When thy days be fulfilled, and thou shalt sleep with thy fathers, I will set up thy seed after thee which shall proceed out of thy bowels, and I will establish his kingdom. He shall build an house for my name and I will stablish the throne of his kingdom for ever. I will be his father and he shall be my son.   [2 Sam. 7.12ff.]

In one sense David was himself a *messiah*, a word that becomes 'Christ' or *Christos* in Greek. It was always believed, however, that another would follow in his footsteps, 'a son of David and a righteous branch of the stem of Jesse'. This vision, coupled with the ancient prophecy of Jacob, kept alive the dream of the 'anointed one' who, one day, would bring back the might and the glory to Israel.

> I saw in the night visions and, behold, one like the Son of man

came with the clouds of heaven, and came to the Ancient of days, and they brought him near before him. And there was given him dominion, and glory, and a kingdom, that all people, nations, and languages should serve him: his dominion is an everlasting dominion, which shall not pass away, and his kingdom that which shall not be destroyed.   [Dan. 7.13ff.]

Crucial to the issue of Mary's identity is: What kind of *messiah* did the Jewish people anticipate? One of the criteria stressed at the beginning of this book is that her biography is inseparable from that of Jesus Christ, the one being the mutually exclusive key to the other. Orthodox Jews probably saw the future in terms of a sacred king, Yahweh's anointed 'Stem of Jesse' who would save his people with Torah in hand. Generally the dream seems to have been of a single heroic *messiah*, although the Essenes thought that a warrior would bring 'death to the ungodly' and defeat 'nations' [IQSb v, 20–29] while a priestly '*messiah* of Aaron' would interpret the law [IQSa 11,20]. In this purely Yahwist vision the mother of the *messiah* would have been a royal Jewish matron, the wife of a sovereign king.

The orthodox image of the *messiah* cannot, however, have been the only one in circulation because the Jews were steeped in the pagan traditions of Canaan and Mesopotamia. These traditions told of the birth of *messiahs* of a different genre. First-century Judaea was a place where, for more than a thousand years, the traditions of Isis and Osiris, Baal and Anat, Tammuz and Ishtar had been firmly accepted beside those of Yahweh. Since the days of Moses, the Jewish rank and file had envied the national success of nations whose prosperity was safeguarded by the sexual inter-course of fertility goddesses and their dying-and-rising sons and lovers. In the climate of persistent Jewish apostasy these heavenly partnerships must have loomed large. The Hebrew people and their descendants must have seen for themselves the ritual drama-tisation of celestial intercourse at times of need. If not, they will have been told of it by travellers to the pagan lands. Mortal sovereigns, the seemingly invincible and god-like rulers of Meso-potamia, mated with the priestesses of the goddess, the sacred prostitutes, and their sexual union bore fruit in the form of sacred kings. Living in Galilee, steeped in pagan tradition, it is likely that this idea about a messianic birth was more familiar to Mary, her friends and family, than the Yahwism of the Pharisees and Sadducees in Jerusalem. It is to what we know of Mary's life, or what we think we know, that the focus of the case now turns.

SIX

The Biblical Mary

The search for the real Mary must properly begin with the records of the men who wrote the books of the New Testament and its apocryphal counterpart. Some of the authors were contemporaries of Jesus and his mother, others were writing of events in the recent past. Unfortunately these records are thin on the ground and many of them are fallible. We should also be aware that lack of reliability is not the only complication: the way in which the New Testament has been interpreted has changed over the years. Meanings have been drawn, not only from what is written, but also from what is not.

Each of the four canonical gospels takes up Mary's brief story, with varying degrees of elaboration. Much of the text in three of these narratives, the works attributed to Matthew, Mark and Luke, all compiled during the second half of the first century CE, is exact or extremely close in its language. The similarity is extraordinary among the literature of the ancient world and because of the way they are written, their comparable content and outlook, they are known as the Synoptic gospels.

Most scholars believe the Gospel of Mark to have been the earliest written, between 60 and 70 CE, about thirty or forty years after the Crucifixion. It has no decisive references to events after 70 CE. Mark was followed about ten years later by the Gospels of Matthew and Luke. These are thought to draw on Mark, though possibly both incorporate material from another unknown origin which is referred to as the *Q* or *Quelle* source. Matthew was in use from about 100 CE. Approximately 90 per cent of Mark is repeated in Matthew and more than 50 per cent in Luke, but neither Matthew nor Luke seem to be related except by way of Mark. Not all theologians go along with the proposal that Mark's gospel is the linchpin: it has been argued that Matthew's was the original gospel, subsequently used by Luke, while Mark alternated between them. Another argument has Matthew copying Mark and Luke copying both! Whatever the finer academic points about who should take the literary honours, the fourth gospel, the work attributed to John the Divine, bears very little similarity to the other three and probably comes from a quite independent source. It is also thought to have been penned not by John but by a group of his students in Rome. Clement, the second-century Bishop of Alexandria, identified it as the 'latest of the four gospels', suggesting that it cannot have been written by a contemporary of Jesus, rather by someone of the next generation, but its exact date of composition is unknown. The separate authorship makes John valuable as a point of reference.

A number of the earliest Christian writings are classed as apocryphal, meaning doubtful or fabulous, and to appreciate the value of these texts it is important to understand that, following the death of Christ, the birth of the Christian movement was far from trouble-free. The new religion spawned all kinds of squabbling factions, each trumpeting its own dogmas to an extent that was never subsequently matched. Jesus may have seen himself as a social reformer and anticipated a following but he left neither rule-book nor mandate for a sect to be formed in his name. So the first two and a half centuries of Christendom saw rival groups squaring up against each other without any sense of orthodoxy or right opinion. Each of the factions argued for different doctrinal views, each robustly defended itself and each, not surprisingly, claimed the moral and theological high ground.

It was not until one faction, based on the Church of Rome, gained the upper hand during the fourth century that any kind of majority opinion came to the fore. This faction took upon itself the role of ombudsman, throwing out all religious texts other than those of which it approved and then insisting that it represented orthodoxy, the pure and absolute truth underwritten by Jesus Christ.

Largely composed from early in the second century CE until the beginning of the Middle Ages, the apocryphal works were considered 'non-orthodox' by the Apostolic Church and were received with varying degrees of disapproval or outright rejection. A high proportion were to be labelled 'heretical' in order to separate them, conveniently, from those styled 'orthodox'. By and large they have become pigeonholed as part of the early record not accepted as being authentic by any measurable section of the Christian movement. Some are published with caveats while others are banned.

The position of the Church of Rome was, however, subjective and not necessarily a genuine apostolic viewpoint. So little appeared about Mary in the canonical texts that her biographical portrait was open to infinite coloration, however far-fetched the embellishment. Writings accepted by the apostolic fathers as orthodox in the early years were often rejected later, resulting in elements being incorporated into Mary's portrait from works which then became anathematised on the grounds that they were heretical. For many decades the *Protevangelium of James*, written in the second half of the second century, was considered worthy of inclusion in the official biblical literature until certain elements concerning details about Mary's life, which we shall examine shortly, became regarded by the Church establishment in Rome as 'unacceptable'. Sometimes the reverse was true, in that material originally condemned became accepted.

In his *History of the Church* the Greek Christian commentator, Eusebius, writing in the third century CE, adopted a typically pedantic attitude towards authors abandoning the official line.

> The demon who hates the good, sworn enemy of truth and inveterate foe of man's salvation, turned all his weapons against the Church. In earlier days he had attacked her with persecution from

without; but now he was debarred from this, he resorted to unscrupulous impostors as instruments of spiritual corruption, and employed new tactics, contriving by every possible means that impostors and cheats, by cloaking themselves in the same name as our religion, should at one and the same time bring to the abyss of destruction every believer they could entrap, and by their own actions and endeavours turn those ignorant of the faith away from the path that leads to the message of salvation. [Penguin edn, p. 158]

Eusebius' uncompromising attitude was echoed by the early Christian Fathers, unswerving in their zeal and resolute in their own narrow view that any doctrinal deviation was tantamount to perversion. Motions of censure fell on all 'unacceptable' interpretations including writings that cast the slightest doubt on Mary, the divinely graced mother, as she is described in the canonical works. Given the machinations that were taking place, how much of the surviving literature is accurate and how much the product of fervent imagination will never be wholly clear.

Eventually, on the issue of what was and was not acceptable as Christian reading, the biblical texts were formalised in a succession of severe papal edicts. The *Decretum Gelasianum*, attributed to the fifth-century Pope Gelasius I but probably compiled in the sixth century, is perhaps the best known. Under the heading *de libris recipiendis*, it lists the twenty-seven books of the New Testament and follows them with a list of sixty condemned works.

The remaining writings which have been compiled or been recognised by heretics or schismatics the Catholic and Apostolic Roman Church does not in any way receive . . . what also all disciples of heresy and of the heretics or schismatics, whose names we have scarcely preserved, have taught or compiled, we acknowledge is not merely to be rejected but excluded from the whole Roman Catholic and Apostolic Church with its authors and the adherents of its authors to be damned in the inextricable shackles of anathema forever.

[*Decretum Gelasianum*]

Most of the detail of Mary's life is to be found in an assortment of these banned narratives which deal with Jesus' infancy. Some are little more than romantic tales. Even the canonical Nativity accounts were authored by anonymous scribes who composed them not less than eighty years after the events they describe. We must assume, therefore, that the biblical and apocryphal biography is an uncertain blend of history and myth. We should also keep in mind that any myth evolves as a totality. In traditional stories the world over, every detail bears some underlying importance and nothing can be brushed aside as 'window-dressing'. Small cameos which have found their way into Mary's biography may appear incidental but they have significance.

The Mary of the New Testament and its Apocrypha was a woman of considerable contradiction. Her childhood, we are told, was spent cloistered in the Temple, an exclusively male preserve. From at least the age of twelve she lived in what was probably the most pagan-minded area of Greater Judaea, Galilee, yet was supposedly a devout orthodox Jew. She was a lifelong virgin who achieved the biologically impossible feat of conceiving and giving birth to a son. Jesus was a social reformer and friend to all, yet seems to have treated her with contempt. Mary is almost central to the Christian faith yet she is one of the most vague figures of the Bible. For Christians, she embodies the renunciation of sex yet was destined to receive the title 'Queen of Heaven', which possesses sexual connotations because it was the title also given to the Mesopotamian fertility goddess.

At least some of the paradox has to do with the complicated political and religious climate both of Mary's world and that of the early Christians under the aegis of the Roman Empire. By the time of her death, and we must assume that if she lived the full biblical span of three score years and ten, this would have occurred in about the mid-first century CE, the Roman world, including the ancient Near East, was poised for a massive upheaval. It was a change as profound as the advances in technology witnessed at the close of the twentieth century, yet this was not a technical revolution but a spiritual one. By comparison, the change from Yahwism or Hebraism, based on the Temple cult and sacrifice, to Judaism, revolving around the synagogue and prayer, had been a much more localised and less radical affair. It had taken place in the climate of the Exile in Babylon where the Jews had been denied a temple in which to practise their cult but it did not involve any fundamental change in religious allegiance.

In the first century CE two religious systems were starting to square up one against the other: monotheism, in the shape of Christianity, and polytheism, which I am treating as paganism. Christians worshipped their own 'Universal God' while denying everyone else's. Pagans were more liberal in their view of other religious systems. The three centuries that followed Mary's lifetime would witness the most profound religious transformation the world had ever known. In order to appreciate how the change was possible we need to return briefly to the time of Mary's birth. In 31 BCE Octavian, the adopted son of Julius Caesar, had become effective ruler of Rome, and Rome ruled the world. Yet Octavian was no ordinary leader because, in 27 BCE, he had taken absolute power and given himself the title *Imperator Caesar (divi filius) Augustus*, meaning that he was the son of a god. When he came to power the Roman world was in a less than stable condition, having been plagued with social upheaval and civil war since the middle of the previous century. The machinery of government had virtually collapsed and the constitution was being ignored by Rome's leaders. Backed by a vast army and the wealth of Egypt, now under imperial control, Octavian found himself with complete authority. This meant that he could establish peace and economic prosperity in the new Empire. He also believed in traditional Roman values and virtue. To many he may have seemed akin to a god.

There was a growing sense that a new 'golden age' was in sight and the poet Virgil (70–19 BCE) summed up the mood of expectation.

Now is come the last age of the song of Cumae; the great line of the centuries begins anew. Now the Virgin [Justice] returns, the age of Saturn returns, a new generation descends from heaven on high.   [*Eclogue* 4.4ff.]

Into this atmosphere of renewal and expectation of 'something different', however, was to march a Christian convert and evangelist, Paul, with his eye strictly on the gentile (meaning pagan) community. Paul preached of a new beginning under the aegis of a 'new' god whose intentions for humanity had been revealed through his martyred semi-divine son. His message possessed the right ingredients to attract pagans from all walks of life, a heady mix of old pagan sentiments directed towards a demigod who had been put to death in the spring of the year and been miraculously restored, the promise of eternal life, and radical social reforms. The problem was that the emperor was also divine and therefore not enthusiastic about the emergence of rival deities. This resulted in the persecution of Christians who would not recognise the emperor to be numinous. But by the time of Constantine's conversion in 312 CE, although the emperors were still calling themselves 'august', they were no longer claiming to be divine and, of great importance, imperial Rome was backing the Christians.

In the end, one system was neatly exchanged for that which was in place at the start of the process. The winner was Christianity but in its triumph it actually came to embrace both systems. This fundamental detail, the fact that Christianity is a hybrid belief, is one which history tends not to record because the historians were, unfortunately, the early Church Fathers and denial was essential to them.

Let us take a close look at Mary's biography stripped of its romanticism. No firm information has survived about her date or place of birth and while the Nativity story places her at a young age in the Judaean town of Bethlehem, her main association is with Galilee. From various events noted in Matthew and Luke, we know that Jesus' birth date was in about 4 BCE, around the time of the death of Herod the Great. Luke states that Mary and Joseph set up home in Nazareth in Galilee. Nazareth was a provincial town in a remote Palestinian region and does not earn even a mention in the Old Testament; to call it a city, as Matthew and Luke have done, probably reflects poetic licence.

In terms of the New Testament, the earliest reference to Mary might seem logically to be in the gospels. We can, however, turn to at least one reference to 'Jesus' mother' from before 60 CE, the earliest date for their composition. In his letter to the Galatians, written in about 51 or 52 CE, Paul made a passing comment.

> When the fulness of the time was come, God sent forth his Son, made of a woman, made under the law.'   [Gal. 4.4]

Paul avoids mention of Mary by name but the expression 'made of a woman' implies that she was a normal person. Significantly, Paul added the words 'made under the law'. He was presumably referring to Mosaic law which meant that Mary, a Jew, conceived Jesus either with her legal husband or, under the Hebrew Law of Levirate, with her brother-in-law. Paul's comments indicate that the fanciful notions about virgin birth which were to arise in the second century, and which became so essential to the Marian cult, did not exist in his day.

The *Protevangelium of James* is the most important of the apocryphal gospels and much of the present-day Marian story can be traced to this book. Popularly known as the 'Birth of Mary, Mother of God', its author claims to be one of the twelve apostles, James the Less, the son of Alphaeus. The claim is doubtful because the author turns out to be ignorant of Jewish customs and of the geography of Palestine with which James and his family would have been familiar, suggesting that the work is neither that of a Jew nor originally composed in Hebrew. It has done much to fill in a biography and background, even though in places it lavishes an excessive amount of adulation on Mary. In the sixteenth century, when the first printed edition was published in Switzerland, it was wrongly assumed that the *Protevangelium* was older than the canonical gospels. It is now thought to have been written anonymously in the latter half of the second century, which still makes it a very early Christian work and, when set beside the paucity of interest in Mary by writers such as Paul, it shows how quickly Marian devotion moved forward.

Mary's parents, named in the *Protevangelium* as Anna and Joachim, had remained childless for many years so that when Anna became pregnant, folklore claimed it was nothing short of divine intervention.

> And behold an angel of the Lord appeared to her and said, 'Anna, Anna, the Lord has heard your prayer. You shall conceive and bear, and your offspring shall be spoken of in the whole world.' And Anna said, 'As the Lord my God lives, if I bear a child, whether male or female, I will bring it as a gift to the Lord my God, and it shall serve him all the days of its life.'   [*Protevangelium* 4.1, ANT]

In return for their boon the couple promised to place the child in the service of the Israelite God by giving her over, at the age of three, to the priests of the Temple.

> And when the child was three years old Joachim said, Call the undefiled daughters of the Hebrews, and let each one take a torch, and let these be burning, in order that the child may not turn back and her heart be tempted away from the temple of the Lord ... and the priest took her and kissed her and blessed her ... and Mary was in the Temple of the Lord nurtured like a dove and received food from the hand of an angel.   [*Protevangelium* 7.2,8.1, ANT]

In reporting this, the author of the *Protevangelium* makes an extraordinary admission and strips away the first significant layer of the brushwork covering the real portrait of Mary. On the face of it the account is implausible because, in Jewish law, women were not permitted to live in the Temple and, significantly, the matter is not reported by the canonical writers. The mere suggestion of a virgin female child raised by male priests would have been socially abhorrent to Jews. Mary should properly have been kept closeted with her mother and the other women of her family, well away from public attention and, particularly, from the eyes of men.

A number of other early apocryphal narratives, mainly of unknown authorship and date, seem to have been drafted with the precise purpose of rectifying the shortfall in the New Testament texts. They may appear to fill in a little more of the Marian biography but their authors often set about romanticising and padding out the canonical comments about Mary. Though they were avidly read by early Christian believers and some were even accepted as orthodox, in reality they were mostly figments of the imagination, short on historical credentials or eyewitness accounts. Several of the apocryphal authors, however, reported the Temple episode, which indicates that it must be taken seriously.

Joining in the burgeoning adoration of Mary, the *Liber de Infantia* or *Gospel of Pseudo-Matthew* was probably written in the eighth or ninth century CE, possibly as early as the sixth, although the earliest surviving copy dates from the eleventh century. It backs up the *Protevangelium* story of Mary's Temple upbringing, as does the *History of Joseph the Carpenter*, thought to have been written in the third or fourth century CE as a counterblast to the many legends placing emphasis on Mary, and a work known as the *Gospel of the Birth of Mary*, the earliest surviving version of which was copied by the fourth-century writer and evangelist, Jerome. Although this probably has a common origin with the *Protevangelium*, it is even more intimate and includes cameos such as Mary, the toddler, climbing the fifteen stairs into the Temple all on her own.

> The Virgin of the Lord in such manner went up all the stairs one after another, without the help of any to lead or to lift her ... the parents having offered up their sacrifice, according to the custom of the law, and perfected their vow, left the Virgin with the other

virgins in the apartments of the Temple, who were to be brought up there, and they returned home. [*Birth of Mary* 4.6,8, ANT]

Such details probably served the need for an 'eyewitness account' rather than strict accuracy but the fact that the anomaly of the Temple upbringing is detailed in more than one of the apocryphal infancy gospels must surely have presented a great problem to the Founding Fathers of the Church. Mary remained in the Temple, we are told, for nine years until she was twelve, or twelve and a half, and was showing the first blossoming signs of adolescence.

When she was twelve years old there took place a council of the priests saying, 'Behold Mary has become twelve years old in the Temple of the Lord. What then shall we do with her lest she defile the Temple of the Lord?' [*Protevangelium* 8.2, ANT]

This offers a clue to the year of Mary's birth. According to the apocryphal *History of Joseph the Carpenter* she was with Joseph for two years before the Nativity, making her fourteen at the time when she gave birth to Jesus, in which case she must have been born in about 18 BCE. The *Gospel of Pseudo-Matthew*, suggests that she was fourteen when she left the Temple, conceiving immediately and giving birth at the age of fifteen. This seems a very young age for motherhood but it was not particularly unusual in an era when many Jewish girls were married off in their early teens.

Several other passing details of Mary's youth found their way into the apocryphal works, some of which also suggest that things were not quite as her 'official' curriculum vitae would have it. According to the *Protevangelium*, Mary was recruited with other virgins to weave curtains or veils for the sanctuary.

Now there was a council of the priests saying, 'Let us make a veil for the temple of the Lord.' And the priest said, 'Call to me pure virgins of the tribe of David.' . . . 'Cast lots to see who shall weave the gold, the amiantus, the linen, the silk, the hyacinth-blue, the scarlet, the pure purple.' The pure purple and scarlet fell by lot to Mary.   [*Protevangelium* 10.1, ANT]

Care of the curtains, which separated the sanctuary of the Temple, was a constant chore. The Mishnah notes that a priest named Eleazar, among a list of higher officials, was in charge of the hangings and that his weavers were obliged to produce two new curtains annually [*Sheq.* 5.1ff.]. By any standard the hangings were substantial, each 'a handbreadth thick' and twenty cubits broad by forty long (where a cubit is roughly the distance from a man's elbow to the tip of his middle finger). This figure is based on an inscription dated to about 701 BCE indicating the length of a tunnel built in Jerusalem by Hezekiah (about 525 metres) as 12,000 cubits. The hangings were woven by eighty-two young girls who operated on a piece-work rota using sizeable looms of seventy-two strands, each strand made up of twenty-four threads.

As such, there is nothing surprising about Mary having been recruited for weaving Temple hangings, although even this activity carried a certain stigma and harks back to the women described in 2 Kings preparing hangings for the *asherah*, the symbolic embodiment of the mother goddess designed like a stylised tree. The real anomaly about Mary's formative years is that she would not have normally been a resident of the Temple. Nothing in the apocryphal texts, or later commentaries, explains the decision to hand her over to the priests in her infancy nor the judiciously arranged 'guardianship' which was decided for her at puberty by these same priests.

Mary was given into the care of the elderly widower, Joseph, described in the *Protevangelium* as a house builder rather than a carpenter. He apparently took on the responsibility for the welfare of this young woman only after strong complaint and the drawing of lots.

And the priest said to Joseph, 'You have been chosen by lot to receive the virgin of the Lord as your Ward.' But Joseph answered him, 'I have sons and am old; she is but a girl. I object lest I should become a laughing-stock to the sons of Israel.'

[*Protevangelium* 9.1ff., ANT]

The author of *Liber de Infantia* tells us a few more passing details about Mary and Joseph but his information is not supported from any other source. Mary's maternal grandfather was Achar and, at the time when Mary was espoused to Joseph, the high priest of the Temple in Jerusalem was Abiathar. More interesting is the revelation that 'Joseph came to a feast with his sons, James, Joseph and Judah, and Simeon, and his two daughters.' Who was their mother? Matthew and Mark, perhaps shrewdly evasive, described them as Jesus' siblings rather than Mary's offspring but some additional details are contained in the *History of Joseph the Carpenter*. The narrative comes as if from the mouth of Jesus.

There was a man whose name was Joseph, descended from a family of Bethlehem, a town of Judah, and the city of King David. This same man, being well instructed with wisdom and learning, was made a priest in the temple of the Lord. He was, also, skilful in his trade which was that of a carpenter; and like all men he married a wife. Moreover he begot for himself sons and daughters, in fact four sons and two daughters – Judas, Justus, James and Simeon – Assia and Lydia ... at length the wife of righteous Joseph, a woman intent on the divine glory in all her works, died.   [ANT, p. 114]

The inclusion of details about Joseph's earlier marriage, and the children of that union, led to the condemnation of several apocryphal narratives. In a series of sermons, the *Catechetical Lectures*, Cyril of Jerusalem (315–386 CE) prepared one of the early lists of books that were acceptable and stated, 'Of the New Testament there are four Gospels only, for the rest have false titles and are harmful.' The ban imposed on the *History of Joseph the Carpenter*, the *Liber de Infantia* and the *Protevangelium* was particularly strong in the West. The observations they contain conflicted with the fierce claims of early Christian commentators, like Jerome and Ambrose, that Joseph had no other marital partner than Mary and that, like her, he remained a lifelong virgin. Yet, perversely, men like Jerome chose not only to publish versions of the apocryphal infancy gospels but to do so including the 'difficult' sections, about Joseph's marriages and the Temple years. The fact that Jerome was not branded a heretic is succinct proof that ideology shifted one way then another in the early centuries of Christianity.

It is at the time of the Nativity that two of the canonical gospels show a limited interest in Mary's story. According to the Luke gospel she had become the 'espoused wife' of Joseph. Whether the expression was introduced diplomatically in preference to 'guardian', or whether marriage to Joseph was actually intended, is not explained. The *Protevangelium* is clear that Joseph was required to keep Mary as his ward. Yet a miraculous event is alleged to have taken place because Mary became pregnant at the age of fourteen or fifteen, miraculous because allegedly no human father was involved.

Matthew states that the relationship was not consummated: 'And he [Joseph] knew her not till she had brought forth her firstborn son.' [Matt. 1.25] The *Protevangelium* makes a similar point by suggesting that Joseph was absent on business at the time when Mary conceived.

> And Joseph said to Mary, 'I have received you from the temple of the Lord, and now I leave you in my house and go away to build my buildings. I will return to you; the Lord will guard you.'
>
> [*Protevangelium* 9.2, ANT]

Luke offers a different scenario carrying the same message, relating that when the angel told Mary that she would conceive of the Holy Ghost, she left Joseph's house hastily and stayed for three months with her cousin, Elisabeth.

Predictably a strong finger of blame was pointed at Joseph who, the *Protevangelium* reveals, experienced a catalogue of emotions –

anger, remorse, fear, uncertainty about what to do and, eventually, awe that a miracle had occurred. Joseph was quickly reported to the high priest by a scribe named Annas and was charged with consummating an unofficial marriage secretly. The author of the *Protevangelium* underlined Joseph's eventual acquittal from charges of sexual misconduct, but only after both Joseph and Mary had been subjected to a curious form of trial known as Drinking the Bitter Waters, the *me hammarim ham'ar rim*. One of the strangest devices in the biblical legal system, this was an ordeal designed to establish the guilt or innocence of someone accused of sexual misconduct. It was the judicial recourse if no decision could be reached after the examination of evidence, or if the accused could not produce witnesses for the defence. Similar rituals, though not necessarily using the bitter waters, were carried out in Babylonia and Assyria. In principle the defendant claimed innocence before God whose judgement was to be made through the swearing of an oath, the so-called 'oath of the Lord' [Exod. 22.11]. To refuse the ordeal was to concede guilt, and perjury by the accused would bring on the curse accompanying the oath. The ordeal is detailed in the Old Testament Book of Numbers.

And the priest shall take holy water and the dust that is in the floor of the tabernacle and put it into the water. And the priest shall say unto the woman, If no man have lain with thee, and if thou hast not gone aside to uncleanness with another instead of thy husband, be thou free from this bitter water that causeth the curse. But if thou hast gone aside to another instead of thy husband, and if thou be defiled, the Lord make thee a curse and an oath among thy people, when the Lord doth make thy thigh to rot, and thy belly to swell. This water that causeth the curse shall go into thy bowels, to make thy belly to swell, and thy thigh to rot; And the priest shall write these curses in a book, and he shall blot them out with the bitter water. And he shall cause the woman to drink the bitter water, and the water that causeth the curse shall enter into her, and become bitter. [Abridged from Num. 5.17ff.]

The priest, who first wrote the curse on a slate, washed it off and then mixed the dirty water with dust from the tabernacle floor, made up the concoction. The water that a guilty woman had been forced to drink was claimed to make her permanently barren, causing 'her abdomen to swell and her thigh to waste away'. The effect was probably not entirely psychological and some potent drug may have been mixed with the dust.

The mention of this trial ordeal in the *Protevangelium* is important for two reasons. The outcome supports claims in the canonical narratives that Joseph played no part in fathering Jesus; it also indicates that, in Jewish eyes, there was a strong suspicion that Mary had experienced sexual relations with an adulterer. These claims are important, as we shall discover, for ideological reasons.

Matthew and Luke differ so markedly in the content and mood of the infancy stories that it is unlikely they were copied from a common source like the rest of the synoptic narratives. On the whole the account in Matthew is the more prosaic. At times the mood is violent, particularly in the dramatic episode of Herod's persecution and the flight of Mary, Joseph and the infant Jesus to Egypt (echoing the birth of Moses in the Book of Exodus). Over the conception and birth of Jesus, Matthew largely agrees with Luke that Mary became pregnant during her 'espousal' to Joseph and, in doing so, left him with an amount of understandable anxiety. Matthew also introduces us to the imagery of the three kings travelling from afar, following a light in the heavens and visiting Mary with the infant Jesus in order to pay their respects to the new-born child.

> And when they were come into the house, they saw the young child with Mary his mother, and fell down and worshipped him.
>
> [Matt. 2.11]

In the genealogy that opens his gospel, Matthew emphasises that it was Joseph, not Mary, who was a direct descendant of the royal Davidic family. This was to be one of the problem areas of

Mariolatry for early Christian commentators. If Joseph had no part in Jesus' conception it became essential to work Mary into the royal lineage since the Messiah, according to tradition, could come only from the house of David.

> Now the birth of Jesus Christ was on this wise: When as his mother Mary was espoused to Joseph, before they came together, she was found with child of the Holy Ghost. [Matt. 1.18]

> The angel of the Lord appeared unto him [Joseph] in a dream, saying, Joseph, thou son of David, fear not to take unto thee Mary thy wife: for that which is conceived in her is of the Holy Ghost.
>
> [Matt. 1.20]

Luke's is the more romantic of the gospel Nativity accounts. It reveals that Mary's cousin, Elisabeth, also pregnant under noteworthy though less contentious circumstances, was the person to whom she turned for refuge when she found that she was carrying a child, a condition that might have led to her shaming as an unmarried mother had she remained with Joseph.

> And it came to pass, that, when Elisabeth heard the salutation of Mary, the babe leaped in her womb ... And Mary abode with her [Elisabeth] about three months, and returned to her own house.
>
> [Luke 1.41,56]

Luke also tells of Joseph's betrothal to Mary and adds the quaint story of an angelic visit to calm her anxieties about unmarried motherhood and to give her the news of her special relationship with God:

> To a virgin espoused to a man whose name was Joseph, of the House of David; and the virgin's name was Mary. And the angel came in unto her, and said, Hail, thou that art highly favoured, the Lord is with thee: blessed art thou amongst women. And when she saw him, she was troubled at his saying, and cast in her mind what

manner of salutation this should be. And the angel said unto her,
Fear not, Mary: for thou hast found favour with God.

[Luke 1.27–30]

In the opening of his first chapter Luke claims the greatest
historical accuracy among the gospel writers and implies that the
others fall short in this respect, but he also conveys a sentimentality
that has largely been the inspiration for the popular Christmas
Nativity scene. Luke's version makes no mention of the three
kings but draws the birth of Jesus in the setting of a manger
beside a roadside hostelry with shepherds from the nearby fields
abandoning their flocks to visit the new-born infant.

And they came with haste, and found Mary, and Joseph, and the
babe lying in a manger.   [Luke 2.16]

Luke's account is the inspiration for the Arcadian, but wholly
fictitious, stable which was first made popular by Francis of Assisi
and which now decorates so many charming Nativity scenes. The
cosy setting is furthered in the late narrative of the *Liber de Infantia*
which introduces the domestic animals, an addition that is clearly
designed to fulfil Isaiah's prophecy that 'The ox knoweth his
owner, and the ass his master's crib' [Isaiah 1.3]. This make-believe
has become ingrained in Christmas traditions but it is far removed
from any reality and it escapes the true and more provocative
setting for the birth of the Messiah. Cattle in biblical Palestine
were not kept in pretty thatched barns. Probably far more accurate
is the description contained in the *Liber de Infantia*.

The time when she should bring forth was at hand; and he [the
angel] commanded Mary to come down from the animal, and go
into an underground cave, in which there was never light, but
always darkness, because the light of day could not reach it ... and
there she brought forth a son.   [*Liber de Infantia* 13, ANT]

The Luke gospel also describes a taxation decree. This actually represents an anachronism because, according to Roman records from the period, it cannot have taken place at the time suggested. It has its purpose, none the less, because the inclusion of the decree conveniently places Jesus' birth in the Judaean city of Bethlehem rather than in Nazareth where Luke had Mary and Joseph living. Old Testament prophecies had told that Israel would be restored by a descendant of the House of David, so Matthew and Luke had to work their stories in such a way that, overlooking divine parentage, Jesus was born into David's line and David's city.

> And it came to pass in those days, that there went out a decree from Caesar Augustus, that all the world should be taxed. (And this taxing was first made when Cyrenius was governor of Syria.) And Joseph also went up from Galilee, out of the city of Nazareth, into Judaea, unto the city of David, which is called Bethlehem (because he was of the house and lineage of David). To be taxed with Mary his espoused wife, being great with child. [Luke 2.1ff.]

Luke attempted to write an account that was materially accurate but he did not have sufficient information to work with. Jesus is reckoned to have been born at about the time of Herod's death in 4 BCE but Quirinius (Cyrenius) did not become governor of Syria until about 6 CE when Archelaus, one of Herod's three sons who succeeded him, was deposed as an unsatisfactory Ethnarch of Judaea. The region then passed into the direct control of Rome and a census was authorised for tax purposes. These censuses were extremely unpopular among Jews and led to riots which have been documented in independent archives, but there is no record of any census encompassing the Roman world taking place under Caesar Augustus at the time of Jesus' birth. By contrast, Matthew places Mary and Joseph as residents of Bethlehem but then introduces a move to Nazareth after their fugitive return from Egypt in order to conform to historical necessity that Jesus was a Nazarene.

Luke has no more to offer apart from an isolated incident: at the age of twelve, Jesus was taken to the Temple in Jerusalem and remained there, unbeknown to Mary and Joseph, until they realised he was missing and began desperately to search for him.

> And it came to pass, that after three days they found him in the temple ... And when they saw him, they were amazed: and his mother said unto him, Son, why hast thou thus dealt with us? behold, thy father and I have sought thee sorrowing. And he said unto them, How is it that ye sought me? wist ye not that I must be about my Father's business? And they understood not the saying which he spake unto them ... but his mother kept all these sayings in her heart. [Luke 2.46ff.]

The first gospel mention of Mary after the Nativity amounts to some anonymous and indirect comments, casual chatter in a crowd at the time when Jesus first returned to his home district of Nazareth to preach in the local synagogue. Matthew and Mark concur.

> 'Is not this the carpenter's son? is not his mother called Mary? and his brethren James and Joses, and Simon, and Judas? And his sisters, are they not all with us?' [Matt. 13.55–56]

> 'Is not this the carpenter, the son of Mary, the brother of James, and Joses, and of Juda, and Simon? and are not his sisters here with us?' [Mark 6.3]

John overlooks this but does record a passing comment of Jesus to his mother during the marriage at Cana, something not picked up by any of the Synoptic authors. The text of John always avoids use of Mary's name, preferring 'mother of Jesus'.

> And the third day there was a marriage in Cana of Galilee; and the mother of Jesus was there ... Jesus saith unto her, Woman, what have I to do with thee? mine hour is not yet come. [John 2.1,4]

In the description of the Crucifixion which, at odds with the synoptic narratives, was witnessed by Mary, the Gospel of John gives a small sketch supporting the idea that John the Divine, known as the 'disciple whom Jesus loved', took Mary into his care after the death of Jesus since the request that he should act as her protector comes pointedly from Christ himself.

> Now there stood by the cross of Jesus his mother, and his mother's sister, Mary the wife of Cleophas, and Mary Magdalene. When Jesus therefore saw his mother, and the disciple standing by, whom he loved, he saith unto his mother, Woman, behold thy son! Then saith he to the disciple, Behold thy mother! And from that hour that disciple took her into his own house. [John 19.25–27]

Aside from the Nativity story, and a single mention at the beginning of Acts, there are no other references to Mary in the orthodox texts of the New Testament. There also appear to be significant omissions in the Synoptic gospels. This is an amazing reflection on the most important female figure in Jewish–Christian history. Where, in the minds of the synoptic authors, was Mary at the time of the Crucifixion? They agreed that a group of Galilean women witnessed Jesus' death but, at odds with John's account, none seems to have considered that his mother was present.

> And many women were there beholding afar off, which followed Jesus from Galilee, ministering unto him. Among which was Mary Magdalene, and Mary the mother of James and Joses, and the mother of Zebedee's children. [Matt. 27.55–56]

> There were also women looking on afar off: among whom was Mary Magdalene, and Mary the mother of James the less, and of Joses, and Salome; (Who also, when he was in Galilee, followed him, and ministered unto him); and many other women which came up with him unto Jerusalem. [Mark 15.40]

> And all his acquaintance, and the women that followed him from

Galilee, stood afar off, beholding these things.   [Luke 23.49]

The *History of Joseph the Carpenter* indicates that Jesus' brothers and sisters were the children of Joseph's first marriage. Given that official Marian ideology insists that she bore no more children but remained a lifelong virgin, the references in Matthew and Mark to the mother of Joseph's children must identify *another* Mary. When Matthew 13.55 describes James and Joses, Simon and Judas as Jesus' brethren, he is more likely to imply the sons of one father. There are numerous biblical precedents for the use of 'brethren' as a euphemism. The Israelites in Egypt were seen as brethren of Joseph. 'And they said, Thy servants are twelve brethren, the sons of one man in the land of Canaan.' [Gen. 42.13] In the New Testament, 'brethren' also tends to imply neighbours or kinsmen who are closely banded together. Paul's letter to the Romans refers to 'my brethren, my kinsmen according to the flesh: Who are the Israelites' [Romans 9.3,4]. On this basis, Mary the Virgin is not named among the slightly disparate cast-lists which both Matthew and Mark drew up of those present at the Crucifixion, while Luke fought shy of including names at all.

Nothing more in the New Testament or its apocryphal literature reveals information of value in the search for Mary during the adult life of Jesus. There is, however, a work called the *Assumption of the Virgin*, openly condemned through the *Decretum Gelasianum*. Its description of her death and burial strips away another layer of the façade, the high regard in which Mary is presumed to have been held.

The *Assumption of the Virgin* seems to be the first known attempt to explain the *transitus*, Mary's alteration at death from an earthly to a celestial state. In spite of hostility towards it, the work had a massive effect on Christian belief and practice from about the fourth century onwards. Some biblical scholars have attributed the standard Greek text to St John the Evangelist but its provenance is largely unknown. It was copied extensively in both Greek and Latin. The story covers the death of Mary in Jerusalem surrounded by the virgins who seem to have attended her throughout her life. It reveals an unusual incident that took place as the funeral party was making its way to the burial ground.

> Various disciples lived with Mary after the Passion, as did Salome and Joanna and the rest of the virgins who were with her ... Jesus made us stand for the prayer, and the virgins also who used to minister in the temple and had come to wait on Mary after the Passion. After she had died Peter and John took the body to the field of Jehoshaphat to a new tomb to watch it for 3 and 1 half days. The Jews heard singing and came out intending to burn the body. But a wall of fire encompassed us and they were blinded and the body was laid in the tomb.   [Coptic text from the *Homily* attributed to Evodius, Archbishop of Rome, ANT, p. 695]

The first Latin version of the event, known as *Pseudo-Melito* (because attributed to Melito, a second-century Bishop of Sardis), names a Jewish priest, Jephonias, as the ringleader of these Jews. It seems a bizarre incident yet it was highlighted in a number of other respectable early Christian discourses, including those of Cyril of Jerusalem (315–386 CE) and Theodosius, Archbishop of Alexandria (536–568 CE). This gives its possible authenticity more weight.

> We carried the body out to the field of Jehoshaphat. The Jews saw it and took counsel to come and burn it. The apostles set down the bier and fled. Darkness came on the Jews, and they were blinded and smited by their own fire.   [*Discourse of Theodosius* 7ff., ANT]

The only other biographical information comes from the historian Josephus, who indicated that Mary lived out her remaining years of life with John in Jerusalem. As for Mary's maligned husband, Joseph, his portrait is even sketchier than that of Mary and he comes across strictly as a bit-part player. He disappears quickly from the canonical texts although some additional details are contained in the *History of Joseph the Carpenter*.

> He [Joseph] returned to Nazareth and fell ill. The dates of his life:
> he was forty when he married, and was married forty-nine years: a
> year alone after his wife's death. Two years with Mary before the
> Nativity.   [ANT, p. 115]

The Marian romance adopts the attitude that if Joseph's was
the bloodline from David, it was an irrelevance. His lineage is,
however, identified in Matthew and Luke although they cannot
agree certain details of his pedigree. According to Matthew he
was the son of Jacob, whereas Luke claims that his father was a
brother of Jacob named Heli. An influential third-century historian, Julius Africanus, explained this anomaly in a letter to a
fellow Christian author, Aristides. The differences, according to
Africanus, can be accounted for because one genealogy is based
on natural fathers and the other on the Hebrew Law of Levirate.

> Matthan, Solomon's descendant, begat Jacob. On Matthan's death
> Melchi, Nathan's descendant, begot Heli by the same woman. Thus
> Heli and Jacob had the same mother. When Heli died childless,
> Jacob 'raised up' offspring to him, begetting Joseph – by nature his
> own son, by law Heli's.   [Eus., *Hist.*, 7.5]

Africanus' contemporary, the Greek Christian writer Eusebius
(263–339 CE), presented the weak argument that Mary belonged
to the same tribe as her husband. He maintained that under Mosaic
law a woman was expected to wed someone from the same town
and the same clan. Intermarriage between different tribes was
forbidden because of the risk that family inheritance would be
dissipated if moved from tribe to tribe. Eusebius, however, mis-
understood the extent of the ban on inter-tribal marriage which,
in fact, only affected heiresses.

> So shall not the inheritance of the children of Israel remove from

tribe to tribe: for every one of the children of Israel shall keep himself to the inheritance of the tribe of his fathers. And every daughter, that possesseth an inheritance in any tribe of the children of Israel, shall be wife unto one of the family of the tribe of her father, that the children of Israel may enjoy every man the inheritance of his father's. Neither shall the inheritance remove from one tribe to another tribe; but every one of the tribes of the children of Israel shall keep himself to his own inheritance.

[Num. 36.7–9]

The statute does not mention towns or clans and it probably endorsed the age-old Jewish sentiment that a man, with his male beneficiaries, should be entitled to live 'under his vine and under his fig tree' [1 Kings 4.25]. Problems arose when the property of a man who died without male heirs passed to his daughters, since a girl marrying outside the family of a peasant landowner who already had the security of male offspring was not entitled to material inheritance. Eusebius' argument is not only negated but is illogical in the context of Mary and Joseph since it does nothing to prove that they *were* of the same clan. On the contrary, Luke identifies Mary through her cousin Elisabeth, the wife of Zacharias, with the priestly tribe of Levi.

If the elders had a real grudge, it was over marriage between Israelites and foreigners, a sensitive issue that comes up regularly in the Old Testament books of Exodus, Deuteronomy and Joshua. It is re-kindled in Ezra and Nehemiah, books authored in the fraught period after the Babylonian Exile.

The land, unto which ye go to possess it, is an unclean land with the filthiness of the people of the lands, with their abominations, which have filled it from one end to another with their uncleanness. Now therefore give not your daughters unto their sons, neither take their daughters unto your sons. [Ezra 9.11–12]

And in those days also saw I Jews that had married wives of Ashdod,

of Ammon, and of Moab ... And I contended with them, and
cursed them, and smote certain of them.   [Neh. 13.23,25]

Philo, a Jewish contemporary of Mary who was born in Alexandria in about 20 BCE, wrote one of the most important and
detailed accounts of life in Palestine during the Herodian era and,
with a keen eye to first-century rabbinical law, he clarified Moses'
rulings on intermarriage.

> Do not either form a connection of marriage with one of another
> nation and do not be seduced into complying with customs incon-
> sistent with your own and do not stray from the right way and
> forget the path which leads to piety, turning into a road which is
> no road ... the anxiety and fear which parents feel for their sons
> and daughters is not slight; for, perchance, they may be allured by
> mischievous customs instead of genuine good ones.
>
> [*De Specialibus Legibus* III.29]

Philo also made the important distinction between tribes and
nations, when he described what the Christian community came
to know as the Old Testament as 'the supreme authority over each
of the tribes of the [Jewish] nation' [*Rewards and Punishments*,
XI.65].

Moving forward in time, one of the few references to Mary, the
mother of Jesus, in the context of the historical period following
that covered by the gospel narratives is to be discovered in the
Apocalypse of Paul. Although using Paul's name, this work was
written towards the end of the fourth century CE and, while
also laying emphasis on her virginity, it includes a brief visionary
mention of Mary having been assumed into the realms of glory.

> I saw a virgin coming from afar and two hundred angels before her
> singing hymns, and I asked and said, 'Sir, who is she who comes in
> so great glory?' and he said to me, 'This is Mary the Virgin, the
> mother of the Lord.'   [*Apocalypse of Paul* 46, ANT]

This is about the full extent of early descriptions of Mary and Joseph. Some became established as part of the official canon, others at various times were rejected with differing degrees of severity. Many more were probably destroyed, lost without trace among the ashes of pedantry and intolerance. Even though books like the *Protevangelium*, in company with many works of a similar style, were officially prohibited, particularly in the West (which explains why there are often no early Latin translations available), they enjoyed tremendous popularity at street level. Over one hundred handwritten Greek copies of the *Protevangelium* have survived to this day, swelled by innumerable translations into languages including Syriac, Ethiopic, Georgian and Armenian. In their time, and for centuries afterwards, they played a strong part in the way Christians envisaged personalities like Mary and Joseph while also padding out the embarrassingly sparse references in the officially approved texts.

An argument against the authenticity of the *Protevangelium*, a work which seems to have provided the inspiration for several others focusing on Mary, such as the *Liber de Infantia*, is that anomalies have resulted from ignorance of Jewish tradition on the part of a foreign author. An odd sense of local geography can certainly be detected in the *Protevangelium*. It is also claimed that the author introduced inaccuracies over religious customs: Mary's father Joachim was forbidden to offer his gifts first in the Temple because 'he had begotten no offspring in Israel'. J. K. Elliott, in his edition of the *Apocryphal New Testament*, based on a translation by M. R. James, picks on this as a blatant mistake confirming suspicions that the author did not understand the finer points of Jewish law. Elliott's criticism, however, is not entirely reasonable. While it may be true that there is no specific Mosaic regulation to the effect, the most important branch of the Hebrew law, the so-called Pentateuch including the five books of Genesis, Exodus, Leviticus, Numbers and Deuteronomy, couples barrenness with sin. In Numbers, for example, the daughters of Zelophehad, bewailing an absence of male siblings, are unequivocal that a man without sons is considered blameworthy in the eyes of God.

> Our father died in the wilderness, and he was not in the company
> of them that gathered themselves together against the Lord in the
> company of Korah; but died in his own sin, and had no sons.
>
> [Num. 27.3]

Elsewhere in the Old Testament, the prophet Job describes how, 'evil entreateth the barren that beareth not: and doeth not good to the widow' [Job 24.21]. On the opposing side of the morality argument, the Book of Deuteronomy places fertility among the divinely dispensed blessings of the covenant reached between God and Israel on Mount Sinai.

> Thou shalt be blessed above all people; there shall not be male or
> female barren among you, or among your cattle.   [Deut. 7.14]

To interpret such small details as mistakes due to the author's ignorance is not sufficiently convincing. More probably there were considered reasons for the addition of some details that were to play a significant part in the developing image of Mary.

In certain instances, omissions also highlight ideological problems that were associated with the presentation of the desired Marian ideology. Mary's childhood, as we have seen, is revealed in various apocryphal works and it is corroborated in the Islamic Koran which shares some of the religious history and mythology of Judaism. Yet this critical chapter is notably omitted from the canonical texts because, from the outset, it was seen to pose awkward questions, not least concerning why Mary was admitted to the Temple.

The dearth of detail about Mary's later life in the canonical and apocryphal writings is echoed by a no less puzzling absence of information in the period that followed. After her death, interest in Mary seems virtually to have disappeared until the second Christian century. In the Acts of the Apostles, written by Luke some time between 60 CE and the end of the first century, Mary gets a brief mention, though not by name, to mark the occasion when she joined the disciples in Jerusalem after the Ascension. As for the earliest Christian writer, the evangelist Paul, apart from his passing comment in Galatians, he ignored her.

The elaborate cult that has grown up surrounding Mary amounts to a combination of little more than ingenious manipulation of Old Testament prophecy and padding out the sparse New Testament detail with popular romance. Behind the popular mythology, however, lies a more profound ideological and political aspiration held by an influential few. In order to expose this, we need first to question in much greater detail the anomalies that emerge from Mary's authorised biography. Only when these are uncovered can we begin the real process of stripping away the layers concealing the original portrait.

SEVEN

Priestesses of the Marriage

The Gospel of Matthew opens with a genealogy and from this emerges a striking flaw in the case for the authorised biography of the mother of Christ. Of the four gospel accounts, only Matthew and Luke include an alleged lineage of Jesus. The purpose in each case (however illogical, given that Joseph is supposed to have played no part in Jesus' fathering) was to offer proof of Joseph's ancestry and thereby link Jesus with the royal house of David. As we saw in the last chapter, the two gospel writers offer different lines of descent from David as well as giving different names to Joseph's father. However, the discrepancies may not be particularly significant. Many Judaean families are known to have held ancestral records, probably in the hope that they might eventually stake a claim to the Jewish throne, and sometimes these records relied on slightly different criteria.

Matthew's list is probably the more accurate because it respects the historical actuality of Judah's and Israel's genealogies contained in 1 Chronicles. Luke tends to pay greater attention to prophecy in Chapter 3 of his gospel, although in fairness he offers a more realistic number of generations. It is thought by biblical analysts, including E. P. Sanders and Margaret Davies in their book *Studying the Synoptic Gospels*, that by opening Jesus' biography with a genealogy the writer of Matthew copied 1 Chronicles. He called his work 'The Book of the Genealogy of Jesus Christ'. Matthew's list starts with Abraham and progresses via David to Jesus. Luke's runs in the reverse direction, from Jesus to David and then on, through

Abraham, to Adam. In each list, however, David provides the pivotal link because the *messiah* was required to be his descendant in order to fulfil prophecies that Israel would be restored through the Davidic line.

> Hear ye now, O house of David ... the Lord himself shall give you a sign; Behold a virgin shall conceive, and bear a son, and shall call his name Immanuel.   [Isa. 7.13,14]

> And there shall come forth a rod out of the stem of Jesse [the father of David], and a Branch shall grow out of his roots.   [Isa. 11.1]

Matthew includes forty-one generations in three distinct sections. Two have fourteen names and the third group has one name missing, which (as has been suggested by Sanders and Davies) needs Jesus to make up a full, evenly divided complement of forty-two. The first group covers the period from Abraham to David, the second from David to the Exile, and the third from the Exile to the birth of Jesus, each marking the major turning-points in Israelite history.

In biblical times, Jewish genealogy needed to conform to a family succession that was strictly patriarchal, the *beth 'ab*, or 'house of one's father'. Inheritance was always in the father's line, the nearest relation being the paternal uncle. Women, rarely mentioned, were treated as property.

> And if a man entice a maid that is not betrothed, and lie with her, he shall surely endow her to be his wife. If her father utterly refuse to give her unto him, he shall pay money according to the dowry of virgins.   [Exod. 22.16–17]

The husband was the *ba'al* or 'master' of the wife, and a father had full authority not only over his own children but even over the wives of married sons. The lack of rights for women could hardly have been clearer in the circumstance of rape.

If a man find a damsel that is a virgin, which is not betrothed, and lay hold on her, and lie with her, and they be found; Then the man that lay with her shall give unto the damsel's father fifty shekels of silver, and she shall be his wife. [Deut. 22.28–29]

Women are mentioned only occasionally in the very extensive list of generations laid out in 1 Chronicles. Luke's genealogy ignores women altogether in the period from Jesus to Adam but Matthew's concise listing includes five women through the generations from Abraham to Jesus. What is particularly surprising are the similarities between them: at least four are known to have been pagans, or had strong pagan links, and enjoyed liaisons with Israelite leaders. In direct consequence of unorthodox and largely unexplained sexual relationships, each of the five bore a son for whom the Davidic throne was subsequently claimed.

The first of these women, Tamar, was picked as a wife for Er, the son of the Patriarch Judah. It is a reasonable guess that she was of Canaanite extraction because Judah had married a Canaanite who became Er's mother. Tamar is identified as a prostitute.

Tamar thy daughter in law hath played the harlot; and also, behold, she is with child by whoredom. [Gen. 38.24]

Through illicit sex with Judah, Tamar conceived his heir, Phares, the ninth generation back from David.

The second woman, Rahab, was an acknowledged Canaanite and a self-confessed prostitute, one of the few Jericho residents to survive its sacking by the Israelites because she gave refuge to two of their spies prior to the attack.

And Joshua the son of Nun sent out of Shittim two men to spy secretly, saying, Go view the land, even Jericho. And they went, and came into an harlot's house, named Rahab, and lodged there. [Josh. 2.1]

In Matthew's genealogy Rahab became the wife or concubine of the Israelite leader Salmon and the mother of Boaz, the great-grandfather of David.

The third is Ruth, a Moabite woman whom Boaz took to his bed under improper circumstances. Their liaison came about after Mahlon, one of the sons of Naomi (whose Judahite husband died in Moab where they had gone to escape famine), married Ruth. When Mahlon died, leaving her widowed like her mother, Ruth insisted on returning to Judah, presumably with the intention of seeking legitimate family support. In Bethlehem, Ruth was encouraged by Naomi to compromise a man by the name of Boaz, a powerful kinsman of Naomi's deceased husband. Irrespective of whether he was a sibling of Mahlon, the circumstance of the liaison was highly irregular under the conditions of Levirate and Ruth's behaviour amounted to prostitution.

> He winnoweth barley tonight in the threshing floor. Wash thyself therefore, and anoint thee, and put thy raiment upon thee, and get thee down to the floor: but make not thyself known unto the man, until he shall have done eating and drinking. And it shall be when he lieth down, that thou shalt mark the place where he shall lie, and thou shalt go in, and uncover his feet, and lay thee down; and he will tell thee what thou shalt do. [Ruth 3.2–4]

Having slept with Ruth, Boaz felt obliged to marry her and Ruth conceived Obed, David's grandfather.

On the return of Ruth and Naomi to Bethlehem, Naomi made the despairing cry, 'Call me Mara: for the Almighty hath dealt very bitterly with me.' [Ruth 1.20] The use of the term *mara* suggests that Naomi had, at some time, undergone the oath of the Bitter Waters, the *me hammarim ham'ar rim*, and failed it, thus becoming barren. In her words, 'I went out full, and the Lord has brought me home again empty' [Ruth 1.20,21]. If Naomi had been a Moabite prostitute it is a fair guess that Ruth followed in the same profession. Evidence will also come to light in due course that the surroundings of a threshing floor for Ruth's tryst hold more significance than passing mention suggests.

The fourth woman in the Matthew genealogy is Bathsheba, the wife of Uriah the Hittite, who effectively prostituted herself to King David. She may not have been a professional harlot but she acted in a sexually provocative manner by undressing and taking a bath more or less under David's nose. He responded by seducing her and arranging for her husband to be assassinated.

> And when the mourning was past, David sent and fetched her to his house, and she became his wife, and bare him a son. But the thing that David had done displeased the Lord. [2 Samuel 11.27]

Although David's existing wives and concubines, including Eglah his first wife, had already provided him with sons it was Bathsheba's eldest child, Solomon, who earned the royal inheritance. The incident has been considered so sensitive and socially damaging that it is one of only three in the entire Jewish canon rejected for public reading in any language.

A considerable time-gap then occurs before the emergence of the fifth name. It is that of Mary, the mother of Jesus. Tradition has it that, in common with Tamar, Rahab, Ruth and Bathsheba, she conceived out of wedlock (in her case with a father claimed to be God) and bore a much-heralded claimant of the royal Davidic inheritance, a *messiah*. Mary's Jewish peers were not slow to level the accusation that she was also a prostitute. We know from the first chapter of the Luke gospel that Mary was so worried about possible repercussions arising out of her condition that she fled to her cousin Elisabeth during her confinement. Her concern was justified because, according to the *Protevangelium*, she and Joseph were subjected to the same trial that Ruth's mother seems to have undergone, the *me hammarim ham'ar rim*, before acquittal of charges of sexual misconduct. Nor did the accusations cease. The work of the second-century orthodox Jewish critic, Celsus, has been lost to posterity, thought to have been destroyed by early

Christian activists. As we saw in the opening chapter, fragments survive only as quotations which the Greek Christian theologian Origen (184–254 CE) used as ammunition in his acidic charge, *Contra Celsum*. According to Origen, Celsus levelled the claim that Jesus had invented his birth from a virgin, a not unfamiliar accusation shared among various early Christian sects including the Ebionites and Valentinians, which I shall discuss in more detail later. Celsus went further, however, by alleging that Mary, earning a meagre income from spinning, had been thrown out of house and home by her carpenter husband on grounds of adultery. She had, Celsus claimed, become pregnant by a Roman soldier cited as Pantherus. This name may not have much significance since 'Pantherus' was a tag sometimes applied to men serving in the Roman legions [*Contra Celsum* I, chs. XXVIII and XXXII]. The accusation might be attributable to unsubstantiated rumour-mongering, except that 'Pantherus' may also be a corruption of the Latin *panderus*, the derivation of the English verb to 'pimp' or 'pander'.

But, to go back to the genealogy, why are the five names included? Clearly, Matthew added them for a purpose since such an eye-catching inclusion cannot have been down to whimsy. Many biblical scholars believe that the authorship of Matthew's gospel is questionable but, whoever he was, the man was clearly sensitive to Jewish criticism of Christians and his response was to show that Jesus fulfilled biblical prophecy. Throughout the Nativity account he confirms that various scriptures have been fulfilled. For example, when discussing the return from Egypt, he is quick to add the qualification, 'that it might be fulfilled which was spoken of the Lord by the prophet, saying, Out of Egypt have I called my son' [Matt. 2.15].

The presence of the names, including that of the mother of Christ, in the Matthew genealogy was an embarrassment over which the early Church found itself facing awkward inquiry. Among the more prominent establishment figures, Ambrose, the 'heavyweight' Bishop of Milan between 373 and 397 CE, was forced to concede that opponents of Christianity had discovered several women of ill repute in Matthew's list [*In Lucam* (iii) 17.p.110.17]. The explanation put forward by the Church today is that Matthew demonstrated the intention of the Israelite God to embrace the gentile or pagan world, but this is nonsense. The Old Testament texts are littered with militant exhortation encouraging the Israelites to slaughter their adversaries with the assistance of Yahweh.

> The Lord thy God shall cut off the nations from before thee, whither thou goest to possess them, and thou succeedest them, and dwellest in their land. [Deut. 12.29]

> Stay ye not, but pursue after your enemies, and smite the hindmost of them; suffer them not to enter into their cities: for the Lord your God hath delivered them into your hand. [Josh. 10.19]

The key to the real significance of the five women probably lies in the timing, because it emerges that all gave birth to leaders who were seen to be the realisation of divine assurances at moments of crisis. Each had been called upon to bear a child in the hereditary chain from Abraham and David, concluding with Jesus. The offspring would become a leader, an anointed one among God's chosen people. We tend to assume that the Jews were only ever promised one *messiah*. But such an individual, an expected king and deliverer of the people from oppression, was promised in varying ways and on many occasions throughout biblical history and the assurances were usually made at times of great national urgency. When the Hebrews were enslaved in Egypt, Joseph told them, 'God sent me before you to preserve you a posterity in the earth and to save your lives by a great deliverance.' [Gen. 45.7] During early Mesopotamian domination, the Hebrews were offered similar salvation in the form of the military leader Othniel: 'When the Children of Israel cried unto the Lord, the Lord raised up a deliverer to the children of Israel' [Judg. 3.9]. From the time of the religious elder, Samuel, late in the eleventh century BCE, the Israelite god was promising deliverance in the shape of kings. After Saul had ignored the commands of God and was rejected, Samuel was told to anoint David, the youngest son of Jesse, as a new deliverer. All of these men appear as part of the lineage from Adam to David in 1 Chronicles.

Of the pregnancies of the women in Matthew's genealogy, two were coincidental with famine in the land. When Judah cohabited with Tamar, Canaan was plagued by starvation which was only alleviated when Joseph, the brother whom Judah had once conspired to kill, sent corn from Egypt. Ruth seduced Boaz on a threshing floor at the beginning of the crucial barley harvest and shortly after a damaging crop failure in Canaan. Two other pregnancies coincided with military operations, the success of which was essential to the Israelites' prosperity. Rahab became wedded to Salmon in a highly charged period when the last of the powerful Canaanite resistance in Palestine was being overcome. David bedded Bathsheba at the time of a strategically vital war against the Ammonites who repeatedly threatened national security from their power base north of the Dead Sea. After the reign of David no more women are mentioned until the addition of Mary, yet her pregnancy also came about in troubled circumstances. Judaea had experienced an abject failure to maintain national sovereignty; its people were under punitive subjugation to the Romans and had suffered massive loss of life during the recent Maccabean revolt.

In the singular worship of Yahweh, although individuals such as Phares, Boaz, Obed and Solomon could not be god-kings in the sense of the divine rulers of Mesopotamia and Egypt, they were undoubtedly seen as leaders sent by God. So too, as far as those Jews sympathetic to his cause were concerned, was Jesus Christ. What, therefore, was special about the mothers of these men? None was wedded to the father of their royal child and merely to have been linked through adultery or commercial prostitution seems inadequate as an explanation.

We must consider the possibility that each of the women named in the genealogy, including Mary, was a sacred prostitute, a *qdesha*, the holy woman who became the high priestess of the Sacred Marriage. At this juncture we run into difficulties because the existence of Jewish priestesses was officially denied. Certainly the Jewish critic Celsus believed that Mary was a prostitute, but he did not identify whether commercial or religious. Even if any of the New Testament writers had concurred, we would be none the wiser as to whether they considered Mary a priestess or a commercial whore since, as we have seen, her biography was composed in Greek, which recognised only the word *porne*. We do, however, have other circumstantial evidence that orthodox Jews probably regarded Mary as a *qdesha*. In reporting her death, the apocryphal writer of the *Assumption of the Virgin* detailed an extraordinary attack on the bier by Jews apparently determined to seize and burn her corpse. It would be easy to put the story down to a guileless Christian attempt to discredit unruly Jewish behaviour. But a number of early spokesmen, including Evodius, Archbishop of Rome, Theodosius, Archbishop of Alexandria and Cyril, Bishop of Jerusalem (315–87), picked up on a hatred of Mary stemming from certain Jewish quarters, suggesting that the report has deeper implications. Under Mosaic law the normal style of punishment for capital offence was stoning but there were two offences which merited the extreme penalty of death by fire. One was the incest of a man who wed both a mother and daughter, the other was prostitution by the daughter of a priest. Since the penalty of burning was demanded when Tamar, not a priest's daughter but named as a *qdesha* or sacred priestess, stood condemned by her father-in-law, Judah, 'daughter of a priest' appears also to have stood as a euphemism for priestess.

> And it came to pass about three months after, that it was told Judah, saying, Tamar thy daughter in law hath played the harlot, and also, behold, she is with child by whoredom. And Judah said, Bring her forth, and let her be burnt.   [Gen. 38.24]

Speculation that a Jewish mob attempted a symbolic 'execution' in order to subject Mary's corpse to the punishment reserved for cultic whoring might be shaky were it not for the fact that we can unearth cases that may bear similarity. In Alexandria in 415 CE a prominent pagan woman, Hypatia, was abducted and hacked to death with the approval of Cyril, Bishop of Alexandria (370–444). Whether her activities included cultic prostitution is not made clear but the mob burned her remains in a manner curiously reminiscent of that in which Mary's corpse had been abused a little over three centuries earlier.

Suggesting that Mary the mother of Jesus was a *qdesha*, or any of the other women in Matthew's genealogy, will carry little advocacy unless we also establish, with reasonable certainty, that the Sacred Marriage was being enacted by Jews within the borders of biblical Israel. The Old Testament is littered with references to pagan practice of a sexual but otherwise undefined nature and a pagan institution so repugnant to orthodox Jews might not seem a suitable candidate for inclusion in the canonical texts. There is no overt biblical admission about the Marriage but in the Old Testament, sandwiched between Ecclesiastes and Isaiah, rests a slim literary masterpiece that provides sufficient evidence. The last of the so-called 'poetic books', the *Canticum canticorum* or Song of Songs, is perhaps better known from its opening lines as the Song of Solomon. Composed not as a single poem but as a collection of verses, its authorship remains unknown. Traditionally, however, it is attributed to Solomon, or to a poet eulogising him, and scholars argue possible dates for the composition between the eighth and the third centuries BCE. It must have been after the ninth century BCE because the Song equates the city of Tirzah in Samaria with Jerusalem in Judah and Tirzah became the northern capital during the reign of Omri (876–69 BCE).

Little in the Old Testament is mere speculation and the Song of Solomon is included for a special reason. An exquisitely lyrical evocation of passion, it cannot be explained as a sanitised allegory on the love of God for his bride, Israel, because its content is too

blatantly sexual. Beautifully composed and bitter-sweet, the poem
is incestuous in nature and translucent in its eroticism.

> My beloved put in his hand by the hole of the door, and my bowels
> were moved for him. I rose up to open to my beloved; and my
> hands dropped with myrrh, and my fingers with sweet smelling
> myrrh, upon the handles of the lock.   [Song of Sol. 5.4ff.]

In the Song 'myrrh' possesses sexual connotations associated with
breasts.

> A bundle of myrrh is my well-beloved unto me; he shall lie all night
> betwixt my breasts.   [Song of Sol. 1.13]

'Hand' is sometimes a prudish substitute for the penis.

> Thou art wearied in the greatness of thy way; yet saidst thou not,
> There is no hope: thou hast found the life of thine hand; therefore
> thou wast not grieved.   [Isa. 57.10]

Hence, the Essenes allegedly at Qumran considered it a punishable
offence to 'expose the hand'.

> Whoever has been so poorly dressed that when drawing his hand
> from beneath his garment his nakedness has been seen, he shall do
> penance for thirty days.   [1QS 7.15]

Nor is the Song an innocent story of human passion. The initiative
in this haunting duet lies with an anonymous woman referred to
only as a Shulamite, which would not have been possible if she
were an ordinary wife or concubine in a male-dominated Jewish
society. The sense and the ordering of sections is confused, elements jumbled by time and pieced together haphazardly by an
anonymous editor. Whatever the identity of the woman, the Song

tells of the coming of spring when the shepherd king, her consort and heart's desire, is sleeping.

> I charge you, O ye daughters of Jerusalem, by the roes, and by the hinds of the field, that ye stir not up, nor awake my love, till he please.
> [Song of Sol. 3.5]

When her king awakens he greets his bride and their love is consummated in a bower beneath the green trees. The words render a sublime counterpoint of softly awakening passions.

> The voice of my beloved! behold, he cometh leaping upon the mountains, skipping upon the hills ... Behold, thou art fair, my beloved, yea, pleasant: also our bed is green. The beams of our house are cedar, and our rafters of fir ... My beloved is like a roe or a young hart: behold, he standeth behind our wall, he looketh forth at the windows, shewing himself through the lattice. My beloved spake, and said unto me, Rise up, my love, my fair one, and come away. For, lo, the winter is past, the rain is over and gone.
> [Song of Sol. 2.8, 1.16ff and 2.9ff.]

Towards the end of the Song an extraordinary fragment of information, so inconspicuous as to be readily overlooked, confirms that this is no ordinary woman. As she wanders the streets in search of her lost lover, the guards of the city stop her.

> I opened to my beloved; but my beloved had withdrawn himself, and was gone: my soul failed when he spake; I sought him, but I could not find him; I called him, but he gave me no answer. The watchmen that went about the city found me, they smote me, they wounded me; the keepers of the walls took away my veil from me.
> [Song of Sol. 5.6–7]

The significance of the passage lies in the wearing of the veil. In Israelite society the veil was not normally an item of apparel for

ordinary women other than occasionally as an article of orna-
mental dress, or when worn by a betrothed maiden before and
during her wedding, as with Rebekah's marriage to Isaac. A prostitute, whether *zona* or *qdesha*, was distinguished because she *did*
wear the veil in public. Like Tamar in her tryst with Judah she
needed to protect her anonymity.

> And she put her widow's garments off from her, and covered her
> with a veil, and wrapped herself, and sat in an open place, which is
> by the way to Timnath ... When Judah saw her, he thought her to
> be an harlot, because she had covered her face.   [Gen. 38.14–15]

Throughout other parts of the ancient Near East during biblical
times the custom was reversed, as it remains today. Out of modesty,
the ordinary woman, and the retired but married cult priestess,
retreated behind the veil when in a public place. Active prostitutes
of both categories left their faces uncovered.

> Neither wives of freemen nor widows nor Assyrian women, who
> go out in the streets, may have their heads uncovered ... a sacred
> prostitute whom a man married must veil herself in the street, but
> one whom a man did not marry must have her head uncovered in
> the street; she must not veil herself. A harlot must not veil herself;
> her head must be uncovered.
>
> [*Middle Assyrian Laws* no. 40, after Meek, 1950]

The Qumran scrolls, the sacred texts dated to the first or second
century BCE, confirm the difference between Judaean and other
Near Eastern prostitutes in that the Judaean prostitute wore a
veil.

> For her ways are the ways of death, and her paths are the roads of
> sin, and her tracks are pathways to iniquity, and her by-ways are
> rebellious wrong-doings. Her gates are the gates of death, and
> from the entrance of the house she sets out towards the underworld.

> None of those who enter there will ever return, and all who possess
> her will descend to the Pit. She lies in wait in secret places ... in
> the city squares she veils herself and she stands at the gates of
> towns. [Scroll 4Q184.5ff.]

Jewish protocol surrounding the wearing of the veil is also
revealed in the apocryphal tale of Susanna, set in the period of the
Babylonian Exile. While bathing nude in her garden, Susanna was
propositioned by two elders who, when she resisted, spitefully
charged her as an adulteress and she was brought before a Jewish
court accused of prostitution. Although intended as a Jewish morality play, Susanna's shaming has distinct parallels with that of
David and Bathsheba, involving an allegedly virtuous wife whose
nude bathing made her the object of lustful attentions. The writer
refers to improper sexual activities 'under a green tree' and charges
both elders with being 'relics of wicked ways, offspring of Canaan
not Judah whose sins, committed in the past, have now come
home'. These small points reinforce the general impression that
sections of the exiled Jewish priesthood were sympathetic to the
Babylonian fertility cult. Accused of prostitution with cultic undertones, Susanna was brought before the court wearing the veil.

> So they sent for her. And she came, with her parents, her children,
> and all their kindred. Now Susanna was a woman of great refine-
> ment and beautiful in appearance. As she was veiled the wicked
> men ordered her to be unveiled, that they might feed upon her
> beauty. [Sus. 30.ff.]

It has been suggested that, after the Exile, Judaea may have fallen
in behind the Arab world on women's dress code. The historian
Josephus, however, notes in his *Antiquities* that if a man suspected
his wife of having committed adultery she was to be taken to the
gates of the temple and her veil removed by a priest [*Antiq.* 3.270].

The Jewish author Philo (*c.*20 BCE–*c.*50 CE) also linked the veil
with prostitution but in doing so separated it from the headdress.

This was an item worn by the respectable woman in the form of a net or cloth designed to tidy the hair rather than to conceal the face and it was removed from the accused as a mark of shame.

> If she be convicted by her own conscience, let her cover her face, making her modesty the veil for her iniquities, for to persist in her impudence is the very extravagance of wickedness.
> [*De Specialibus Legibus* III.X.54]

> The priest shall take away from her the headdress on her head, that she may be judged with her head bare, and deprived of the symbol of modesty.
> [*De Specialibus Legibus* III.X.56]

The headdress was not the only article of clothing taken away by a law court. In the Mishnah, where a woman is condemned for 'going out with her hair flowing loose' [*Ket.* vii.6], implying that ordinary women were expected to cover their hair, the veil goes without mention. The duty of an adjudicating priest, however, included seizing the woman's clothing and ripping it from her 'until he bares her breast' [*Sot.* (i).5.E]. The evidence confirms that, in Jewish society, veiling was a mark of prostitution. A woman charged with adultery was obliged to cover her face as a mark of shame but was then exposed before the judiciary.

Almost throughout, the Song of Solomon echoes details of the Mesopotamian Sacred Marriage. In the third part the bride wanders the city streets at night searching for her lost lover until she finds him.

> It was but a little that I passed from them, but I found him whom my soul loveth: I held him, and would not let him go, until I had brought him into my mother's house, and into the chamber of her that conceived me.
> [Song of Sol. 3.4]

Her words reflect the Babylonian drama as the *entum* priestess leads her consort and king into the house of the goddess. These

verses are filled with imagery that is not Israelite but Mesopotamian, its origins known from cuneiform texts to be at least a
thousand years older than the earliest realistic date for composition
of the Song. The house they refer to is a strong reminder of the
giparu of the goddess in Babylon and the imagery of harts and roes
may also be traced back to Babylonia and Assyria, although it
became widely copied in the ancient world. In the late 1950s the
archaeologist M. E. L. Mallowan found, among the ruins at
Kalakh, the Calah of Genesis, fragments of fretted ivory depicting
a deer standing before a latticed tracery of branches, which almost
exactly emulates the account in the Song.

The Song of Solomon is a description of the Sacred Marriage
and it can only have found its way into the Jewish canon because
it reflected an important part of an unorthodox Jewish tradition.
The decision of the Christian editors of the Old Testament to
carry such a contentious piece of poetry through into the new
tradition can only suggest that they too were faced with pressure
from elements within the Christian movement to retain pagan
elements as part of its official canon. The inclusion of the Song in
the biblical Old Testament resulted in considerable ideological
'wriggling'. By the early centuries of the Christian era, sexual
interpretations were being fiercely denied and trend-setting
bishops like Origen and the early-third-century writer, Hippolytus, were making the ridiculous claim that the Song represented
a brilliant metaphor on the pristine love between Christ and the
Church. By the dawn of the medieval period, however, a more
extraordinary twist was to emerge which would come close to
bringing the matter full circle: the woman of the Marriage was to
be identified as the Virgin Mary.

It is possible to understand the pressure on the biblical editors
to retain the Marriage only when one appreciates its massive
popularity. The ritual was followed with great devotion throughout the Near East and its influence extended far beyond the
boundaries of Mesopotamia. Canaanite records found at Ras
Shamra, the site of the ancient city of Ugarit, confirm that the

cult of Baal and Asherah involved a similar rite. Almost invariably in the mythology, and not infrequently in the dramatic enactment of the myth, it involved incest. In Mesopotamia the intercourse was between the mother goddess and her son. In Canaan, Baal had sexual intercourse with his sister, the virgin goddess Anat, in order to consummate the natural world and ensure its prosperity.

He is passionate and takes hold of her vagina,
She is passionate and takes hold of his testicles,
Baal makes love by the thousand with the virgin Anat.
[Gordon, 1949]

There is occasional evidence that the incest theme even permeated Christian folklore. During the first century, for example, a rumour spread in Alexandria that Mary had conceived incestuously with an unnamed brother [Nourry-Warner].

The Song was not the only account of the Sacred Marriage which Christians drew from the Jewish canon and attempted to sanitise. The apocryphal legend of Joseph and Asenath, mentioned in Genesis, was romanticised in the third century CE apparently with the intention of justifying the Christian link between sin, sex and sorrow. In the story, a love-affair between a priestly son of Jacob and the eighteen-year-old daughter of the Egyptian priest, Asenath is drawn as a virginal fertility priestess, surrounded by other virgins and worshipping idols in a tower high above her father's house. When Asenath sees Joseph she becomes infatuated but is still fiercely proud of her cult status. Joseph, vowing to remain a virgin, rebuffs her but prays for her conversion; her passion for him is gratified spiritually after she has suffered numerous personal hardships, renounced her pagan idols and converted to Judaism. The story becomes an allegory on the richness and spiritual reward of life devoted to Yahweh after denouncing paganism, which can only result in desolation and death. The ingredients, however, remain pagan. The virgin priestess sleeps ever alone on an ornate golden bed in a guarded chamber. She wears a tiara and veil which, for a Jewish writer, marked her as a prostitute and partakes of a ritual meal accompanied by 'a great wealth of oil' to celebrate the arrival of her intended consort – both strongly pagan elements. The story is another thinly disguised account of the Sacred Marriage.

The Song of Solomon is, nevertheless, the clearest indication that the Sacred Marriage was celebrated by the Jews, in which case it needed its players. This brings us back to Mary because the accumulated evidence suggests that she was a partaker of the Marriage. But it is not only the fact that Mary is included in Matthew's genealogy that links her with ritual prostitution, it is also her name.

EIGHT

What's in a Name?

If Mary was a *qdesha*, then clearly she could not be named as such. Jewish writers were unwilling to use the term and the mere inference that Mary might have been associated with cultic prostitution was anathema to orthodox Christians. Yet the profession existed in the first century and therefore its sorority must have been identifiable.

During biblical times in the Semitic world, names carried more significance than they do today and the use of name-codes to identify people became a vogue. The Book of Proverbs urges that 'a good name is rather to be chosen than great riches'. A name did not simply identify a person but frequently hinted at personality or position in life. In Genesis, Eve is called the 'mother of all living things' because of popular links between *hawwa*, her name in Hebrew, and *hayya* meaning 'to live'. Tradition also once placed *hawwa* in the same etymological box as the ancient Semitic word for a serpent, suggesting the primeval progenitor of life. Given names which evoked a person's character were not always complimentary. At the dawn of the Israelite Kingship 'David' became a by-word for good government, but a wealthy individual who declined to pay King David protection money at the time of his political rift with Saul was given the name 'Nabal', which means 'a fool'.

> And it came to pass, after they went forth, that David behaved himself more wisely than all the servants of Saul; so that his name was much set by.
> [1 Sam. 18.30]

Let not my lord, I pray thee, regard this man of Belial, even Nabal:
for as his name is, so is he; Nabal is his name, and folly is with him.

[1 Sam. 25.25]

A name could also express hope or religious conviction. Joshua,
which in Greek translation becomes the more familiar Jesus, means
'Yahweh will save'. A name sometimes revealed personal habits so,
when Josephus refers to a man called Bannus in his autobiography,
The Life, it is to be read as someone with a fetish for bathing.

On hearing of one named Bannus, who dwelt in the wilderness,
wearing only such clothing as trees provided, feeding on such
things as grew of themselves, and using frequent ablutions of cold
water, by day and by night, for purity's sake. [*Life* 11]

If meaning is anything to go by, one of the most curious choices
of name in the Bible is Maryam (rendered as Miriam in the Old
Testament) which became anglicised to Mary. Before the Herodian
era, Miriam or Maryam can be found only once in the fifteen-
hundred-year time-span of Jewish biblical history and elements in
the make-up of the woman concerned probably reflect the
meaning of the name.

Lack of detail in the biblical texts makes Miriam, the sister of
Moses and Aaron, a shadowy character, described in the Book of
Exodus as a prophetess who accompanied the Israelites fleeing
from the Egyptians. At face value she seems unimportant but she
is mentioned in the Levitical, or priestly, genealogies of Numbers
and Chronicles and more of her story may have been lost than has
survived the process of editing and political correction. Small
details in the canonical text, however, coupled with a single piece
of archaeological evidence, hint that she may have had pagan
leanings and been devoted to leading a cult of women among the
refugees.

And Miriam the prophetess, the sister of Aaron, took a timbrel in her hand; and all the women went out after her with timbrels and dances. And Miriam answered them, Sing ye to the Lord, for he hath triumphed gloriously; the horse and his rider hath he thrown into the sea.   [Exod. 15.20–21]

In terms of her role among the Hebrews and her family relationships, Miriam's real identity cannot be ascertained from the Old Testament. She is not, however, an older sister of Moses. The second chapter of Exodus has her intervening in his rescue from the bulrushes because, according to Chronicles, generally regarded as being the most faithful to historical accuracy of the Old Testament texts, Moses was Jochebed's first-born child.

In the early 1930s, during the excavation of a third-century CE Jewish synagogue at the Roman settlement of Dura Europos in Syria, a mural was uncovered that sheds more light on Miriam. It appears to link Moses' rescue with a local fertility goddess, Anahita, who later became transposed into Aphrodite. Women identified as Miriam, Jochebed and two midwives look on (Leach and Aycock, 1983) as the Pharaoh is seen giving orders to destroy the Hebrew first-born. In the foreground the naked figure of Anahita, bearing a faceless infant, rises from the water on which floats an object looking like a miniature Roman sarcophagus. Three other female figures behind the goddess bear gifts and a kneeling figure, thought to be the princess, completes the picture.

The composition seems to tell a death-and-renewal story. Moses shared certain features with the god-kings, including his birth from an incestuous relationship, since Exodus [6.20] identifies his mother, Jochebed, as her husband's aunt. His death is symbolised by the sarcophagus and the nakedness of the goddess who restores him suggests that she is associated with fertility. Since Miriam serves no obvious purpose in the mural, she may have been included because she was the priestess of Anahita. As we have discovered, the place of Miriam's burial also reveals a possible connection with fertility cults because it is identified with the moon god, often portrayed as the father of the fertility goddess.

Miriam was a woman to whom the epithets 'rebellious' and 'bitter' might well be applied. She challenged Moses for the leadership of the Israelites, a moment of rashness for which she was 'punished' by God with the deadly disease of leprosy. She was forced to live out her remaining time in isolation and never saw the Promised Land.

> And, behold, Miriam became leprous, white as snow: and Aaron looked upon Miriam, and, behold, she was leprous. And Aaron said unto Moses, Alas, my Lord, I beseech thee, lay not the sin upon us, wherein we have done foolishly, and wherein we have sinned. Let her not be as one dead ...   [Num. 12.10ff.]

There have been conflicting claims that Miriam's name derives from 'myrrh' (a term which has sexual connotations since the Song of Solomon associates it with breasts) or that it links etymologically with Akkadian words meaning 'stubborn' and 'fattily plump'. The fourth-century Italian Christian scholar, Jerome, responsible for the first translation of the Bible from Latin to Hebrew, was keen to trace it to *stilla maris*, meaning 'a drop of the ocean'. The most probable origin, however, is from the Hebrew root *mara*, מאר, a term that crops up in various places in the Old Testament. Hebrew has tended to borrow from Mesopotamian sources and *mara* is a loan-word derived from the Akkadian verb *mararu*, 'to be bitter'. Although *mara* can convey personal traits of rebellion or audacity, the Old Testament writers used it to describe bitterness and the word generally appears in the context of warnings about illicit sex and the perils of carnal knowledge. Such biblical caveats were regularly aired in a world where temptation in the form of prostitutes and adulteresses constantly awaited men. In the Book of Proverbs, the fate of the female seductress was 'bitter (*mara*) as wormwood, sharp as a two-edged sword' [Prov. 5.4]. A similar caution is delivered in the Book of Ecclesiastes whose author uses the word again in connection with prostitution.

> I find more bitter (*mara*) than death the woman, whose heart is
> snares and nets, and her hands as bands: whoso pleaseth God shall
> escape from her; but the sinner shall be taken by her.   [Eccl. 7.26]

The juxtaposition of words and subject matter in various passages
such as these suggests that *mara* is a euphemism for someone who
has experienced the Ordeal of the Bitter Waters. The title of the
me hammarim ham'ar rim, set by law for a woman accused of
prostitution and adultery, is based on the word *mara*. The Book
of Ruth seems to provide confirmation of the argument in the cry
of Naomi, made barren through the will of God (the fate of a
guilty woman subjected to the Ordeal), when she returned to
Bethlehem and encouraged her daughter into prostitution.

> Call me not Naomi, call me Mara: for the Almighty hath dealt very
> bitterly with me.   [Ruth 1.20]

In spite of these negative associations, we find an extraordinary
dichotomy in the use of Maryam in the New Testament. The
apparently stigmatised name of the mother of Christ is also given
to no fewer than six other women directly associated with Jesus.
One of the most influential spokesmen of early Christianity, Cyril
of Jerusalem, apparently believed that the term *maryam* was a
job description. In his pseudepigraphal Coptic work (ascribed
to biblical characters but not judged genuine by scholars), the
Twentieth Discourse, he placed words in the mouth of Mary, the
mother of Jesus, indicating that she herself viewed her name more
as a common denominator.

> I am Mary Magdalene, because the name of the village wherein I
> was born was Magdala. My name is Mary of Cleopa. I am Mary of
> James, the son of Joseph the Carpenter.

As an orthodox Christian, Cyril would, of course, have vigorously
denied any inference that it indicated cultic prostitution. If,

The Immaculate Conception (Diego Velasquez 1609–1660). The stars of heaven and the fiery clouds of creation surround Mary as she stands on the globe of the world arising from a dark sea. The Counter-Reformation artist has subtly interwoven Christian and pagan imagery.

(*Opposite*) In this immense and spellbinding study of *The Two Trinities* (Bartolome Murillo 1617–1682), the artist arranges the light to fall onto the timelessly enigmatic face of Mary and her son, whilst God and Joseph take second place.

Michaelangelo's *Pieta* is an unfinished work in the Duomo in Florence. It depicts the dead Christ half lifted by Joseph of Arimathea and a young woman, while Mary presses her face into her son's hair.

(*Opposite*) *La Maddalena* (Nicolo Donatello 1386–1466). The grotesque wooden sculpture of Mary Magdalene caricatures the Christian dogma that portrays sexuality as a sin linked with physical decay and death.

(*Above*) In the *Madonna della Rondine* (Carlo Crivelli c.1430–1495) Mary is dressed in the regalia of a queen but possesses the more accessible face of a young mother with her child, while a swallow perches above her head.

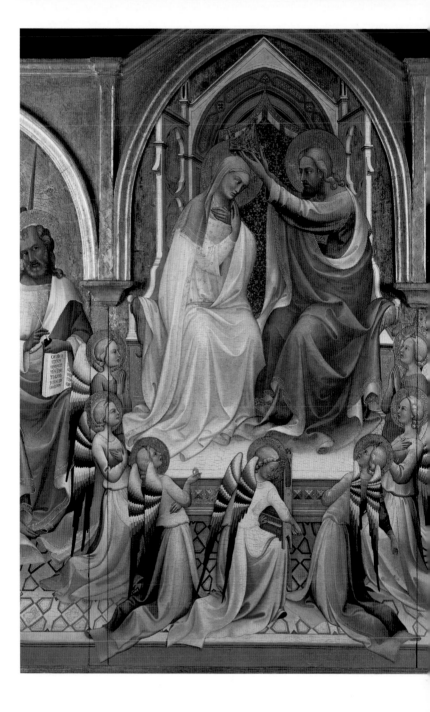

(*Opposite*) *The Coronation of the Virgin* (Lorenzo Monaco *c.*1370–1425). This formal 15th-century Florentine study is one of many following the popular theme of Christ crowning his bride and mother as the Queen of Heaven.

(*Right*) Lourdes, situated at the foot of the French Pyrenees, is a pilgrimage centre for Roman Catholics seeking miraculous cures at the grotto where Bernadette Soubirous claimed to have been visited by the Virgin Mary in 1858.

(*Below*) A bas relief in gypseous alabaster from the throne room in the northwest Palace at Kalakh (Nimrud) reveals the 9th-century Assyrian king Assur-nasir-apli II worshipping the sacred tree, a symbol of the mother goddess Ishtar.

(*Above*) *The Adoration of the Golden Calf* (Nicholas Poussin 1594–1665) reveals the strong pagan leanings towards the fertility god Baal by the Israelite tribes under Moses and Aaron.

(*Right*) In *The Crucifixion* by Quinten Massys (1465–1530), Mary, the mother of Jesus, Mary of Magdala and Mary of Bethany are depicted attending the crucifixion.

however, the Marys amount to a sisterhood, then others who portrayed them may have let slip small details of its nature.

Christ's mother has probably enjoyed greater fame among artists than any other religious figure. She has been drawn, painted, sculpted and modelled *ad infinitum*, but it has been popular to place her in a trio with Mary of Magdala and Mary of Bethany, the two whose personalities stand out among her namesakes.

Mary of Magdala, or Mary Magdalene, was one of Jesus' closest supporters. She came from the western end of the Sea of Galilee north-west of Tiberias, a village named Magdala (from the Aramaic *migd la*, meaning 'tower') where the modern town of Mejdel stands. She is described as a pagan woman who helped with Jesus' finances [Matt. 27.55–6; Luke 8.2–3] and she was present at the Crucifixion and burial. According to John, it was she alone who witnessed the risen Christ [John 20.14]. The *Twentieth Discourse* also reveals that she was the person to whom Mary the Virgin turned, on her deathbed, to nominate as her successor. Cyril's homily not only provides rare written evidence of a special link that existed between Mary the Virgin and Mary of Magdala; it also confirms that a clique of special women surrounded the mother of Christ throughout his life.

> One day the Virgin bade John summon Peter and James; and they sat down before her, and she addressed them, reminding them of the life of Jesus. She went on to say that Jesus had come to her and warned her that her time was accomplished. 'I will hide your body in the earth,' he had said; 'no man shall find it until the day when I raise it incorruptible. A great church shall be built over it. Now therefore summon the virgins.' It was done. Mary took the hand of one of them, Mary Magdalene, now very old, and committed the others to her charge. [*Twentieth Discourse*]

Mary of Magdala, as will be revealed in the next chapter, also enjoyed a more intimate relationship with Jesus Christ than the canonical texts allow. Furthermore, the comparative richness of information about her has been a source of much irritation to the Church when set against the serious paucity of colour in the biography of the mother of Jesus. When Matthew, Mark and Luke speak of the women who 'followed Jesus from Galilee', and where groups of Marys are named, it is Magdala who invariably heads the list. Particularly awkward is the absence, in all but the John gospel, of Mary the Virgin from the Crucifixion or the moment of resurrection. Matthew and Mark state that Mary of Magdala was witness to both events and, according to Mark, she was the first person to greet the risen Christ (though not the only one, as stated in John). John Chrysostom, Patriarch of Constantinople (398–404), was offended by this, to the point of complaining publicly that Christ should have appeared to his mother in his ascendant glory. From the second century onwards it became an embarrassment for Christian leaders that the Synoptic gospel writers had claimed this privilege for Mary of Magdala. Origen was one of many who remonstrated that she was wholly unsuited to such an exalted position.

The authors of the canonical gospels might, however, have looked with some incredulity at Mary of Magdala's subsequent character assassination because they had written so little about her that was detrimental. Yet to judge her from art and romantic fiction is to be led down various false trails. She is probably cast in the worst light in the famous wooden sculpture known as *La Maddalena*, created by the fifteenth-century Florentine artist, Donatello. The work is expressively grotesque, a reflection of all that the uncompromising propaganda machine of the Church was to make of Mary Magdalene. Although modern biblical historians have conceded that much of the calumny heaped upon her is entirely unsubstantiated, for centuries she was marked down as the 'penitent whore' whose corruption had brought the unwelcome stench of an early physical decay. Donatello's *Maddalena* thus depicts a hideous withered crone, long hair covering her emaciated limbs, who, as medieval literature explains, spent long years of fasting and denial in ineffectual self-chastisement for her sins. Less brutal are the portraits which draw her as a beautiful, beguiling, flame-haired, if somewhat chastened harlot.

The information we have on Mary of Bethany, who listened to Jesus' teaching, is sparse compared with that on Mary of Magdala. She lived in a village a few miles to the east of Jerusalem in the foothills of the Mount of Olives and she was the sister of Martha and Lazarus. While Martha played hostess and housekeeper [Luke 10.38,40; John 12.2], Mary was the staunch spiritual acolyte [Luke 10.39]. In the apocryphal *Book of the Resurrection*, allegedly composed by Bartholomew the Apostle, she is named in the party of women attending the tomb on Easter morning. The *Epistle of the Apostles*, written anonymously towards the end of the second century CE, corroborates this but identifies her as the daughter of Martha.

On the face of it they may appear to have little in common, other than being disciples of Jesus, but certain factors link these two Marys. Both gained reputations of a questionable nature with tags including 'sinner' and 'possessed of evil spirits', and both appear to have anointed Jesus. This coupling demands closer examination because the act of anointing carried various connotations in the ancient world, some of which were associated with fertility rites and, therefore, ritual prostitution.

All of the gospel writers drew attention to anointing but variation of detail in different accounts has led to confusion about who performed it and whether it was carried out on more than one occasion. Following the gospels in sequence, Matthew described an anonymous woman who incurred the displeasure of the disciples by anointing Jesus' head in the town of Bethany in the weeks immediately before the Last Supper:

Now when Jesus was in Bethany, in the house of Simon the Leper, There came unto him a woman having an alabaster box of very precious ointment, and poured it on his head, as he sat at meat. But when his disciples saw it, they had indignation, saying, To what purpose is this waste?   [Matt. 26.6ff.]

Mark echoed the incident, without naming the woman, and also
signalled the negative attitude of the disciples, but his narrative is
more specific in that it has only *some* of Jesus' immediate circle
objecting.

> And being in Bethany in the house of Simon the leper, as he
> [Jesus] sat at meat, there came a woman having an alabaster box of
> ointment of spikenard very precious; and she brake the box, and
> poured it on his head. And there were some that had indignation
> within themselves, and said, Why was this waste of the ointment
> made?   [Mark 14.3–4]

Luke placed the incident in an earlier period of Jesus' life, when
he was at the beginning of his ministry and at the home of Simon
the Pharisee in the town of Nain some five miles south-east of
Nazareth. Luke's narrative also varies in that he had the woman
anointing Jesus' feet, not his head.

> And, behold, a woman in the city [of Nain], which was a sinner,
> when she knew that Jesus sat at meat in the Pharisee's house,
> brought an alabaster box of ointment, And stood at his feet behind
> him weeping, and began to wash his feet with tears, and did wipe
> them with the hairs of her head, and kissed his feet, and anointed
> them with the ointment.   [Luke 7.37–38]

The non-Synoptic account attributed to John is of considerable
importance because it appears to name the anonymous woman
described in Matthew and Mark as Mary of Bethany.

> Now a certain man was sick, named Lazarus, of Bethany, the town
> of Mary and her sister Martha. (It was *that* Mary which anointed
> the Lord with ointment, and wiped his feet with her hair, whose
> brother Lazarus was sick.)   [John 11.1ff.]

John's explanation is not entirely satisfactory. He complicates the issue by drawing attention to Jesus' feet, whereas Matthew and Mark referred to anointing the head. It is also difficult to reconcile an event that allegedly took place in Bethany, in the house of Simon the leper, with the description of an earlier act of anointing that Luke placed in Nain.

Luke's use of the term 'sinner' has fuelled a tradition that the woman was Mary of Magdala because, in a separate description, he positively identifies Magdala as a woman possessing 'evil spirits': in the minds of many Christians, these shortcomings have been indistinguishable.

> And it came to pass afterward, that he went throughout every city and village, preaching and shewing the glad tidings of the kingdom of God: and the twelve were with him, And certain women, which had been healed of evil spirits and infirmities, Mary called Magdalene, out of whom went seven devils. [Luke 8.1–2]

The last observation is reiterated in Mark.

> Now when Jesus was risen early the first day of the week, he appeared first to Mary Magdalene, out of whom he had cast seven devils. [Mark 16.10]

The similarity in the acts of anointing, assisted by the vagueness surrounding Mary of Bethany in the Synoptic gospels, has sometimes been used to support a claim that Mary of Magdala and Mary of Bethany are one and the same person. This, however, is improbable because Mary of Magdala does not make her debut in Luke until the chapter *following* the description of the woman of Nain. It is now generally accepted among biblical scholars that Bethany and Magdala were two distinct individuals in Jesus' circle and that Luke's woman of Nain is an anachronistic reference to Mary of Bethany, in which case *she* becomes identifiable as the sinner. Yet there is no ready explanation of why Mary of Bethany should be identified as a sinner and, by implication, a prostitute.

Was Mary of Magdala also a prostitute? Being possessed of 'evil spirits' does not necessarily make her one, although she is traditionally described as the 'penitent whore'. But in the next chapter a more conclusive indictment will be brought concerning her sexuality. The canonical texts reveal nothing overtly but it is of critical interest that both women are linked through anointing Jesus. This act brought a hostile response and we need to consider why the disciples objected to it. Matthew and Mark merely dismissed the action as a waste of a valuable item which could have been sold to raise funds for the poor. According to Luke, the objection was because the woman was a sinner; and in the language of the Bible, the misdemeanour is usually of a sexual nature when a woman is equated with sin, in other words prostitution or adultery.

> Now when the Pharisee which had bidden him saw it, he spake within himself, saying, This man, if he were a prophet, would have known who and what manner of woman this is that toucheth him: for she is a sinner.   [Luke 7.39]

Biblical commentators attempt to justify the anointing as an act of dedication to Jesus and, from his viewpoint, a symbolic preparation for death and burial, a foretaste of the purpose in returning to the tomb after the Crucifixion.

> And when the Sabbath was past, Mary Magdalene and Mary the mother of James, and Salome, had brought sweet spices, that they might come and anoint him.   [Mark 16.1]

Anointing was an old-established part of Near Eastern tradition and was practised extensively among the Jews in Palestine, both in times of celebration and during the rites of the dead. It was also a gesture of dedication and consecration symbolising royalty. The practice continued into the Christian era and today it still accompanies the coronation of a new king or queen in England. To a person of pagan persuasion, however, anointing also carried a meaning that was intimately associated with fertility rites and the cult of the dying-and-rising god. It provided an allegory on insemination. The act of the fertility god coupling with his goddess was frequently referred to in Mesopotamian poetry as anointing. In this instance Inana (Ishtar) bewails the absence of Dumuzi (Tammuz):

For the far removed there is wailing
Ah me, my child, the far removed
My Damu [Dumuzi] the far removed
My anointer the far removed.

Drawings of Mesopotamian rites involving sacred trees, symbols of the goddess and perhaps of her consort, often show the king or his courtier dipping a pine cone into a bucket of what may have been holy oil and then pointing it phallus-like. Sometimes it is directed at the tree, sometimes at the king. In Babylon it was the convention that oils and scented unguents were offered so that the spirit of the dying-and-rising god-king could absorb the essence of these substances. We have separate evidence of the anointing of the Canaanite *massebah* representing the phallus of Baal. Esoteric meaning may also lie in the reference to anointing Jesus' feet because, in biblical times, 'feet' were employed as a euphemism for the male genitalia. The most notable example from the Old Testament comes on the occasion when Ruth compromised Boaz.

And when Boaz had eaten and drunk, and his heart was merry, he went to lie down at the end of the heap of corn: and she came softly, and uncovered his feet, and laid her down. And it came to pass at midnight, that the man was afraid, and turned himself: and, behold, a woman lay at his feet. And he said, Who art thou? And she answered, I am Ruth thine handmaid: spread therefore thy skirt over thine handmaid.   [Ruth 3.7ff.]

We have now established threads that link two of the Marys (aside from Jesus' mother), one of them a confirmed pagan, first to prostitution and then to anointing, an act that formed a key element of sexually-orientated rites involving priestesses of the fertility cult.

The four other Marys offer little by way of useful information since they emerge in varying degrees of importance as 'bit-part' players. Joseph's first wife, the mother of his older children, went under the name of Mary. We have scant detail about her beyond the fact that she bore James the younger, Joseph (or Joses) and Salome. According to the writers of Matthew and Mark, she was one of the women who attended Jesus' Crucifixion and burial and visited the tomb on Easter morning [Matt. 27.56; 28.1; Mark 15.40,47; 16.1]. She is referred to as the 'other Mary' among the group of women who reported the resurrection of Jesus to the apostles [Luke 24.10]. If these claims are correct, they confound reports that Joseph was a widower; however, even if one abandons the idea of perpetual virginity, it is unlikely that this woman was the mother of Jesus who, it is claimed, was also present at the Crucifixion [John 19.25]. It is also improbable that she was the sister of the Virgin Mary since James and Joses would then become Jesus' cousins, not his stepbrothers.

Mary, the wife of Clopas or Cleophas (sometimes claimed to be Alphaeus, the father of the apostle James the Just), is referred to only once [John 19.25]. The historian Eusebius cites lost evidence from the historian Hegesippus that Clopas was Joseph's brother, making this Mary the sister-in-law of the mother of Jesus, and James the Just Jesus' cousin. The relationship appears even more tangled because, according to the *Liber de Infantia*, Mary the mother of Jesus had a sister, also called Mary, who was the daughter of Cleophas.

A fifth Mary, identified as the wife of Zebedee, is named in one of the surviving manuscript copies of the *Liber de Infantia* although she does not appear in other medieval copies, of which over one hundred and thirty exist in Latin.

And when Joseph, worn out with old age, died and was buried with his parents, the blessed Mary lived with her nephews or with the children of her sisters; for Anna and Emerina were sisters. Of Emerina was born Elizabeth the mother of John the Baptist. And as Anna, the mother of the blessed Mary, was very beautiful, when Joachim was dead she was married to Cleophas by whom she had a second daughter. She called her Mary and gave her to Alphaeus to wife; and of her was born James the son of Alphaeus and Philip his brother. And her second husband having died, Anna was married to a third husband named Salone [sic] by whom she had a third daughter. She called her Mary likewise and gave her to Zebedee to wife; and of her were born James the son of Zebedee, and John the Evangelist. [ANT, p. 98fn]

No other Marys are mentioned in the gospels but, in Acts, passing mention is made of a sixth, the mother of John Mark, whose private house was used as a meeting place for the early Church [Acts 12.12ff]. Moderately affluent, employing at least one servant, some traditions claim that she played hostess at the Last Supper and the Pentecost incident described in Acts when the Spirit allegedly came upon the disciples, allowing them to speak in foreign tongues.

A seventh Mary is to be discovered, not in the canonical or apocryphal narratives but in the *Panarion*, an anti-heretical work by the fourth-century Bishop of Salamis, Epiphanius. This was the mother of Rufus and Alexander, the sons of Simon the Cyrenian, the man ordered by the Roman military to bear the Cross after Jesus staggered under its weight [Mark 15.21].

Mary Magdalene stood by the cross, and Mary the wife of Cleopas, and Mary the mother of Rufus, and the other Mary, and Salome and the other women.

It is worth mentioning that these seven Maryams add up to a number that carries mystical significance in both Christian and pagan tradition where we regularly find mention of seven vestal virgins, and seven devils. The seven Stations of the Cross are a Christian adaptation of the seven gates of the underworld through which the goddess Ishtar passes in a mythical confrontation with death. The design of the *palmette* leaf on the Sacred Tree of Mesopotamia is thought by ancient Near Eastern scholars to equate with the seven lobes once believed to make up the human uterus.

Jesus Christ was not the only first-century claimant to Kingship of Israel who attracted Maryams. The Jewish historian Josephus describes a further six Mariamnes or Mariammes who were either born, or married, into the Herodian dynasty within a few decades of Jesus' death and the biographies of some of these women also indicate links with prostitution. The most influential became the second wife of Herod the Great. Rumour spread that she had conducted an improper relationship with Joseph, the husband of her sister-in-law, Salome, and Herod also thought that she had slept with others including Antony, the co-respondent in a well-publicised tryst with Cleopatra of Egypt. Herod had his straying wife assassinated some time between 35 and 29 BCE but subsequently married another Mariamne, identified by Josephus as a daughter of Simon, the high priest. A third, the daughter of Olympias who was a child of Herod the Great by his Samaritan wife Malthace, became the wife of another Herod, the King of Chalcis, a city of the Lebanon valley. Josephus also mentions Mariamne, the wife of Julius Archelaus who vetted his work for accuracy, and a fifth namesake who was the daughter of Aristobulus, son of Herod and Mariamne, and Berenice, the daughter of Salome.

The sixth, a daughter of the Jewish King Agrippa I (41–44 CE) and the sister of Drusilla and Berenice, went through two unremarkable marriages. A more significant feature of her story comes after the death of her father when, Josephus noted, the people of Caesarea and Sebaste (Samaria) 'went off to their homes and seizing the images of the king's daughters carried them with one accord to the brothels, where they set them up on the roofs and offered them every possible sort of insult, doing things too indecent to be reported' [*Antiq.* XIX, 357].

If the images were models of the trio of sisters, the incident makes little sense because Agrippa I was an extremely pious and modest Jew who barred his own image from coins minted in Jerusalem, although those from other cities occasionally bear his image or that of the emperor. Agrippa, we are told, 'neglected no rite of purification, and no day passed for him without the pre-scribed sacrifice' [*Antiq.* XIX. 331]. The idea that he put up statues of his daughters, in a religious climate that proscribed such things, is highly improbable. Another objection lies in the fact that, at the time of their father's death, Berenice was a young married woman aged sixteen, but Mariamne was only ten and Drusilla six. Fur-thermore the rooftops, where the images were subject to a variety of indecencies, were time-honoured places for worship of the mother goddess. It seems likely that the images to which Josephus referred were of the *asherah*, raising the distinct possibility that one or more of the sisters served as priestesses or at least as child noviciates of the fertility cult.

In the wake of the crucifixion of Jesus, one can find various cases of Jewish antagonism towards women named Mary. We have already identified a hatred of the mother of Christ, resulting in a mob of irate Jews attempting to burn her corpse, the execution of Herod the Great's second wife for adultery, and the serious abuse directed towards Herod Agrippa's daughter. Elsewhere Josephus denigrates the conduct of a Maryam who, during the siege of Jerusalem by the Romans in 70 CE, is alleged to have killed her own child, cooked it, eaten some of the flesh and eventually handed out what was left to partisans.

While famine coursed through her intestines and marrow and the fire of rage was more consuming even than famine, impelled by the promptings alike of fury and necessity, she proceeded to an act of outrage upon nature. Seizing her child, an infant at the breast,

'Poor babe,' she cried, 'amidst war, famine and sedition, to what end should I preserve thee? With the Romans, slavery awaits us, should we live till they come; but famine is forestalling slavery, and more cruel than both are the rebels. Come, be thou food for me, to the rebels an avenging fury, and to the world a tale such as alone is wanting to the calamities of the Jews.' With these words she slew her son and then, having roasted the body and devoured half of it, she covered up and stored the remainder.

[Josephus, *Bello Judaica* VI.206ff.]

Taking into account the common factors among the five women in the Matthew genealogy, the evidence begins to suggest that, by the first century, Maryam had become a euphemism for a *qdesha*. Her title was shunned because officially her vocation did not exist!

The theory is strengthened by the discovery of another Mary from the early Christian centuries, not directly associated with Jesus but whose story, ironically, became manipulated into a medieval Christian morality play: Mary of Egypt. Born in Alexandria in about 344 CE, she earned her living as a child prostitute. At the age of seventeen she decided to embark on a pilgrimage to the Holy Land and, having insufficient funds, offered her services to the ship's crew *gratis* in lieu of buying her passage. When she finally reached the Holy Sepulchre in Jerusalem she caught sight of an icon of the Virgin Mary which brought instant repentance and led her to abandon her professional career. She then made her way to a remote part of the desert to live as an ascetic and recluse for forty-seven years until she was given holy communion by a mendicant priest who happened to be passing by, shortly after which she died [Warner, 1976, p. 233].

Today these are details which the Christian Church ignores or glosses over as being of little consequence because they raise awkward questions about the true identity and role of Mary, the mother of Jesus. Yet, in scratching away at the surface of the portrait, we are beginning to discover hidden layers beneath. We find that she was one of an extraordinary number of women in

Jesus' circle who all possessed the same name, one that, when its etymological roots are explored, appears synonymous with ritual prostitution. One of the namesakes, through being identified as a sinner, is linked with either prostitution or adultery in the gospels. Another carries out anointing, which was also widely associated with sacred prostitution. It could be argued that when the Church, with unreasonable bias, targeted Mary of Magdala as a whore, they turned her into a convenient scapegoat for all these women. I indicated at the outset that we could not find the real Mary by considering her portrait in isolation. It is to the Nativity, Jesus' relationship with his mother, and the association of both with Mary of Magdala, that we must now look in order to strip away more of the deception.

NINE

Brides of Christ

The case against Mary's official biography must now turn to her role as Jesus' mother. This needs careful examination because unusual elements and anomalies in her relationship with her son appear from an early stage of Jesus' life, none of which have been satisfactorily explained by Christian theologians.

Oddities begin with the place selected by Mary for the birth of Jesus. The apocryphal *Liber de Infantia* identifies the Nativity 'stable' as a grotto to which, it is claimed, Mary was directed by a spectral being.

> The angel ordered the beast to stand, for the time when she should bring forth was at hand; and he commanded Mary to come down from the animal, and go into an underground cave, in which there was never light, but always darkness.   [*Liber de Infantia* 13, ANT]

This description tells only part of the story. The true nature of the place came to light thanks to the preservation of a letter from St Jerome (*c.* 342–420 CE), the Italian biblical scholar who lived in Bethlehem during later life. According to Jerome, who we have to assume was writing on the basis of firm evidence though we have nothing to corroborate his claim, the cave was far from being an innocuous rock shelter for domestic stock. It was a pagan sanctuary dedicated to Tammuz, the dying-and-rising god of the ancient Near East, who took over from Baal as the son and lover of the fertility goddess in the affections of the Israelites.

Bethlehem, which now belongs to our faith and is one of the most sacred places in the whole world, lay formerly under the shadow of a grove dedicated to Tammuz, that is to say Adonis, and the very grotto where the infant Christ uttered his first cries resounded formerly with lamentations over the lover of Aphrodite.

[*Patrologie Cursus Completus*, XXII, col. 581]

If this information is true, it is difficult to imagine that Mary's decision to give birth in a pagan temple can have been due to casual coincidence. More significantly, it does not appear in the canonical texts, which either means that the authors of the Matthew and Luke gospels chose not to divulge it or that anonymous editors excised it fairly quickly. Jerome's private correspondence reveals that the matter was known to at least some Christians of his time but the fact that his is the only source to have survived, allows for the probability that the early Christian Fathers decided to suppress sensitive information about the birthplace.

Jesus' subsequent attitude towards Mary is not that which might be expected of a son towards his mother. When, aged twelve, he had gone missing and Joseph and Mary found him in the Temple, Mary complained that he had been unreasonable but received a curt response: 'How is it that ye sought me? wist ye not that I must be about my Father's business?' [Luke 2.49] This was only the first of several cold exchanges that give the impression of an unusual relationship. A similar attitude is revealed by Jesus' reaction to his mother during the unidentified marriage at Cana when he retorts, 'Woman, what have I do to with thee?' [John 2.4]

The Gospel of John reveals a similar instance. At the time of the Crucifixion Jesus said to Mary, referring not to himself but to John the Divine, 'Woman, behold thy son!' Rather than treating Mary intimately, he addressed her as 'woman' in much the same impersonal, even derogatory, manner that Paul used in his letter to the Galatians when he referred to Christ's birth as being 'made of a woman'. Many scholars pass over this anomaly but it has received no convincing explanation.

The canonical texts provide no answers as to why Jesus, the compassionate friend to all, adopted this cold attitude towards Mary. More is to be found among the 'lost' codices of the Gnostics, a branch of Christianity that permitted much greater freedom of expression than orthodoxy allowed. The so-called Gnostic gospels were brought to light after excavations at Nag Hammadi in Upper Egypt in 1945. One of the most important of these early apocryphal texts, the *Gospel of Thomas*, may shed light on the mystery. This is a collection of Jesus' sayings allegedly written down by the apostle Didymos Judas Thomas but probably composed some time before 200 CE by anonymous Gnostic sectarians. Many of these sayings are also found in the canonical narratives, suggesting derivation from a common source. *Thomas* is among the works condemned in the *Decretum Gelasianum*, the earliest comprehensive list of books banned by the ecclesiastical authorities on the pretext that they contained heretical material. The absence of copies of the *Gospel of Thomas*, other than the single complete manuscript found at Nag Hammadi, suggests that serious efforts were made to destroy evidence contained in the text. The papyrus on which it was written has been damaged but the codex contains a particularly unusual comment. The words in brackets are those assumed in deciphering.

> Whoever does not hate his father and his mother as I do cannot become a disciple to me. And whoever does [not] love his [father and] his mother as I do cannot become a [disciple to] me. For my mother [...], but [my] true [mother] gave me life.   [NHL, p. 137]

If the gaps are filled, the verse is thought by one of the foremost scholars of Nag Hammadi, James Robinson, to read, 'My [earthly] mother gave me death but my true mother gave me life'. The implication is extraordinarily far-reaching if this saying is authentic: Jesus, a Jew whose religion insists on the singular presence of a male deity in the heavens, claims two mothers. Only one of these matrons is earthly, so, by implication, the other (his true mother) has to be a goddess.

The equivalent verse in Luke is not the same.

> If any man come to me, and hate not his father, and mother, and wife, and children, and brethren, and sisters, yea, and his own life also, he cannot be my disciple.   [Luke 14.26]

Comparing the two, we can see that the apocryphal text has gained words which distinguish between a 'true mother' and an 'earthly mother'. Whether the anonymous writer of the *Gospel of Thomas* was responsible for an addition, or whether this is the accurate version (suggesting that words were deliberately excised from the Luke narrative), remains unknown. The extra words clearly amounted to a heresy in the eyes of the early Church Fathers because they implied that Jesus had a *heavenly mother* as well as a heavenly father, anathema to a religious belief based on monotheism and recognising one universal god.

If the fuller comments cited in *Thomas* are accurate, Jesus recognised Mary as the earthly stand-in for his heavenly mother. In the context of the Sacred Marriage tradition, this can only suggest that he viewed her as a priestess of the goddess, offering her womb as a mere receptacle for the semen of the god. The words of Jesus open up the critical question of whether he perceived himself to be cast in the mould of the sacred kings, the earthly embodiments of the dying-and-rising gods, that had gone before him in the ancient Near East. The evidence from *Thomas* could explain Jesus' attitude towards Mary who, once she had served her function in conceiving and bearing the sacred king, continued in the role of a *qdesha* or *maryam*.

Another of the apocryphal texts found at Nag Hammadi, the *Gospel of Philip*, describes Jesus as having three close female companions, each a *maryam*.

There were three who always walked with the Lord: Mary his
mother and his sister and Magdalene, the one who was called his
companion. His sister and his mother and his companion were
each a Mary.   [NHL, p. 145]

In order to explore fully the possibility that the *maryams* surrounding Jesus were priestesses of the fertility cult, we need to
examine more carefully Jesus' relationship with at least one of
those named in *Philip*: Mary of Magdala. Whoever and whatever
she was in real life, she was not the grotesque figure that medieval
artists dreamed up, epitomised in Donatello's *Maddalena*. If the
canonical gospel authors cannot be accused of painting Mary of
Magdala alternately as a withered hag and a warm-hearted Christian 'tart', they were certainly guilty of side-stepping her more
credit-worthy distinctions.

Mary of Magdala's unique standing among the ranks of the
exalted male disciples is not advertised in the New Testament, nor
is the intelligence that gave her a splendid academic grasp of such
ethereal topics as the origins of the world. The gospel writers
awarded her a favoured position in the lists of Jesus' companions,
but they wholly omitted to mention the value placed by Jesus upon
her friendship and intellect.

The reluctance of the canonical authors to praise Magdala may,
in part, reflect the endemic Christian reluctance to acknowledge
that women played an influential role in Jesus' life; it may also
have been in deference to the other disciples. The response of the
male apostles, when they were told of the miraculous happening
at the sepulchre, is typical of the dismissive attitude towards
women that prevailed in the emergent Christian community.

It was Mary Magdalene, and Joanna, and Mary the mother of
James, and other women that were with them, which told these
things unto the apostles. And their words seemed to them as idle
tales, and they believed them not.   [Luke 24.10–11]

The *Gospel of Thomas* reveals that the chief architect of antagonism towards Mary of Magdala was Peter, a hard-line Yahwist to whom Jesus responded with no less typical Jewish prejudice.

> His disciples said to him, 'When will the kingdom come?' 'It will not come by waiting for it. It will not be a matter of saying here it is or there it is. Rather the kingdom of the father is spread out upon the earth, and men do not see it.' Simon Peter said to them, 'Let Mary leave us, for women are not worthy of life.' Jesus said, 'I myself shall lead her in order to make her male, so that she too may become a living spirit resembling you males. For every woman who will make herself male will enter the kingdom of heaven.
>
> [*Gospel of Thomas* 1.13ff., NHL]

The antagonism between Mary and Peter is brought into sharp focus in the fragmentary surviving remnants of another Nag Hammadi work, the *Gospel of Mary*, but here the kind of misogynistic rhetoric found in *Thomas* is not repeated. It perhaps reflects more accurately the real relationship between Jesus and Magdala: she is placed in an unambiguous position as the beloved pupil who has received teaching about visions and revelations going far beyond anything divulged to the male disciples.

> Peter said to Mary, 'Sister, we know that the Saviour loved you more than the rest of the women. Tell us the words of the Saviour which you remember – which you know [but] we do not, nor have we heard them.' Mary answered and said, 'What is hidden from you I will proclaim to you.'
>
> [*Gospel of Mary* 10.1 ff., NHL]

Mary begins to explain visions of the universe and the rise of the soul, irrelevant to our investigation, upon which two of the disciples, Andrew and Peter, set out to undermine her.

> But Andrew answered and said to the brethren, 'Say what you [wish to] say about what she has said. I at least do not believe that the

Saviour said this. For certainly these teachings are strange ideas.'
Peter answered and spoke concerning these same strange things
... 'Did he really speak with a woman without our knowledge [and]
not openly? Are we to turn about and listen to her? Did he prefer
her to us?' Then Mary wept and said to Peter, 'My brother Peter,
what do you think? Do you think that I thought this up myself in
my heart, or that I am lying about the Saviour?'

[*Gospel of Mary* 18.8 ff., NHL]

The strongest evidence of Magdala's favoured status and of the
rift between her and some of the male disciples is uncovered in
another Gnostic work, the *Pistis Sophia*. The setting is the Mount
of Olives eleven years after the Crucifixion, when the risen Christ
is instructing the apostles. It is Magdala who asks the most per-
tinent and intelligent questions about the 'higher mysteries' of the
cosmos and it is she who receives the greatest accolade for doing
so. From forty-six questions posed to Christ in the *First Book of
Pistis Sophia*, no fewer than thirty-nine fall to Magdala, and she is
also the first to respond when the disciples are asked their opinions.

Now it happened when Mariam heard these words as the Saviour
was saying them, she stared for one hour into the air and said, 'My
Lord, command me that I speak openly.' Jesus, the compassionate,
answered and said to Mariam, 'Mariam thou blessed one, who I
will contemplate in all the mysteries of the height, speak openly,
thou art she whose heart is more directed to the Kingdom of
Heaven than all thy brothers.'   [*Pistis Sophia* 17, NTA]

Magdala is praised as being 'beautiful in her speech' and her
intelligent reactions prompt glowing responses such as, 'Excellent
Mariam. Thou dost ask well with an excellent question and thou
dost seek everything with certainty and with accuracy.' In the *Pistis
Sophia* the accolade is unequivocal.

Now it happened when Mariam finished saying these words, he

said, 'Excellent, Mariam. Thou art blessed beyond all women upon earth, because thou shalt be the *pleroma* [divine being] of all *pleromas* and the completion of all completions ... speak openly and do not fear. I will reveal all things which thou seekest.'

[*Pistis Sophia* 19, NTA]

Peter, the orthodox stalwart, denies the idea of esoteric revelation and then heatedly rejects the authority of women to contribute to the debate.

It happened now, when Jesus finished saying these words to his disciples, he said, 'Do you understand in what manner I am speaking with you?' Peter leapt forward, he said to Jesus, 'My Lord, we are not able to suffer this woman who takes the opportunity from us, and does not allow any one of us to speak, but she speaks many times.'

[*Pistis Sophia* 36, NTA]

Pistis Sophia also alludes to the close relationship between Magdala and Mary the Virgin when she, too, offers her opinions.

Jesus answered and said, 'Thou also, Mariam, thou hast received form which is in the Barbelo [one of the cosmic powers] according to the matter, and thou hast received likeness which is in the Virgin of the Light according to the light, thou and the other Mariam, the blessed one. And for thy sake the darkness exists and furthermore, from thee has come forth the material body in which I exist, which I have cleaned and purified.'

[*Pistis Sophia* 59, NTA]

That Mary of Magdala's status ranked close, if not equal, to that of Peter, and that it caused great rancour among several of the male disciples, is a point on which the authors of the *Gospel of Philip*, the *Gospel of Mary* and the *Pistis Sophia* concur. An altogether different scenario begins to emerge from these apocryphal writings. Far from playing a 'walk-on part' in the Christian drama, Mary of Magdala came to dominate the group of disciples with her intellectual superiority. Yet the relationship apparently went further than this: the Gnostic gospels indicate that she and Jesus were involved in a sexual relationship.

The *Gospel of Philip* lays bare Jesus' sentiments towards Mary of Magdala with refreshing candour and it does much to belie some of the deprecating nonsense that was subsequently written about her. It indicates, however, that their association was deeper and on a more physical level than that of teacher and disciple – an intimacy that was bitterly resented by some of the other disciples.

> And the companion of the [Lord was] Mary Magdalene. [He loved] her more than [all] the disciples [and used to] kiss her [often] on her [mouth]. The rest of [the disciples protested]. They said to him, 'Why do you love her more than all of us?' The Saviour answered and said to them, 'Why do I not love you like her? When a blind man and one who sees are both together in darkness, they are no different from one another. When the light comes, then he who sees will see the light, and he who is blind will remain in darkness.'   [*Gospel of Philip* 63.34ff. and 64.1ff., NHL; bracketed words indicate where damaged sections of the codex have been restored.]

The question of Jesus' sexuality and to whom exactly it extended (according to evidence from the early texts) is one of extreme sensitivity to the Christian establishment and needs careful scrutiny. Paul, in his correspondence with the Christian Church in Corinth, made an unusual observation.

> It is reported commonly that there is fornication among you, and such fornication as is not so much as named among the Gentiles, that one should have his father's wife.   [1 Cor. 5.1]

The letter prompts an important question. Were Christian cells abusing the moral code and permitting wholesale incest between sons and mothers or stepmothers? If Paul was commenting in a purely secular context, the relationships he criticises smack of the decadence normally associated with the decline of a movement, rather than its pioneering days which are more often steeped in moral zeal. On the other hand, was he alluding to acts of ritual sex? I believe it much more probable that he was. Paul may have supported candour but he could not bring himself to advertise matters such as the Sacred Marriage, and his reticence is indicated by use of the phrase, 'as is not so much as named'. The Sacred Marriage was still being enacted in Paul's day and it seems unlikely that he did not know about it. It may have waned in popularity among Europeans, where agricultural rites were become *passé* as people living in towns and cities took on a new urban chic, but it was not eliminated. The cult of the old gods was officially prohibited by Constantine the Great in 383 CE.

Although Paul recognised Christianity's exclusivity, the restriction was not imposed because he wished to reduce paganism, but rather to curb the magical aura that superstition gave to certain priests and to end the objectionable practice of blood sacrifice. The Roman aristocracy, however, (including most of the Senate) and especially the Roman armed forces, actually held out against the ban until at least the sixth century; in rural areas the feeling for the land and its sacred strength also remained strong. Roman records reveal that, in the Syrian city of Edessa, near Harran, celebration of the Roman version of the Marriage continued until the end of the fifth century. Other records show that as late as 494 CE the sexually charged rites of Attis and Kybele, the Phrygian fertility god and goddess whose cult had been brought to Rome, were celebrated each year on 27 March, to the chagrin of Pope Gelasius I. In the Near East, the cult of the fertility goddess and her consort was upheld particularly among the Sabaeans and, as late as the tenth century, a Christian Arab traveller, Abu-Sa'id Wahb Ibn Ibrahim, wrote:

> In the middle of this month is the feast of Al-Baqat, that is of the Mourning Women; and this is the Ta'uz feast which is celebrated

in honour of the god Ta'uz. The women bewail over him, lamenting
that their Lord has been so cruelly slain. [Briffault, 1927]

The implication in Paul's messages to the Corinthians is that
sects within the Christian movement were celebrating both the
Marriage and other rites associated with the mother goddess and
her dying-and-rising son and lover. Paul's accusations are supported in the General Epistle of Jude, the final correspondence in
the New Testament. The writer claims to have been the brother
of the disciple James but he writes of the apostolic period in
the past tense and biblical scholars incline to the view that the
authorship of the work composed around 90 CE, is anonymous.
The epistle is not directed towards any particular Christian group
and it constitutes an unremitting attack on heretics. Some scholars
have argued that the focus is on an early branch of Gnosticism but
the charges are so loosely worded that they could apply to many
other Jewish-Christian or Gentile-Christian factions.

The epistle describes 'ungodly men, turning the grace of our
Lord into lasciviousness, and denying the only Lord God, and our
Lord Jesus Christ'. It goes on to mark these individuals as 'spots in
your feasts of charity, when they feast with you, feeding themselves
without fear' [Jude 4,12]. 'Feasts of charity' is a euphemism for the
agape, the early Christian 'love feast' (from the Greek word for love).
According to Tertullian, the third-century Bishop of Carthage, this
event 'permits no vileness or immodesty. The participants, before
reclining, taste first of prayer to God. As much is eaten as satisfies
the cravings of hunger.' [*Apology* 38] Tertullian's comments have a
defensive ring and there may have been more to the *agape* than
his blandishment conveys. It was an event that earned considerable
condemnation among critics of the Christian movement.

In his *History of the Church*, Eusebius, Bishop of Caesarea, frequently quoted from other early Christian authors whose correspondence he had studied. Eusebius detailed an issue first raised
by Irenaeus, the vociferous Bishop of Lyons, who championed the
cause of orthodoxy in the second half of the second century. This

concerned the behaviour of the Carpocratians, followers of the doctrine of Carpocrates, a Christian pioneer who did much to advance the cause of Gnosticism. The Carpocratians were said by critics, including Irenaeus, to be radicals with a penchant for licentious behaviour. They were the first Christians of the second century, for example, known to pray before cultic images of Christ. Irenaeus had conceded, in the context of an attack on the Carpocratians, that certain Christians 'practised unlawful intercourse with mothers and sisters and took part in unhallowed feasts' [Hist 7.10]. We thus find reference among Christian writings of the first and second centuries to a feast enjoyed by members of the movement but which was condemned by critics as an excuse for sexual licence. We also have Paul and Irenaeus conceding that Christians were being branded as incestuous. The correspondence of Irenaeus links the *agape* with incest.

The accusations were levelled at conduct reminiscent of the practices of several pagan cultures associated with the Sacred Marriage. In the mythology of Mesopotamia, dramatised in the Marriage rite, Tammuz, the dying-and-rising god, was the lover of the fertility goddess Ishtar and also her son. In comparable Canaanite myths, Anat was the sister of Baal while Asherah was his mother. We know from Assyrian and Babylonian records that the Sacred Marriage in those countries included a feast. We also find in the records that rulers who played the part of the god appointed their own daughters as the priestesses of the Marriage. The sexual intercourse between the priestess playing the part of the fertility goddess and the sacred king taking the role of the dying-and-rising god who was killed for his people and then restored again is, therefore, known to have been incestuous.

In about 346 CE Firmicus Maternus, a Roman senator who had converted to Christianity, compiled a pamphlet in support of the suppression of paganism in which he attacked various cults. He confirmed that in his day the Sacred Marriage rites were still commonplace throughout Mesopotamia and Syria and that their influence had spread west through the Mediterranean.

The Jewish writer, Philo (c.20 BCE–50 CE), reported that the birth of sovereigns from such incestuous liaisons was widely recognised, to the extent that he included specific warnings against such practices.

> It [the law] commands men not only to abstain from the wives of others, but also from certain relations, with whom it is not lawful to cohabit; for the magistrates [in a biblical context the term can mean a hereditary ruler] of the Persians marry even their own mothers, and consider the offspring of such marriages the most noble of all men, and as it is said, they think them worthy of the highest sovereign authority.   [*De Specialibus Legibus* 3 (13)]

The Psalms of Solomon added to the concern of the Jewish community of the first century, by making strong accusations of undercover sexual irregularities, including incest, among the priesthood.

> God exposed their sins in the full light of day; the whole earth knew the righteous judgements of God. In secret places underground was their lawbreaking, provoking [him], son involved with mother and father with daughter; everyone committed adultery with his neighbour's wife; they made agreements with them with an oath about these things.   [Ps. Sol. 8.8ff.]

The observation that the rites took place 'underground' suggests a growing reliance among forebears of the Jewish Christians on discreet caves and grottoes. This occultism seems to have continued even after the unorthodox practice became outlawed among Christians. In his diary, the tenth-century medieval traveller Ibn Fadlan noted the prevalence of remote cave sanctuaries in Cyprus where such rites were celebrated.

Other information has also emerged that levels a potential body-blow against Christian tradition, in the light of what we already know of the sexual partnership of mother goddess and son in pagan culture and the incestuous rites allegedly practised by first-century Jews. The anti-heretical work *Panarion* was compiled by Epiphanius, Bishop of Salamis, with the intention of exposing and cataloguing non-orthodox sects within the Christian movement.

Epiphanius wrote of a lost apocryphal work, the *Genna Marias* (Questions of Mary), of which any direct trace has now vanished, an indication that all copies were removed from circulation and hidden away or destroyed. He noted that two distinct texts were incorporated into the *Genna Marias* and he referred to these as the 'Greater Questions' and the 'Lesser Questions'. It is believed by experts who have studied the Nag Hammadi codices that the 'Greater Questions' probably equated with a surviving codex, the *Pistis Sophia*, since Epiphanius' comments on the text of the 'Greater Questions' make it apparent that the sections of both works are the same. From his limited description of the 'Lesser Questions', however, it seems clear that none of this section is included in any existing versions of the *Pistis Sophia*.

Epiphanius drew attention to a part of the 'Lesser Questions' claiming that Jesus was 'the revealer of obscene practices, which constitute rites of redemption'. This was an idea peculiar to the Gnostics and one that the apostolic succession would no doubt have condemned as heretical since it identified Jesus in the same context as obscenity.

> For in the so-called 'Greater Questions of Mary' they have forged 'Lesser' ones too – they suggest that he [Christ] revealed it to her after taking her aside on the mountain [Mount of Olives], praying, producing a woman from his side, beginning to have intercourse with her, and then partaking of his emission, if you please, to show that 'This we must do that we may live' ... And when Mary was alarmed and fell to the ground, he raised her up and said to her, 'O thou of little faith, wherefore did'st thou doubt?'
>
> [*Panarion* II.(26) 8.1(2ff.)]

The conclusion that might be drawn from casual analysis is that

174 BRIDES OF CHRIST

Jesus took Mary of Magdala aside and had sexual intercourse with her. Magdala, however, is clearly not the subject of Jesus' attentions but is only a third-party observer. The key to the true identity of the woman with whom he had intercourse lies in the expression 'producing a woman from his side'. It is a phrase taken from the Genesis story of the creation of Eve.

> And the rib, which the Lord God had taken from man, made he a woman and brought her unto the man.   [Gen. 2.22]

Epiphanius, however, in common with many of his contemporaries, understood the *alter ego* of the first woman, Eve, to be Mary the Virgin.

> But there is another marvel to ponder in connection with these women, Eve and Mary. Eve has become the occasion of human deaths, for 'Death entered the world through her'. But Mary, through whom life was born for us, is the occasion of life.
>
> [*Panarion* 7.18.5]

In the sense familiar to Epiphanius (and presumably to the writer of the *Genna Marias*) 'producing a woman from his side' was a euphemism that applied to Eve or Mary. Since, in the context of Jesus' activities, the author of the *Genna Marias* was clearly not referring to Eve, he can only have been stating that Jesus committed incest with his mother and that Magdala was the startled bystander. Epiphanius' disclosure presents a specific allegation, albeit couched in veiled terms and drawn from a work that is only reported second hand, that Jesus engaged with Mary in a Sacred Marriage rite.

We should remember that the main purpose of the Marriage in the Mesopotamian cultures had been to invoke, annually, the fertility god and goddess through a dramatised rite of regenesis in order that the natural world might flourish again after the depletion of crops and livestock in the dry season. It was conducted between a god-king (whose role was also that of high priest) and his high priestess and this liaison also, from time to time, generated new god-kings. Evidence from the Old Testament and from Matthew's genealogy suggests that the Hebrews enacted the Sacred Marriage on a regular basis because many of them believed that it would bring them prosperity and end their perennial subjugation to foreign powers. At times of crisis the rite was also employed to raise up a new anointed king or *messiah*.

In summary, the inference gained from piecing together evidence in early Christian texts is that Mary was initiated into the Temple as a priestess of the fertility cult and that she engaged in a Sacred Marriage. This took place in circumstances which accorded with the Patriarch Jacob's prediction of messianic arrival and, as it had with the other women named in Matthew's genealogical list, at a time of crisis in Jewish history. Ostensibly the Marriage should have been consummated with Joseph who was singled out as a legitimate claimant to the throne of the deposed royal house of David. Joseph, we are given to understand, was too old to father more children and therefore it must be assumed that Mary consummated the Marriage with a high priest, identified as Abiathar, standing proxy. We have seen that sections of the Jewish priesthood were corrupt in Mary's time, with members up to senior level involved in pagan practices which included celebration of the Marriage. Various reports indicate that early Christian sects were similarly involved and suggest that this took place in a ritual context, perhaps associated with the *agape* or 'love feast'. The lost text of the *Genna Marias* apparently reported that Jesus had celebrated the Sacred Marriage in a 'high place' (a mountain) with one of the Marys. Through its use of words and phrases drawn from the Book of Genesis, the section of text described by Epiphanius alluded to this having been an incestuous consummation between Mary, the mother of Jesus, and her adult son.

Works such as those that have been touched on in this chapter, containing highly sensitive details about Mary, were particularly vulnerable to 'stigmatisation' in the orgy of censorship that reached its peak during the third and fourth Christian centuries. Influential voices in the early Church, including Irenaeus, Jerome, Ambrose, Origen and Tertullian, had already pinpointed the risks in ideological division and were determined to present a solid front. Irenaeus saw particular necessity to eliminate schisms and it was he who introduced the term 'orthodox', although it did not come into common currency until the fourth century of Christianity. Any suggestion that Jesus or Mary was involved in sexual practices was anathema because it conflicted with one of the central tenets of what was fast becoming the accepted or orthodox Christian dogma: that sex equals sin equals death.

The Emperor Constantine's miraculous conversion to the Christian faith before the Battle of Milvian Bridge in 312 CE undoubtedly had a profound effect on the centralisation of the movement. Having allegedly seen a fiery cross in the night sky emblazoned with the words *In hoc signo vinces* (In this sign is victory), it was he who set about targeting all non-orthodox groups. It has been said that nothing counted after Constantine but the newly triumphant faith. The Roman Empire had become the Christian empire and, as Ramsay MacMullen put it, 'Paganism, no more than a spongy mass of tolerance and tradition, so it might seem, was confronting a growing number of people determined to do away with that mass utterly, so as to replace it with what was enjoined upon them by the tremendous will of one God.' [1997, p. 2]

After Constantine's death, religion and politics became even more entangled and increasingly harsh attitudes developed towards the old religious organisations and institutions. From 397 CE onwards, fringe Christian sects and pagans alike became targets for imperial law under Theodosius, who had been proclaimed head of the eastern wing of the empire in Constantinople, and the authorities started to clamp down with increasing severity on pagan practice. Theodosius' Christian zeal was, however, to some extent forced upon him. In 390 CE, in retaliation for the slaying of the garrison commander of Thessalonica by Christians, Theodosius ordered a massacre that resulted in a thousand civilians losing their lives. Bishop Ambrose demanded public penance before he was prepared to readmit Theodosius to Christmas communion and Theodosius demonstrated his gratitude by renewing the offensive against paganism. On 24 February 391 CE he issued a law forbidding any pagan cult and even prohibiting visits to temples. These draconian statutes led to the destruction of pagan shrines and sanctuaries including the huge Sarapis Temple in Alexandria, razed in the wake of bloody disturbances led by Christian fanatics.

Any books that hinted at heresy or pagan beliefs became a fair target. This explains why so few have survived the passage of time. Cyril of Jerusalem (315–386 CE) once thundered with pious fervour:

> Of the New Testament there are four Gospels only, for the rest have false titles and are harmful ... receive also the Acts of the Twelve Apostles; and in addition to these the seven Catholic Epistles of James, Peter, John and Jude; and as a seal upon them all, and the latest work of the disciples, the fourteen epistles of Paul. But let all the rest be put aside in a secondary rank. And whatever books are not read in the churches, do not read these even by yourself, as you have already heard me say concerning the Old Testament apocrypha. [*Catechetical Lectures* 4.36]

Whether or not all these works have been totally lost is another matter. Today, the Vatican Archive of Secret Briefs contains at least seven thousand bound volumes dating from 1566 to 1846. There is also an incomplete, though scarcely less extensive, catalogue of earlier works dating back to the first centuries of the Christian era. Many of these catalogues, of which the *de libris recipiendis* (writings received) of the *Decretum Gelasianum* is one of the first, refer to decisions on which books should constitute forbidden reading within the Vatican's more exclusive library.

The case put forward in Mary's authorised biography, that she carries no stain of sexuality, is clearly riddled with inconsistencies. It presents a picture of chastity that amounts to a wholly unsubstantiated, fairy-tale invention. Yet hidebound insistence that she never experienced sexual relations and that she delivered Jesus via an intact hymen was to become the central plank on which Marianism and much of the Roman Catholic dogma developed.

TEN

The Virginity Debate

In the two canonical texts that relate the story of Jesus' birth, those of Matthew and Luke, Mary is described as a virgin who conceived through the will of God. In the words of Matthew, Mary 'was found with child of the Holy Ghost' [Matt. 1.18]. He seems to have been unwilling to identify her directly as a virgin and instead draws on an erroneous Greek translation of the prophecy in Isaiah: 'Behold, a virgin shall be with child and shall bring forth a son.' [Matt. 1.23] Luke refers to Mary as a 'virgin espoused to a man whose name was Joseph' [Luke 1.27]. The angel Gabriel is said to have offered her reassurance in the face of the daunting prospect of divine conception.

> And the angel said unto her, Fear not, Mary: for thou hast found favour with God. And, behold, thou shalt conceive in thy womb, and bring forth a son, and shalt call his name Jesus.   [Luke 1.30–1]

These comments are highly significant in the search for the truth about Mary. It is on the strength of the Matthew and Luke narratives that the entire, impassioned Roman Catholic ideology of Mary's lifelong celibacy and her unique position among women has arisen. Yet the claim of virginity implied by Matthew in a single verse (and presumably copied by Luke) is based on a fundamental literary error: the Isaiah prophecy on which the proposition hangs does not identify a virgin. Even if it had done so, the meaning of virginity has changed since biblical times and in ancient Near

Eastern mythology there was also nothing unique in divine conception.

The first area of critical examination must be exactly what Isaiah predicted in the eighth century BCE.

> Therefore the Lord himself shall give you a sign; Behold, a virgin shall conceive, and bear a son, and shall call his name Immanuel.
>
> [Isaiah 7.14]

Sadly, both for credence and for romantic tradition, virgin birth was never proposed by Isaiah. Early Hellenic Jewish translators, working on the original Aramaic in the third to second century BCE, played around with Isaiah's text. In their Greek version (known as the Septuagint because seventy scribes allegedly came up with identical translation copies) Isaiah's words were adulterated. In place of the original Aramaic word *'almah*, describing a young woman of marriageable age, the scribes used the term *parthenos*, meaning 'virgin'. This substantially alters the thrust of the Isaiah prophecy, which properly rests not on divine impregnation but on the coming of a future Davidic king. It is, however, the Greek Septuagint translation of Isaiah that Matthew and Luke appear to have drawn from.

During the first hundred years of Christianity there seems to have been little interest in Mary's virginal state or in the immaculate conception of Jesus. If Paul's comment, made to the Galatians in about 52 CE, is anything to go by ('God sent forth his Son, made of a woman, made under the law') she was regarded much as an ordinary mother who had borne an extraordinary son.

The myth of Mary's virginity *in partu* combined with a belief in her perpetual virginity (during and after the birth of Jesus) probably found its way into a written text with the composition of the *Protevangelium of James*. From the second century onwards, however, a number of Christian spokesmen began to recognise that the Immaculate Conception aspect of the official dogma of Mary had both strengths and weaknesses. They could see the

Church facing problems in justifying the inaccurate translation of *'almah*. In a massive polemical work, *Against All Heresies*, directed mainly against what was regarded as the scourge of Gnosticism, Irenaeus, the second-century Bishop of Lyons, was among the first to defend the Greek rendering of the word in the Septuagint. Irenaeus insisted that it counted as 'incontrovertible proof' of Christ's birth from a virgin.

> God, then, was made man, and the Lord did Himself save us, giving us the token of the Virgin. But not as some allege, among those now presuming to expound the Scripture, [thus:] 'Behold, a young woman shall conceive, and bring forth a son,' as Theodotion the Ephesian has interpreted, and Aquila of Pontus, both Jewish proselytes. The Ebionites, following these, assert that He was begotten by Joseph; thus destroying, as far as in them lies, such a marvellous dispensation of God, and setting aside the testimony of the prophets which proceeded from God.   [*Adv. Haer.* 3.21]

By the beginning of the third century, sceptics were challenging the claims of a virgin birth but, not surprisingly in a growing climate of bigotry and intolerance, their opinions were soon to be suppressed. One of those scathingly critical of the growing dogma about the Nativity was the Jewish critic of Christianity, Celsus. The Church authorities responded in typical fashion by destroying his writings and a weighty riposte, *Contra Celsum*, was published by Origen (born 184 CE), an Alexandrian-born author who was rapidly becoming one of the most outspoken of the hard-line Christian Fathers of his time. Origen called on the wisdom of the Hebrew Patriarchs for a less than convincing vindication of Jesus' miraculous conception.

> Now, if a Jew should split words and say that the words are not 'Lo, a virgin', but 'Lo, a young woman', we should reply that the word *'almah* which the Septuagint have rendered by 'a virgin' and others by 'a young woman' occurs in Deuteronomy as applied to a

virgin in the following connection.

In his *History of the Church*, the Greek Christian writer Eusebius (263–339 CE) backed the arguments of Irenaeus by applauding the Greek interpretation and then vigorously berating anyone who had the temerity to point out that the accurate translation was 'young woman' not 'virgin' [*Hist.* 8.9]. Romance may have been circulating about Mary but so, too, was distortion.

Once the incorrect translation had become accepted, the opportunity to report a miraculous *virgo intacta* birth was taken up enthusiastically by other writers in the early Christian movement who saw in it a great propaganda coup. It freed Mary from sexual sin but also, and this was to cause major divisions in the Church, it gave Jesus some of the credentials of a divinity. Some writers, including the anonymous author of the *Protevangelium*, made virginity claims not only on behalf of Mary but also of her mother, Anna. They suggested an absolute rejection of sexual activity running through more than one generation of Mary's family. The *Protevangelium* writer set a scene comparable to that of Mary's husband, Joseph, being away on business at the time of Jesus' conception by claiming that Joachim, Anna's husband, had departed to the wilderness for forty days when Mary was conceived.

> Anna his [Joachim's] wife sang two dirges and gave voice to a twofold lament: I will mourn my widowhood and grieve for my childlessness ... and behold an angel of the Lord appeared to her and said, Anna, Anna, the Lord has heard your prayer. You shall conceive and bear, and your offspring shall be spoken of in the whole world. *[Protevangelium* 1.2.1ff., ANT]

The Pseudepigrapha on the Old Testament (so-called because although largely written in the third or fourth centuries CE, they were claimed by their authors to be of ancient provenance) include an assortment of inventive variations on the theme of virgin birth by immaculate conception. The *Apocalypse of Adam* refers to someone called the 'Illuminator' who is clearly to be interpreted as Jesus Christ, even though he is placed anachronistically in the reign of Solomon in 970 BCE.

> He came [from a virgin ... Solomon] sought her, he and Phersalo and Samuel and his armies which had been sent out. Solomon also sent his army of demons to seek the virgin. And they did not find the one they sought, but the virgin who was given to them was the one they fetched. Solomon took her. The virgin conceived and gave birth to the child there. She nourished him on the border of the desert. When he had been nourished, He received glory and power from the seed from which he had been begotten. And thus he came to the water. [*Apocalypse of Adam* 79, NHL]

Prophetic Christian legends anticipating the unusual conception of Jesus were frequently offered as a kind of archaic testimonial lending spurious authority to biblical accounts of the Nativity and its miraculous nature. To press home their claims, many writers took advantage of the popular belief that if matters had been predicted by the ancients they must have been preordained.

> Adam said to Seth, his son, 'You have heard, my son, that God is going to come into the world after a long time, conceived of a virgin and put on a body, be born like a human being and grow up as a child.' [*Testament of Adam* 3.1, OTP]

> Then will come Jesus the Messiah from your descendants out of a virgin named Maryam. And God will become incarnate in him until the completion of a hundred years.
> [*Testament of Isaac* 3,17–19, AOT]

> And I saw a woman of the family of David the prophet whose name was Maryam, and she was a virgin and was betrothed to a man whose name was Joseph, a carpenter, and he also was of the seed and family of the righteous David of Bethlehem in Judah ... and

he did not approach Mary, but kept her as a holy virgin although
she was pregnant.' [*Vision of Isaiah* 11.2ff., NTA]

None of these early Christian predictions, however, was considered to be an authentic 'qualification' of the virgin birth of
Jesus. That distinction remains with Isaiah.

There were in fact many spokesmen in the early Church of the
second and third centuries who positively rejected any notions of
a miraculous birth. Among the more prominent Western commentators were Jovinian, Bonosus and Helvidius, each of whom
poured scorn on belief in such a fanciful idea. Helvidius was an
obscure individual who became Bishop of Sardinia and composed
one of the many polemical pamphlets of the day. He claimed
that the observation in Matthew, '[He] knew her not till she had
brought forth her first-born son' [Matt. 1.25] was ample proof
that Joseph had merely postponed sexual relations with Mary until
after Jesus' birth when the relationship became sexually intimate.
Helvidius drew the comparison with a passage in Genesis where
the writer points out that the Patriarch Judah, after Tamar's pregnancy was discovered, 'knew her again no more' [Gen. 38.26] and
suggested, tenuously, that Judah had only kept his distance from
Tamar's bed, as was the custom, during her confinement.

The second important issue to arise from the gospel accounts
lies in the meaning of the term 'virgin'. A modern dictionary
defines it as a girl or woman for whom there has been no experience
of sexual intercourse, but in biblical times it was sometimes understood differently. Among Babylonian texts detailing religious convention and morality, discovered in the ruins of the Assyrian city
of Nineveh, there is some salutary advice on marriage.

Marry not the virgin whose lovers are many,
Nor a harlot who has been consecrated to Ishtar,
Nor a votary whose humiliation [of thee] will be manifest.
She will not lift thee from thy sorrows,
She will ridicule thee in thy quarrels [with her]

Fear and humility are not with her.
If she comes into a house, lead her away
If her attention be turned towards a stranger's house,
it shall be the undoing of that house
and he that marries her shall not prosper.'

[After Langdon, 1916]

'Virgin' did not necessarily describe a chaste woman but a person of independent, feisty spirit. One of the clearest illustrations of the sense in which the term was applied can be found in the descriptions of the Canaanite goddess Anat, the sister of Baal. She is described as a lady of considerable sexual prowess who 'makes love by the thousand', yet in the same context she is identified as 'the virgin Anat' [Gordon, 1965].

Although the biblical texts make no such claim, the Church tends to convey the impression, with pious conviction, that Mary's experience was unique. Cyril of Alexandria, for example, clamoured during the Council of Ephesus in 431 CE that Mary was 'exalted forever in the Catholic Church above all creatures, above Cherubim and Seraphim and set at the right hand of the Son'. In truth, the claim of a virgin birth was not peculiar to Christianity. Threading back through Hebrew culture we can discover a catalogue of miraculous pregnancies in Jewish lore, most involving women who were apparently barren but then conceived against expectations.

Abraham's wife, Sarah, was geriatric when, in her nineties, she became the biologically improbable mother of Isaac after God had promised a child to herself and the even more aged patriarch.

And God said unto Abraham, As for Sarai thy wife, thou shalt not call her name Sarai, but Sarah shall her name be. And I will bless her, and give thee a son also of her: yea, I will bless her, and she shall be a mother of nations; kings of people shall be of her. Then Abraham fell upon his face, and laughed, and said in his heart, Shall a child be born unto him that is an hundred years old? and shall

Sarah, that is ninety years old, bear? [Gen. 17.15–17]

A little later in biblical history, Rebekah, the beautiful but barren wife of Isaac, was rewarded after twenty fruitless years with the birth of the twins, Jacob and Esau. Jacob's own wife Rachel, who also appeared to be barren and was madly jealous of her sister Leah's pregnancies, was eventually favoured by God with a son, Joseph. The wife of Manoah, the anonymous mother of the strong man Samson, had been childless before divine providence intervened. In all cases it was believed that the Israelite God had been responsible for ending chronic infertility while keeping the human husbands at arm's length.

Sometimes events demanded that angels be on hand to lend encouragement. Abraham, for example, was met by a trio of celestial envoys at the time of Sarah's pregnancy.

And the Lord appeared unto him in the plains of Mamre: and he sat in the tent door in the heat of the day; And he lift up his eyes and looked, and, lo, three men stood by him: and when he saw them, he ran to meet them from the tent door, and bowed himself toward the ground. And said, My Lord, if now I have found favour in thy sight, pass not away, I pray thee, from thy servant.

[Gen. 18.1ff.]

Manoah's wife also reported a supernatural visit at the time of her conception.

A man of God came to me, and his countenance was like the countenance of an angel of God, very terrible: but I asked him not whence he was, neither told he me his name: But he said unto me, Behold, thou shalt conceive, and bear a son. [Judg. 13.6]

The Hebrews borrowed these ideas from their neighbours and we can continue tracing the theme to the virgin birth of god-kings in cultures that were essentially pagan. The provenance of the rulers of these societies – Canaan, Assyria, Babylonia and later in Jewish history, Greece – was expected to be somewhat out of the ordinary. Among the peoples of the ancient Near East and then of the European classical world, who were attracted by tradition, 'virgin birth' had been a favourite theme of heavenly obstetrics in company with anomalies including over-long pregnancies and fully grown deities being delivered in bizarre manner. Few gods and demigods have ever been born normally.

In myth, virgin birth was sometimes claimed because the child's father was dead. The Egyptian goddess Isis, grieving for her murdered consort and brother Osiris, reassembled his shattered and scattered parts and managed to become pregnant with Horus while doing so. In other traditions, divine paternity simply remained anonymous. An inscription to the Akkadian king, Sargon the Great, opens with a statement, 'My mother was of lowly birth; my father I knew not.' This may seem innocuous but it is typical of a style of inscription popular in the ancient world to explain the fathering of a ruler by a god. Parthenogenesis – reproduction other than by means of a fertilised ovum – has been another favoured option. The Phrygian god, Attis, was born to the demi-goddess Nana after she placed a ripe almond seed in her bosom and the divine Persian hero, Mithra, the god of light, emerged from a rock, the so-called *petra genetrix*, beside a sacred stream. Many of these pagan birth traditions from Western Asia migrated and found their way into the classical mythologies of Greece and Rome. Athena appeared fully armed from the superhuman forehead of Zeus, while Dionysos, the 'twice born' son conceived but not fully gestated in the ill-fated Semele, popped out of Zeus's thigh. Some of the Greek stories then came full circle to influence Mary's generation of Galilean Jews.

The principle of virgin birth also held good for men of legendary stature outside the mythological arena. Pythagoras and Alexander the Great were reputed to have been conceived with the help of a divine spouse. The writer Plutarch, in his *Life of Alexander*, mentions that 'to the barbarians, he [Alexander] would demand the grovelling due to an oriental despot and would claim the title of Son of God.' Since Egyptian, Canaanite, Assyrian, Babylonian and Hellenic myths played a strong part in Jewish thinking, it is not surprising that stories of virgin birth associated with messianic or God-given leadership slipped easily into the Old Testament writings.

During the early Christian era, virgin birth was being claimed for a motley assortment of personalities. The *Apocalypse of Daniel* was written some time between 780 and 815 CE during the reign of the Empress Irene in Byzantium but it draws on much earlier Christian traditions concerning the coming of the Antichrist. It claims that the Antichrist was believed ready to arrive on earth by similar, bizarre means.

> A virgin girl will buy the fish [into which the Antichrist has come]. Her name is Injustice because the son of injustice will be born from her. And her surname will be Perdition. By touching the head of the fish she will become pregnant and will conceive the Antichrist himself. And he will be born from her after three months. And he will suckle from her for four months. He comes in to Jerusalem and becomes a false teacher. [*Apocalypse of Daniel* 9, OTP]

Simon Magus, a self-proclaimed Samaritan magician who peddled his brand of miracle-working at the time when the apostles were preaching their Christian gospel, was believed by many to be an Antichrist. He attributed claims of virgin birth to himself in a widely publicised exercise that was reported by several early writers, including Clement, Bishop of Alexandria.

> Do not think that I am a man of your race. I am neither magician nor lover of Luna, nor son of Antonius. For before my mother Rachel and he came together, she, still a virgin, conceived me, while it was in my power to be either small or great, and to appear as a man among men.

Set against all these accounts, Mary's virgin birth becomes another instance of story-telling that stems, ultimately, from time-honoured pagan traditions. They are woven as myths and none can be taken literally. None the less, the orthodox Church Fathers chose to ignore all the precedents and argued that Mary's immaculate state was a matter of fact, unique, divinely inspired and beyond question. They took an exceptionally strong line about her permanent celibacy, linking it with prejudices against women in general and, particularly, the physical act of sex. Clearly they were determined to distance Mary from any taint of carnality and the very fact that this emphasis arose so strongly suggests a defensive position. Their preoccupation can be compared, in principle, with the perennial focus in the Old Testament on attacking pagan practice. If sexuality had presented no threat to the Christian Fathers it would not have merited attention. The reality was that early Christianity was beset with similar problems to those faced by the Jewish elders. The Christian movement was a hybrid that wrestled with conflicting ideologies.

The evidence for ideological divisions based on whether or not sex constituted a fundamental part of ritual is to be found in many references, made by early Christian authors, to heretical factions within the movement. St Paul was the earliest of the commentators to identify these problems. His mission lay with the gentiles, to whom Christians would apply the term *pagani* or pagans, and his concerns about pagan practice among Christians is first voiced in Acts in the context of letters to recently converted gentile communities.

> My sentence is, that we trouble not them, which from among the Gentiles are turned to God: But that we write unto them, that they abstain from pollutions of idols, and from fornication, and from things strangled, and from blood. [Acts 15.19–20]

If the emphases in Paul's writings are any measure, he became obsessed by what he saw as clandestine ceremonies of a sexual nature being performed in the name of Christianity. A nagging disapproval of these permeates much of his correspondence to the emerging churches in Europe and Asia Minor. When discussing sexual licence, Paul was fairly candid. Fornication was the issue under discussion and fornication was what it should be called. In the Jewish context (and Paul was of Jewish upbringing), fornication meant adultery or prostitution associated with idolatry. One of his most revealing observations comes in the letter to the Church in Corinth, a city lying just below the neck of land connecting the Peloponnesian peninsula with mainland Greece. Paul painted a thoroughly gloomy picture of the Corinthian Church, riven by internal feuding and theological divisions.

> It hath been declared unto me of you, my brethren, by them which are of the house of Chloe, that there are contentions among you.
>
> [1 Cor. 1.11]

Its fledgeling churches had committed what Paul considered to be an unacceptable list of abuses, for which he held a substantial part of the new congregation responsible.

> Know ye not that your bodies are the members of Christ? shall I then take the members of Christ, and make them members of an harlot? God forbid. What? Know ye not that he which is joined to an harlot is one body? for two, saith he, shall be one flesh ... Flee fornication. Every sin that a man doeth is without the body; but he that committeth fornication sinneth against his own body.
>
> [1 Cor. 6.15ff.]

Paul felt obliged to remonstrate with the Corinthians a second time when much of his worry revolved around the spread of heretical teachings.

> For I fear, lest, when I come, I shall not find you such as I would ... And lest, when I come again, my God will humble me among

you, and that I shall bewail many which have sinned already, and have not repented of the uncleanness and fornication and lasciviousness which they have committed.   [2 Cor. 12.20ff.]

He was scarcely less critical of the Christian communities in Galatia, Ephesus and Colossus, invariably placing fornication at the head of the list of misdemeanours. For the Christians in Thessalonia he had the same uncompromising message.

For this is the will of God, even your sanctification, that ye should abstain from fornication.   [1 Thess. 4.3]

Paul's letters reveal that many of the Christian sects were torn by sexual practices which, from the way he criticises them, were much more than mere dalliances. He was not alone in voicing concern. Sexually driven rites, including Sacred Marriages, feature strongly among complaints made by other early Christian Fathers. In the last decade of the second century, critical attention was paid to the Nicolaitan sect, whose founder was charged by Clement, Bishop of Alexandria, with sexual malpractice.

This man [Nicolaus], we are told, had an attractive young wife. After the Saviour's Ascension the apostles accused him of jealousy, so he brought his wife forward and said that anyone who wished might have her. This action, we are told, followed from the injunction 'the flesh must be treated with contempt'; and by following example and precept crudely and unquestioningly the members of the sect do in fact practise utter promiscuity.   [*Miscellanies* 3]

The Bishop of Lyons, Irenaeus, fingered another Christian group, the Valentinians, making the accusation that 'Some of them fit out a bridal chamber and celebrate a mystery with invocations on those being initiated, declaring that what they are doing is a spiritual marriage.'

In the *Panarion* Epiphanius, Bishop of Salamis, catalogued an impressive list of groups, mainly Gnostic, which paraded under the Christian banner but were strikingly pagan in their practices. He criticised the Valesians for castrating their disciples, alleging that the act was carried out to thwart sexual arousal. It is also possible that these men had committed themselves to keeping alive masochistic rites associated with the cult of Attis and Kybele.

> Most were members of the Church until foolishness became known and expelled. All but a few are eunuchs. When they take a man as a disciple, he does not eat meat while still uncastrated, but when they convince him of this or castrate him by force, he may eat anything because he is out of the struggle and runs no such risk of being aroused to the pleasures of lust by what he eats. [*Panarion* 38]

Much of the criticism was directed at the Gnostics. In his *History of the Church*, Eusebius writes of dealing with 'the names and dates of those who through a passion for innovation have wandered as far as possible from the truth, proclaiming themselves the founts of knowledge falsely so called [Gnosticism] while mercilessly, like savage wolves, making havoc of the Christian flock.' [*Hist.* 1.1] Of Simon Magus, the first-century Christian Samaritan preacher, and his followers, Eusebius wrote, 'For whatever could be imagined more disgusting than the foulest crimes known has been out-stripped by the revolting heresy of these men, who make sport of wretched women, burdened indeed with vices of every kind.' [*Hist.* 13.3] In another section of the book he quotes from *Promises* by Dionysius, Bishop of Alexandria, dealing with the heresy of the Cerinthian Gnostic sect. 'He [Cerinthus] filled the heaven of his dreams – unlimited indulgence in gluttony and lechery at ban-quets, drinking bouts, and wedding feasts (to call these by what he thought more respectable names), festivals, sacrifices and the immolation of victims.' [*Hist.* 28.2] Epiphanius went on to accuse the Manichaean sect of similar behaviour.

Criticism came not only from within the Christian movement. In one of his literary attacks on Celsus, all of whose writings have been destroyed, Origen made an interesting comment.

> He [Celsus] wished to bring into disrepute what are termed the
> love feasts of the Christians, as if they had their origin in the
> common danger and were more binding than any oaths. He
> thought to bring vast discredit upon our system of morals. He
> endeavoured to slander the secret doctrines of Christianity seeing
> he does not correctly understand its nature.
>
> [*Contra Celsum* 1.1; 1.4; 1.7]

Christian apologists have identified the *agape*, the so-called
'love feast', as a communal meal during which Christian devotees
exchanged nothing more reprehensible than spiritual tenderness
and charity. Yet can we be sure? Among the traditions of the
fertility religions, a ritual meal also took place alongside the act of
intercourse and we know from the prophet Jeremiah, writing at
the time of the Babylonian Exile, that pagan-orientated Jews were
well versed in its preparation. It is entirely possible that Christian
Jews carried on the tradition.

> Seest thou not what they do in the cities of Judah and in the streets
> of Jerusalem? The children gather wood, and the fathers kindle the
> fire, and the women knead their dough, to make cakes to the queen
> of heaven, and to pour out drink offerings unto other gods.
>
> [Jer. 7.17ff.]

The broader thrust of Origen's criticism was that Celsus equated
various Christian practices with those of the pagan Greeks and
that the Christians' stubborn reluctance to divulge details of their
more esoteric cult left them open to accusations. To a degree, this
hostility must have been down to knock-about tactics but it also
probably contains some uncomfortable truths about Christian and
pagan syncretism.

There is some archaeological evidence in support of accusations
of sexual misconduct. Recently, near the city boundary of Rome,

a cave with a natural spring was discovered. Originally used as a bathing pool, it was taken over as a shrine that, according to contemporary records, was in active use until the time of the Emperor Justinian (527–65 CE), long after the Christian conversion of the Roman Empire by Constantine in 312 CE. Thousands of lamps had been placed in the cave as offerings, encouraging the popular tourist label 'Fountain of the Lamps'. Many of the caves were decorated with erotica, indicating that the place had been home to popular rites with a sexual purpose.

More to the point in confirming that there were strongly divergent views over who and what Mary represented, Epiphanius criticised a Gnostic female cult, the Collyridians, for worshipping Mary as a goddess. They must have had considerable influence, covering a substantial territory, because he identifies them as having established a base of operations in Thrace to the west of the Black Sea and then spreading northwards and east to Upper Scythia before expanding as far as Arabia.

> I have heard that others, who are out of their minds on the subject of the holy Ever-Virgin, have done their best and are doing their best, in the grip both of madness and of folly, to substitute her for God. For they say that certain Thracian women there in Arabia have introduced this nonsense and that they bake a loaf in the name of the Ever-Virgin, gather together, and both attempt an excess and undertake a forbidden, blasphemous act in the holy Virgin's name, and offer their sacrifices in her name with women officiants.
>
> [*Panarion* vol. 2, no. 79]

Epiphanius took this information and used it to launch a furious attack against women in general.

> Where has this new story come from? From women's pride and female madness? What has nourished the wickedness that – through the female once more – pours the female habit of speculation into our minds ... with adulterous intent they have rebelled

against the one and only God, like a common whore who has been excited to the wickedness of many relations and rejected the temperate course of lawful marriage to one husband.

[Against Collyridians, *Panarion*, no. 79]

The Collyridians were not the only sect to share an interest in a Christianised mother goddess. According to Epiphanius, other Gnostics had been promoting the idea that a dominant female presence called Sophia (Wisdom) existed in the heavens. He also described sects known as Marcosians and Ossaeans who were either practising Sacred Marriages or engaging in aspects of goddess worship. The Marcosian priests 'prepared a bridal chamber, initiated their candidates with certain invocations, and claimed that their rite is a spiritual marriage in the likeness of the *syzygies* [opposites or marital partners] on high'. Until the time of the Emperor Constantius (293–306 CE), the father of Constantine the Great, the Ossaean sect allegedly worshipped as goddesses two sisters named Marthur and Marthana.

Epiphanius alleged that communities such as the Origenists were enjoying comparable sexual rites behind closed doors and 'soiled their bodies, minds and souls with unchastity'. He reported that some of their members adopted the ritual practice of ejaculating on to the earth while they 'masqueraded as monastics and their women companions as female monastics'. He claimed that the Samaritans were another Christian sect not following good orthodox principles and confirmed that their ancient sanctuary at Gerizim was still active in his day.

This sect is continually idolatrous in itself without knowing it, because the idols of the four nations are hidden in the mountain they quibblingly call Gerizim.   [*Panarion* 9]

The people at whose doors all these accusations were laid were professed Christians, and it is clear from the literary records that two opposing doctrines ran in parallel within early Christianity.

One followed the orthodox line that hoped to distance the movement from the pagan cults, the other pursued acts of ritual sex and acknowledged a mother goddess. Unfortunately for the orthodox establishment, an assortment of factors linked Mary, the mother of their inspirational founder, with the pagan cult. As we have discovered, these included the meaning of her name and the fact that she shared it with four prostitutes in the genealogy of Jesus, the matter of her irregular upbringing in the Temple, and rumours of adultery surrounding the conception of Jesus and his birth in a pagan sanctuary. To these elements can be added the documentary evidence that Mary performed an incestuous sexual act with her son and the behaviour of orthodox Jews at the time of her death in trying to burn her corpse.

Who Mary was, and what she stood for became a highly contentious issue. Paul and the other early Christian Fathers, determined to lure converts away from paganism with its sexual rites of devotion to the fertility goddess, would have been obliged to address these 'difficult aspects' of her biography. The response of the orthodox establishment to her pagan colours appears to have been to fight fire with fire.

It is arguable that the permanent celibacy of Mary was invented, and then promoted with such passion, as a counterblast to pagan-leaning sectarians who may, logically, have wished to promote her as a sexually-charged high priestess of the fertility goddess. Due to the destruction of heretical literature under censorship of the Church of Rome, evidence of the beliefs and activities of these sects has only reached us in the polemics of opponents. But if links between Mary and paganism can still be detected today, we can be reasonably sure that much more information was available to the leaders of the early Church.

From the time of Irenaeus (130–200 CE) the fatal parallel was drawn between Mary and Eve, and it is clear from the writings of the early Church Fathers that they viewed Mary as having reversed the misdemeanours that led to the Fall. The argument paved the way for neat contrasts to be drawn between the two women: one succumbed to sexual temptation, the other did not. The linking of Eve with original sin, however, is exclusive to Christian dogma. The Psalms of Solomon make clear that Jews of the first century saw women as being at risk of falling into sinful ways and they regarded ritual prostitutes as 'honeytraps' for the devout male. Original sin seems to have been placed at the door of male deities. In a mythological context, the apocryphal 1 Enoch takes up the Genesis theme of the sons of God, *bene elohim*, who had intercourse with the daughters of the people, producing a corrupt race of giants, the *nephilim*, which was then obliterated in the Deluge from which Noah, his family and his menagerie escaped. Fragments of this work, composed in Aramaic and believed by scholars to have been compiled as early as the Maccabean period in the second century BCE, were found among the Dead Sea Scrolls produced allegedly by the Essene community at Qumran.

> In those days, when then children of man had multiplied, it hap-pened that there were born unto them handsome and beautiful daughters. And the angels, the children of heaven, saw them and desired them; and they said to one another, 'Come, let us choose wives for ourselves from among the daughters of man and beget us children' ... they went in unto the daughters of the people on earth, and they lay together with them – with those women – and defiled themselves, and revealed to them every [kind of] sin ... and God said, 'Make known to those who fornicated with the women that they will die together with them in all their defilement.'
>
> [1 Enoch 6.1ff.; 7.1ff.; 9.1ff., OTP]

The second-century BCE Book of Jubilees emphasises the con-nection between sin and fornication.

> And there is no greater sin but the fornication which they commit upon the earth because Israel is a holy nation to the Lord his God, and a nation of inheritance and a nation of priests, and a royal nation and a special possession. And there is nothing which appears

which is as defiled as this among the holy people.   [Jubilees 33.20]

Tub-thumping evangelists of the calibre of Justin the Martyr, writing in the middle of the second century, launched the argument that 'Adam came into being from two virgins, from the Spirit and from the virgin earth. Christ therefore was born of a virgin to rectify the Fall which occurred at the beginning.' A few decades later, this level of cant was encouraging other Christian firebrands. St Jerome, the fourth-century monastic scholar, and his contemporary Ambrose, Bishop of Milan, began to market pithy catch-phrases such as, 'By a woman came death, by a woman came life.'

The Bishop of Carthage, Tertullian (160–225 CE), was another who railed that women are cursed with the sin of Eve.

Women should dress in mourning garments and neglect the exterior, acting the part of mourning and repentant Eve in order to expiate more fully by all sorts of penitential garb that which woman derives from Eve – the ignominy, I mean, of original sin and the odium of being the cause of the fall of the human race.

[Apparel of Women 1.1]

The novel dogma on original sin, and Mary's celibacy providing the antithesis to Eve's wantonness, was not adopted widely or immediately but the Roman Catholic Church began to emphasise the 'virginity factor' from around the beginning of the fourth Christian century. It became extended into an analogy for the purity of the Christian doctrine. When covering the excesses of Marcus Aurelius (161–180 CE) against the Christian martyrs, Eusebius started to describe the Church as the 'Virgin Mother', a phrase which conveniently made Mary a symbol of the purity and power of the Church. It has stood the test of time because modern Christians still talk of 'Mother Church'.

The belief that Mary remained a virgin, even if untrue, served the bigotry of such men as Jerome, Augustine and Ambrose, a fourth-century Bishop of Milan who effectively promoted Marian devotion in the West, since it allowed them to establish several fundamentals of the new religion: God had rejected sex; Mary's denial of carnality separated her from the rest of womanhood; and Jesus was born free from the taint of both original and actual sin. Typical of the rhetoric was that of Ambrose, who took steps to quell a popular rumour that Mary had subsequently borne other children (which we now suspect to be those of Joseph's first wife).

> Imitate her, holy mothers, who in her only dearly beloved Son set forth so great an example of maternal virtue; for neither have you sweeter children [than Jesus], nor did the Virgin seek the consolation of being able to bear another son.   [*Letters* 63.111]

Epiphanius once made the incisive statement, 'She [Mary] would not have sexual relations with a man' and in 392 CE Pope Siricius I, in correspondence with one of his bishops, hammered home the same insistent argument.

> You had good reason to be horrified at the thought that another birth might issue from the same virginal womb from which Christ was born according to the flesh. For the Lord Jesus would never have chosen to be born of a virgin if he had ever judged that she would be so incontinent as to contaminate with the seed of human intercourse the birthplace of the Lord's body.
>
> [*Letter to Bishop Anysius*]

In explaining how Mary came to be described as Joseph's wife, Jerome had gone so far as to make the dogmatic and radical assertion that the term in the ancient scriptures did not refer to a marital state but actually meant 'betrothed'. He specifically attacked the position of men like Helvidius and the Milanese monk, Jovinian, both of whom denied Mary's perpetual virginity and were expelled from the Church.

We must call upon the Lord Jesus to preserve free of all suspicion of copulation the inn of that sacred womb wherein He dwelled for ten months. We must also invoke God the Father, Himself, to prove that the mother of His Son, who was a mother before she was wed, remained a virgin after she brought forth her Son.

[*Contr. Helv.* 2]

Reading Jerome's comments, one gets some idea of the vehemence and hypocrisy with which the benefits of celibacy were argued. Among his typically misogynistic attacks, he made the distorted observation that marriage was only acceptable because it served to generate more virgins! [*Contr. Helv.* 19] Men of the calibre of Augustine took a similar position about marriage.

Because it is not materially different from fornication, [it] is so deeply infected with sin, that sin is committed, not indeed by the partner who consents, but by the partner who demands, even when it is done for the purpose of avoiding adultery.

[Bonaventura and Thomas Q49, Art 4–6]

The impression given by the early Christian Fathers is that they believed an intact hymen to be a God-given state. A woman who abandoned her maidenhood for sexual intercourse was defacing the excellent work of her Creator; and only by holding on to virginity could a woman escape the punishment earned by Eve at the Fall.

The obsession with linking women and sin sometimes reached ludicrous proportions. In a discussion of women's dress, Tertullian began to adopt tones of censure that approach fanaticism.

We use the word dress when we refer to what they call womanly grace, whereas make-up is more fittingly called womanly disgrace. Articles of dress are considered gold and silver and jewels and clothes, whereas make-up consists in the care of hair and of skin and of those parts of the body which attract the eye. On one we level the accusation of ambition; on the other that of prostitution.

[*Apparel of Women* 4.2]

Ironically, although celibacy had become a peculiarly Christian virtue, virgin birth was a pagan concept and early Christian spokesmen were concerned that the lore about Mary should not incline too far towards the supernatural. Both Origen and Jerome were scathing in their criticism of an apocryphal work *The Gospel of the Hebrews*, a second-century pamphlet thought to have originated in a Jewish-Christian sect. All traces of the work have been lost, other than those cited by its critics, and we must presume that they were destroyed early in the Christian era by the Church Fathers in Rome and elsewhere. The *Gospel of the Hebrews* raised questions about whether Christ was born of a normal earthly mother, to which Origen responded acidly that some Christians were trying to endow Mary with magical attributes beyond anything that was officially claimed for her.

If any should lend credence to the Gospel according to the Hebrews, where the Saviour himself says, 'My mother, the Holy Spirit, took me just now by one of my hairs and carried me off to the great Mount Tabor,' he will have difficulty in explaining how the Holy Spirit can be the mother of Christ. [Origen, *On John* 2.12]

Some of the ammunition fired off by the polemicists admittedly was obtained at second hand. Irenaeus alleged that the followers of Carpocrates, led by the Christian heretic Marcus, were guilty of practising indiscriminate sex with women who became Marcus's priestesses but it is generally conceded that Irenaeus had no direct contact with these people so he could only have gained his information through rumour.

He [Marcus] devotes himself especially to women, and those such as are well-bred, and elegantly attired, and of great wealth, whom he frequently seeks to draw after him, by addressing them in such seductive words as these: '... Adorn thyself as a bride who is expecting her bridegroom, that thou mayest be what I am, and I what thou art. Establish the germ of light in thy nuptial chamber. Receive from me a spouse, and become receptive of him, while thou art received by him.   [Irenaeus, *Adv. Haer.* 1.13.3]

It would be difficult, however, to find one of the Christian Fathers between the second and fourth centuries who did not level accusations of sexual impropriety against some of his brothers in Christ. Charges of moral laxity and rampant promiscuity became more or less routine, aimed with monotonous frequency at opponents whose defence seems to have gone unrecorded or been thoroughly obliterated by the Church. The accusers placed constant emphasis on Mary as the bastion of celibacy whose unsullied life exemplified the benefits of virginity and rejection of sexual desires. Yet this image, which is not reflected in the biblical texts, was almost wholly an invention. The sheer strength and persistence of criticism is evidence enough that other forces were at large within the Christian movement, promoting sexual rites and, perhaps, a somewhat contrasting picture of Mary.

By the fifth century, differences of opinion about this projected image of Christ's mother – exclusively blessed Yahwist matron or personification of a pagan fertility goddess – had become the focus of a fierce debate that was to erupt into open hostility between opposing factions. It revolved around the issue of whether or not Mary, the mother of Jesus, could legitimately be referred to by the contentious title, Mother of God.

ELEVEN

Deception

As Ramsay MacMullen put it, when commenting on the veracity of the early Christian record in *Christianity and Paganism in the Fourth to Eighth Centuries*, 'The truth left little mark. We may fairly accuse the historical record of having failed us not only in the familiar way, being simply insufficient, but through being also distorted ... what was written in the past had to be transmitted from generation to generation across succeeding centuries, and those centuries, as everyone knows, constituted a differentially permeable membrane: it allowed the writings of Christianity to pass through but excluded those of Christianity's enemies.' [pp. 3–4] MacMullen's statement needs amplifying in terms of the parameters of 'Christianity's enemies'. The dominant ecclesiastical forces of the time not only attacked the writings of non-Christians but also anything that they viewed as heretical inside the Christian movement. When sectarian disputes took place, the ideology of one side would invariably be declared heterodox and measures would be taken to eradicate any record of its existence other than what survived in the comments of its victorious critics.

Irenaeus, appointed Bishop of Lyons in 178 CE, was largely responsible for setting in motion the process of 'heretic bashing' through his massive work *Adversus Haereses* (Against the Heresies). Irenaeus' approach was to be shared by his contemporary, Tertullian, the third-century Bishop of Carthage. Both men took the position that heretics within the Christian communities were preaching something highly offensive. Irenaeus opened his attack with these words:

Inasmuch as certain men have set the truth aside, and bring in lying words and vain genealogies, which, as the apostle says, minister questions rather than godly edifying which is in faith, and by means of their craftily-constructed plausibilities draw away the minds of the inexperienced and take them captive, I have felt constrained, my dear friend, to compose the following treatise in order to expose and counteract their machinations. [*Adv. Haer.* 1, Preface]

Frequently this kind of criticism carried familiar undertones, equating heresy with sexual promiscuity.

The 'most perfect' among them addict themselves without fear to all those kinds of forbidden deeds of which the Scriptures assure us that, They who do such things shall not inherit the kingdom of God ... others of them yield themselves up to the lusts of the flesh with the utmost greediness ... some of them, moreover, are in the habit of defiling those women to whom they have taught ... as has frequently been confessed by those women who have been led astray by certain of them, on their returning to the Church of God, and acknowledging this along with the rest of their errors. Others of them, too, openly and without a blush, having become passionately attached to certain women, seduce them away from their husbands, and contract marriages of their own with them. Others of them, again, who pretend at first to live in all modesty with them as with sisters, have in course of time been revealed in their true colours, when the sister has been found with child by her [pretended] brother. [*Adv. Haer.* 1.6.3]

The Synod of Laodicea, convened in about 363 CE, was one of several that reinforced the message. Canon 59 of the synod states, 'No psalms composed by private individuals nor any uncanonical books may be read in church.' If one was forbidden to read non-canonical works, then clearly owning such books also carried its risks. Cyril of Jerusalem's *Catechetical Lectures* includes the homily, 'Whatever books are not read in the churches, do not read these even by yourself.' In short, the absence of surviving literature may not accurately reflect what was in circulation at the time.

We do not know how much of the writing about Mary in those early centuries was categorised as 'bringing in lying words'. It is clear, however, that apart from a few apocryphal texts like the *Protevangelium of James* Mary seems to have been excluded from theological writings between the date of the Crucifixion and the end of the second century. The dearth is striking, and it remains unanswered whether literature about Mary simply did not exist or whether it has been eradicated. We can compare the marked lack of discussion, irrespective of the cause, with a virtual absence of observation about such major personalities as Mozart or Napoleon Bonaparte until the end of the twentieth century.

The approach of the influential Christian writer Eusebius is also not untypical of the sparse sources that remain. He began compiling his exhaustive *History of the Church* at the beginning of the Emperor Diocletian's reign in 284 CE. The work spans the period from the birth of Jesus in about 4 BCE to the early decades of the fourth century, yet Mary is mentioned just four times. Eusebius gave Mary no credentials other than through recognising the doctrine of the virgin birth.

> Then there was James, who was known as the brother of the Lord; for he too was called Joseph's son, and Joseph Christ's father, though in fact the Virgin was his betrothed and before they came together she was found to be with child by the Holy Ghost, as the inspired gospel narrative tells us. [*Hist.* 2.11]

Irenaeus adopted a similar attitude. He mentioned Mary in *Adversus Haereses* for the first time after seven chapters and then only in passing. Like Eusebius, he introduced Mary into the discussion in order to hammer home the significance of the virgin birth of Christ and to emphasise Mary's immaculate and unique nature.

The Virgin pointed out the place of Ecclesia. And thus, by a special dispensation, there was generated by Him, through Mary, that man, whom, as He passed through the womb, the Father of all chose to [obtain] the knowledge of Himself by means of the Word.

[*Adv. Haer.* 15.3]

A 'sea change' took place when, after about two hundred years, there was a surge of interest in Mary that included a more liberal interpretation of her life. Perhaps the process began when Christians found the opportunity for self-analysis in the relative calm that followed the horrific persecutions of Christians by Marcus Aurelius (170 CE) and his son Commodus (176–192 CE), the last of the hard-line Roman emperors. Although the struggle between Church and empire would re-emerge briefly under the Emperor Diocletian (284–305 CE) it did not affect the enthusiasm, either officially or at a popular level, for putting together the framework which would become Marian dogma. Whether this verve was always present, or whether it simply came out of the closet, is unclear.

More or less from the end of the second century the apostolic bishops were drawing not only on canonical but also on apocryphal writings, such as the *Protevangelium of James*, to lay down what may be described as a 'publicly accountable' Marian doctrine. If the extraordinary compromise that this doctrine reveals is any measure, the cult of Mary seems to have been developing on two distinct levels reflecting the hybrid nature of the origins of Christianity. On the one hand, it was moulded by the apostolic ideology that outlawed fleshly desires. This is the side of Marian ideology that has come down to us as official Christian dogma. On the other hand, a less well-publicised conservatism flourished, favouring the old, pagan side of Jewish and gentile religion, based on a mix of Christian and pagan ideals where sex and sexuality were important features of ritual. In other words, Mariolatry was beset by much the same ideological division that was experienced by Jews in first-century Palestine. Elements of the new Christian congregation were pressing to wipe the slate clean and establish Mary as the Christian Immaculata without so much as a whiff of paganism, while others envisaged her as an old-style pagan *diva*. The embellishments in works such as the *Protevangelium*, including biographical details of Mary's miraculous birth (though not her immaculate conception), her genealogy, formative years and marriage, were fairly innocuous and could be exploited by both sides.

Some other apocryphal texts conveyed a more disturbing message. The writers of the *Gospel of Philip* and the *Genna Marias* included a side to the relationship between Jesus and the Marys which was unequivocally sexual. Others, such as *Origin of the World* and *Thunder, Perfect Mind*, evidenced interest in a dominant female presence in the heavens. These works are largely known through the discovery of the so-called Gnostic manuscripts, buried at Nag Hammadi in about 400 CE and preserved in the desert sands. Thought to have been written by unknown authors early in the fourth century, perhaps in Alexandria, they include alien concepts which were resisted by the orthodox lobby. Eusebius made some fierce comments in his *History of the Church*.

> Nothing could be further from apostolic usage than the type of phraseology employed, while the ideas and implications of their contents are so irreconcilable with true orthodoxy that they stand as revealed as the forgeries of heretics. It follows that so far from being classed even among the spurious books, they must be thrown out as impious and beyond the pale. [*Hist.* 25.2]

Coupled with the obstinate, often vitriolic attacks in the major anti-heretical works such as Origen's *Contra Celsum* and Epiphanius' *Panarion*, works such as the Nag Hammadi manuscripts constitute the only evidence of the unorthodox side of the Marian perspective. The extent of their influence is, however, manifest in the awkward compromise that was reached over Mary's official portrait, a melting-pot of various mythical elements.

Before examining the development of Mariolatry in the early Christian centuries we need to understand a little of what was happening to Christians at that time, in a more general sense. To some extent, due to the paucity of canonical record, and also due to the way in which Christianity developed after its arrival in Rome, Mary was not launched on to the public stage straight away. Christianity began as a Jewish experience in Jerusalem. It is reasonably certain that it was established there as a splinter group within the Jewish synagogue community. In the dispersal caused by foreign domination of Palestine, some Jews came to Rome where they set up synagogues within which Christian cells no doubt developed. Outside the Jewish community, Paul seems to have been the dominant figure in establishing Christian churches and we know from Roman records that both he and Peter died as martyrs in Rome under the rule of Nero from 54 to 68 CE. For about two centuries thereafter, Christianity was run from private houses as a small, exclusive club. The movement was gaining its converts mainly from the middle and lower classes. There were no churches in the sense that we would recognise today and no evidence survives of any kind of fixed Christian altars being built until the fifth century. Ceremonies, mainly the Eucharist, were apparently simple, without appeal to the emotions: the overriding concern seems to have been to dodge the scrutiny of outsiders, many of whom were unsympathetic to the Christian cause.

The writer Arnobius summed up the mood of much of Rome's citizenry towards the end of the third century when he belittled Christians for having no temples, altars, statues or effigies of divinities and blamed them for the general decline of Roman influence in the world.

Ever since the Christians have been on the earth, the world has gone to ruin; many and various scourges have attacked the human race; and the celestial beings themselves, abandoning the care with which hitherto they have watched over our interests, are banished from the regions of the earth.　　　　[*Adversus Nationes*, 1.1]

Rome's pagan conservatives were not alone in their chagrin. Problems quickly became apparent inside the Christian community because, while the movement maintained a low profile, it was also rubbing shoulders with the more liberally-minded of the pagan citizenry. To some extent this was attributable to an imbalance in the gender make-up of early Christian communities. We know from various contemporary sources that, in the third century, Christian women outnumbered Christian men. In his book *Pagans and Christians*, Robin Lane Fox notes that a church in North Africa, seized in a persecution of 303 CE, contained sixteen men's tunics against eighty-two ladies' dresses and forty-seven pairs of women's slippers. According to Tertullian, Christian wives frequently took pagan husbands and dangers were clearly inherent in the match.

> The handmaid of God dwells amid alien labours; and among these, on all the memorial days of demons, at all solemnities of kings, at the beginning of the year, at the beginning of the month, she will be agitated by the odour of incense. And she will have to go forth by a gate wreathed with laurel and hung with lanterns, as from some new consistory of public lusts; she will have to sit with her husband oftimes in club meetings, oftimes in taverns.
>
> [*To His Wife* 2.6]

Close contact between pagans and Christians in the major urban centres of the empire was a permanent irritation and worry to the hard-line evangelists because it had no small part to play in keeping the melting-pot of ideology warm. Serious concern lay in the potential ease with which Christian converts could be lured back into pagan ways. Children were brought up according to whatever beliefs their parents considered natural and profitable. The family and marital situation turned into an almost exact *déjà vu* of the intermarriage problems that had bedevilled early Israelite history where an Israelite might take a foreign wife with different religious beliefs. In effect, far from becoming established as a clear-cut

radical movement, the line between emerging Christian orthodoxy and old-fashioned paganism was, for a while, progressively
more blurred. Christianity remained unpopular with a large slice
of the population: many civilians saw little attraction in what it
had to offer and, although there were Christian units within the
Roman military, the army by and large detested it. In 299 CE the
Emperor Diocletian went so far as to order a purge of Christians
from the army.

The catalyst for change, and the moment for Christianity to
come out of the closet, clarify its doctrine and stamp its authority,
was the miraculous conversion of the Roman Emperor, Constantine, in 312 CE, when he is alleged to have witnessed a fiery
Christian emblem in the night sky before the Battle of Milvian
Bridge against his rival Maxentius. Constantine's conversion did
not, however, put an end to the blurring at a domestic level. The
Christian Fathers became so concerned about the situation that,
two years after Constantine's switch of religious allegiance, the
Council of Arles threatened excommunication to anyone who
married out of the new faith. The warning was largely ignored
even when Theodosius I, who became emperor in 378 CE, rubber-
stamped Christianity as the official imperial cult and started the
process of enforcement against pagan worship.

The fourth century saw Marian ideology take on a more defined
shape, including both orthodox and heterodox thinking. During
this period, Mary's allegedly permanent virginity remained the
most strident message and it encouraged a level of extremism
among the Church's misogynists. Men such as John Chrysostom,
Patriarch of Constantinople, took an uncompromising Pauline
view of wedlock. It was only fit for people who, through personal
weakness, could not abstain from sex and the same argument was
used to justify the imposition of austere restrictions on what went
on in the Christian bedchamber. Chrysostom was among those
who considered that the story of the fall of Adam and Eve provided
a proper lesson in morality. Sexual activities could, and should, be
dispensed with altogether. The bigotry revealed in his *Homily on*

Virginity, which lacked forward planning for humanity's future, included the puritanical claim that 'Where there is death, there is sexual coupling; and where there is no death, there is no sexual coupling either ... do you see where marriage took its origin?' Out of the bizarre logic arose the dogma that, since a normally conceived child is the product of sin, it is automatically tainted with evil from the moment of its birth and can only recover its innocence through the rite of baptism.

While not all Marian devotees can have taken this extreme view, the growing band, determined to promote Mary as a wholly chaste virgin, feasted on the developing belief that she had been the product of immaculate conception on the part of her mother, Anna. From this, it could be claimed that Mary had never been tainted with sin and was therefore able, uniquely, to give birth to a sinless baby. The ideology led to the harsh treatment of Christian women accused of sexual impropriety. A comment by St Jerome some time in the late fourth century CE indicates that he endorsed the practice of allowing women to be beheaded if they were caught participating in extramarital sex. This contrasts markedly with the pagan sense of justice in comparable situations. A revealing record of the same period from Thebaid in Egypt details how, when a prostitute was murdered, her attacker was executed and the victim's mother, whose poverty had necessitated her daughter turning to whoring, inherited a tenth part of the killer's property. Jerome was a fanatical advocate of celibacy, and there is a degree of irony in the fact he was one of the most convincing Church leaders of his day, providing evidence that Christians of every rank and calling were indulging in scandalous activity. Much of his *Letter to Eustochium*, for example, is taken up with details about the sexual behaviour of fellow Christians.

If even real virgins, when they have other failings, are not saved by their physical virginity, what shall become of those who have prostituted the members of Christ, and have changed the temple of the Holy Ghost into a brothel? Straightway shall they hear the

words: 'Come down and sit in the dust, O virgin daughter of
Babylon, sit on the ground; there is no throne, O daughter of the
Chaldaeans: for thou shalt no more be called tender and delicate.
Take the mill-stone and grind meal; uncover thy locks, make bare
thy legs, pass over the rivers; thy nakedness shall be uncovered,
yea, thy shame shall be seen.'   [Jerome, *Letters* 22.6]

The moral superiority regarding celibacy, claimed by the Christian establishment, actually rested on shaky foundations. One of
the factors fuelling the argument of Christians determined to
retain aspects of Mary's biography which identified her with a
pagan mother goddess, was that views about the value of virginity
were shared by others. In pagan Rome, the Vestal Virgins and the
priestesses of the great goddess Pallas Athene were considered the
moral and social equals of their Christian counterparts and their
chastity was dedicated to the well-being of the state [Ambrose, *De
Virginibus* (I) 4.14–15]. Even Plato had argued that the salvation
of the soul could best be achieved by refraining from passion and
through the regular use of prayers. Nor was the Christian view –
of a virgin being impregnated by a god before giving birth to a
great leader – unique. Romans considered the Phrygian goddess
Kybele, who became their *Magna mater*, to be a virgin mother. It
was also widely held in both Greek and Roman traditions that the
mythical founder of Rome, Romulus, the twin brother of Remus,
was born to a mother who had been impregnated by the god Mars.
In Rome the cult of Mithraism had been imported from India
via Persia as a powerful influence which blended well with the
monotheistic religion of Zoroastrianism: the god Mithras was
known to have been born from a rock, symbolising the sun rising
from behind mountains. Virgin deities like Vesta, the hearth
goddess, were also revered and frequently invoked.

The Christian establishment may have targeted unofficial
Marian biographies like the *Protevangelium of James* and the
Assumption of the Virgin as unacceptable reading in the churches
but their prohibition did not stop such literature from spreading,

nor did it prevent the arbitrators of Mariolatry from drawing on it. These works became immensely popular, evidenced by the fact that, today, over one hundred early copies of the *Protevangelium* in Greek survive, some dating from the third century. Within a few decades of its publication it was translated into various other languages. The fact that the Church Fathers were using material which, at other times, they denounced suggests that they were faced with some pressure to incorporate contentious elements into Mary's portrait. Through this liberalisation the seeds of an extraordinary transformation were being sown that would change Mary the Jewish mother into a celebrity, and grant her a new personality.

The transformation of Mary was not without its problems. Many of the Church Fathers remained deeply misogynist and were able to resolve the paradox of their veneration of Mary only by separating her, physically and spiritually, from the rest of mortal womanhood on which they continued to cast unremitting scorn. St Augustine of Hippo (354–430 CE) was at the forefront. He laid great emphasis on the sinfulness of humanity, including the saints, but pointedly excluded Mary. In some of his more moderate writings Augustine fell short of the outright argument that sexual relations within marriage were sinful.

> I admonish both men and women who follow after perpetual con-
> tinence and holy virginity, that they so set their own good before
> marriage, as that they judge not marriage an evil: and that they
> understand that it was in no way of deceit, but of plain truth that
> it was said by the Apostle, Whoso gives in marriage does well; and
> whoso gives not in marriage, does better; and, if thou shalt have
> taken a wife, thou hast not sinned; and, if a virgin shall have been
> married, she sinneth not, and a little after, But she wilt be more
> blessed, if she shall have continued so, according to my judgement.
> Whoso therefore shall be willing to abide without marriage, let
> them not flee from marriage as a pitfall of sin; but let them surmount
> it as a hill of the lesser good, in order that they may rest in the

mountain of the greater continence. [*On Holy Virginity* 18]

Elsewhere, however, Augustine revealed more extreme sentiments when he asserted that a child born of sexual intercourse was a child born in sin.

> He [Jesus] only was born without sin whom a virgin conceived without the embrace of a husband, not by the concupiscence of the flesh, but by chaste submission of her mind. She alone was able to give birth to One who should heal our wound, who brought forth the germ of a pure offspring without the wound of sin.
>
> [*Merits and Remission of Sin* 57]

It was through Augustine that the peculiarly Christian link between sin and procreation was forged and he served the misogynist dogma well with his rhetoric. Physical desire and sexual contact were not, in his argument, healthy biological parts of the human psyche but aberrations attached firmly to the weak shoulders of women. He was, however, by no means the first of the Christian Fathers to advocate celibacy. Tertullian also placed strong emphasis on the desirability of spinsterhood.

> In that it is written, To marry is better than to burn, what, pray, is the nature of this good, which is only commended by comparison with evil, so that the reason why 'marrying' is more good is merely that 'burning' is less? Nay, but how far better is it neither to marry nor to burn? [*To His Wife* 1.3]

Tertullian had a particular message concerning Christian women who had renounced marriage.

> They have laid hold for themselves of an eternal gift of the Lord; and while on earth, by abstaining from marriage, are already counted as belonging to the angelic family. Training yourself to an emulation of constancy by the examples of such women, you will

by spiritual affection bury that fleshly concupiscence, in abolishing the temporal and fleeting desires of beauty and youth by the compensating gain of immortal blessings. [*To His Wife* 1.4]

Augustine of Hippo echoed the uncompromising message of Jerome and Ambrose: that Eve had brought death through her curiosity and weakness for apples and that Mary, the antithesis of Eve, brought life by rejecting all sensuality and conceiving through faith rather than an impious human agency. Humanity's salvation, Augustine thundered, lay in Mary whose rejection of sex had reduced the special penalties of the Fall. In a superstitious age, his argument was potent.

Church Fathers, including Augustine, Origen and Ambrose, extolled Mary's immaculate life as a paradigm for all to emulate, and argued that her absolute virginity conferred power. They promoted extreme claims, fuelled by the romantic fiction in the burgeoning apocryphal texts, that Mary's virginity lasted from cradle to grave. The virginity of her mother Anna had been unsullied. Even Joseph had been a perpetual virgin. Mary and her mother were paraded as the unusual exceptions among women until, gradually, virgin birth ceased to be a subject for debate and became an incontrovertible fact of Christian tradition.

The fast-developing fictional colours washing over Mary's portrait at a popular level also included the desire to promote her as the embodiment of a goddess. This left some of the ecclesiastical establishment less than euphoric. The desire, however, emanated not only from the minority groups such as the Collyridians, but came, as we shall see, from mainstream ecclesiastical heavyweights. This suggests that powerful influences within the Christian movement were keen to recognise Mary as a goddess, either because they were genuinely sympathetic to the idea or had succumbed to pressure from pagan elements. If they were looking for an exercise in damage limitation (given the clearly pagan nature of the idea) the justification was found not in a debate over Mary, but Jesus.

Within the Christian orthodox 'think-tank', interest in Mary was titillated, in no small part, by the emergence of a long-running controversy on the subject of Christ's nature, otherwise known as Christology. Clarifying the true nature of Christ would not only provide a justification for the unique identity that apostolic bishops wanted to give Mary; it would also satisfy the more discerning requirements of the Church's scholastic lobby who considered that any apocryphal claims needed some theological justification.

Christology agonised over whether Jesus was human, divine or something of a hybrid. It was a puzzle which occupied the minds of Christian intellectuals during most of the fourth century. A number of the early sects, particularly the Jewish Christians or Ebionites (from the Hebrew word meaning 'poor') who were later condemned as heretics, regarded Jesus Christ as a perfectly ordinary man who became extraordinary only through the growth of his character. Ebionites ridiculed the story of the virgin birth; as far as they were concerned, the mother of Jesus was irrelevant.

Casting back to the latter half of the second century, three schools had emerged within mainstream Christian thought. A group known as the Adoptionists maintained that Jesus was made of flesh and blood and, at some point in his life, probably at his baptism but maybe at his Crucifixion, that he was adopted by God. By and large they discounted the ideas either that Jesus was born of a virgin or that he had previously existed in a spiritual form. The Adoptionists, one of whose strongest proponents in the third century was the Bishop of Antioch, Paul of Samosata (subsequently denounced as a heretic), claimed to echo the views of Jesus' earliest followers. This claim has some justification because the Adoptionists' arguments, implying that Christ's divinity was only gained at the time of his death, can be found in the opening of the Epistle to the Romans. Allegedly the author was St Paul, but the style in which the letter is written indicates that he was not the correspondent. The language is non-Pauline and it contains greetings to various people whom Paul had never visited, suggesting that it may even have predated the books of the New Testament.

Concerning his son Jesus Christ our Lord, which was made of the seed of David according to the flesh; And declared to be the son of God, with power, according to the spirit of holiness, by the resurrection from the dead.   [Rom. 1.3–4]

The second philosophical movement was known as Separationism. It followed a similar line but argued that, at his baptism, the human Jesus was granted divinity in order to empower him for his ministry. This divine power was withdrawn from Jesus prior to the Crucifixion since, as a divinity, he could not have 'died' in this way. The third school, Doceticism (from the Greek word meaning 'to seem or appear'), was the most radical. It owed its inspiration to the Gnostic teacher, Valentinus of Rome, who lived during the second century and whose philosophy followed that of Plato. Docetics rejected the argument of any genuine incarnation, claiming that Jesus possessed only the appearance of a human being. He was actually God, innocently disguised, who had descended to earth with the purpose of redeeming his chosen people.

The Christians who eventually took the moral and intellectual high ground and became the voice of 'orthodoxy', decided it was safest to sit on the ideological fence and argue that, in some way, Jesus was both human and divine. The impossible paradox spawned a new rash of pundits who, with great personal conviction, managed to tie themselves in knots by denying and, at the same time, agreeing with everything! These apologists opposed anyone who claimed that Christ was man but not God, or that he was God but not man, or that he was two distinct beings, one divine and one human. One of the most vociferous in this convoluted argument was to be St Augustine.

The Father, and the Son, and the Holy Spirit intimate a divine unity of one and the same substance in an indivisible equality; and therefore that they are not three Gods, but one God: although the Father hath begotten the Son, and so He who is the Father is not the Son; and the Son is begotten by the Father, and so He who is the Son is not the Father; and the Holy Spirit is neither the Father nor the Son, but only the Spirit of the Father and of the Son, Himself also co-equal with the Father and the Son, and pertaining to the unity of the Trinity. [*On the Trinity* 1.4.7]

Christianity had saddled itself with responsibility for preserving the thrust of Old Testament Jewish religion, which emphasised monotheism, but it also had to deal with two divinities, God and Jesus Christ. If the Church was to distance itself from paganism, which was virtually synonymous with polytheism, and to defend monotheism, how could it also argue that the Son was distinct from the Father?

Within the Christian community, most of the early ideological arguments were thrashed out in the eastern wing of the Roman Empire. 'East' and 'West' had tended to separate along cultural lines, a division that was exacerbated because the two regions spoke different languages – Greek in the East and Latin in the West. Western Christianity was essentially gentile and was promoted by Paul and his followers, while the East inclined towards conservatism and maintained faith more strongly, and for longer, with some of the old Judaic traditions. The Christology dilemma led to ideological rifts between two rival camps, Antioch in modern Turkey and Alexandria in North Africa.

The Antiochian Church had taken the old-style monotheistic and Judaic view: Jesus Christ might have spoken of God as a triad of Father, Son and Spirit, but these remained aspects of the One and although Christ himself was both divine and human, God, in the opinion of the Antioch school, was definitely on his own.

The Alexandrian school promoted a philosophy known as pluralism. God was indivisible but also an abstract. In the early part of the third century the Alexandrian Church was strongly influenced by Origen, one of the giants of early Christian thinking whose work *De Principiis*, 'On First Principles', is arguably the earliest great compendium of Christian principles under one title. Origen argued that the material world could not have been created by an abstract without an intermediary, the *Logos* or Word, which became flesh in the form of a Son who died for the world's redemption. The Holy Spirit completed the triad.

One of the local quarrels fermenting over the Trinity was between Alexander, Bishop of Alexandria (313–28 CE), and Arius, one of his presbyters. Arius contrived to put the heretical cat firmly among the clerical pigeons by preaching the message of Alexandrian pluralism in such an extreme manner that it almost seemed that there were three gods, one supreme, God, and two inferior, Christ and the Spirit, linked by the Word. The argument became known as the 'Arian Heresy'. In a pamphlet, *Deposition of Arius*, St Athanasius (296–373 CE) cited a passage from a letter that Arius had written to Eusebius, Bishop of Nicomedia.

> The Father remains ineffable to the Son, and the Word can neither see nor know His Father perfectly and accurately ... but what He knows and sees, He knows and sees in the same way and with the same measures as we know by our own powers.
>
> [*Ep. ad episc. Aeg et lib* 12]

Arius was excommunicated by a synod in 321 CE. Open sectarian warfare over Christ's identity was now threatening the stability of the Church and it was decided that a special assembly of bishops should convene in Nicaea to resolve the matter. The council took place under direction of the Emperor Constantine in May 325 CE and out of the proceedings came the familiar imagery of the Trinity: Father, Son and Holy Spirit. The council proceedings also amounted to an ambivalent compromise over the nature of Christ both incarnate and divine. The delegates worked into the 'Nicene Creed' the key word *homoousios*, meaning 'consubstantial' or 'of one substance' with the Father.

> We believe in one God, the Father almighty, maker of all things both visible and invisible; and in one Lord, Jesus Christ, the Son

of God, only begotten of the Father, that is of the substance of the Father, God of God, Light of Light, very God of very God, begotten not made, of one substance with the Father; through whom all things were made, both things in heaven and the things on earth.

[Appendix to *De decret. Nic. syn.*, St Athanasius]

The Christology wrangle inevitably influenced how Mary was perceived. If Christ was born human and only gained divinity at a later date, which was effectively the Antiochian argument, then Mary was scarcely more than a simple Jewish matron. But according to the Alexandrians, since the birth of a god could not be through the normal human process, his mother could not be a normal human being either. The Antioch school was less than impressed by the suggestion that Mary was the superhuman mother of a divinity and promptly threw the idea out. It was this new source of rancour which led to the introduction of the most controversial part of the Marian dogma, that of the *Theotokos*, the 'Mother of God'. Hauling Mary into the debate was, at face value, illogical since Mary was not a Christian and in her lifetime Christology was something for the future. But what emerged from the debate may, ironically, be closer to the truth than the Church establishment intended.

Although the *Theotokos* argument probably began in the second century, the earliest recorded use of the word is by Alexander, Bishop of Alexandria. He argued that, since Christ was God incarnate, Mary must be afforded the title 'Mother of God' instead of *Christotokos* or 'Mother of Christ'. The vogue became increasingly widespread so that, by about 360 CE, it was part of a general, though strictly unofficial, religious currency. At around the time of the Council of Nicaea the bishops of Alexandria, including Athanasius [*Four Discourses against the Aryans* 3.29], were challenging the Adoptionists and Separationists by connecting Mary with the idea of *Theotokos*. In later decades their arguments would be supported by such weighty defenders as Ambrose, Jerome and particularly Augustine, who did much to promote Mary's image in the West.

Once the *Theotokos* claim had gained the upper hand, Mary would be transformed officially into a Christian character who was, however, indistinguishable in the eyes of many from a pagan mother goddess, the diametric opposite of much that Yahwism and Christianity stood for. The conflict of opinion about Mary not only made for bitter arguments, it led to actual tampering with biblical texts. None of the original gospel manuscripts has survived and there is a considerable gap between these and the earliest handed-down manuscripts written in Greek and Latin by anonymous scribes between the fourth and sixth centuries CE. It is from various Greek copies that the first published New Testament text was prepared by Erasmus in 1515 CE. A similar procedure, though with closer attention to provenance, was adopted for such well-known English translations as the Authorised (King James) Version of 1611 and the modern Revised Standard Version completed in 1952. The manuscripts from which any copies of the New Testament have been drawn are, however, virtually impossible to authenticate. The sheer extent of copying resulted in inadvertent text changes. Furthermore, neither the ideological leanings nor the level of education of the scribes is known. There is firm evidence, none the less, that some of the early manuscript copies were deliberately altered for ideological reasons. Attempts were made to cut the virgin birth from the opening chapters of the gospels of Matthew and Luke. The King James translation of Matthew reads, 'Joseph the husband of Mary, of whom was born Jesus, who is called Christ.' [Matt. 1.16] A thousand years earlier the anonymous scribe of a fifth-century manuscript, discovered in St Catherine's Monastery on Mount Sinai and written in Syriac, had made the sentence read: 'Joseph, to whom was betrothed the Virgin Mary, begot Jesus, who is called the Christ'. Similarly, while the King James Version reads, '[Joseph] knew her [Mary] not till she had brought forth her firstborn son: and he called his name Jesus' [Matt. 1.25], the Syriac text claims that 'Mary bore to him [Joseph] a son'.

We can find evidence of more severe doctoring. Several Christian Fathers, among them Papias writing in the first third of the second century and Jerome in the fourth century, reported that the Ebionites, for whom the virgin birth was a nonsense, had written a gospel based on a form of Matthew from which the entire opening Nativity chapters had been deleted. The evidence has long since been destroyed so we only have the words of these early commentators to rely on. These adulterations of New Testament text are further proof that the shaping of the Marian legend was proving controversial.

The *Theotokos* debate came to a head in the fifth century as ecclesiastical in-fighting shifted even more strongly towards Mary. The catalyst was an Antiochian priest named Nestorius, a hard-line champion of orthodoxy with impressive powers of oratory who had recently been appointed Bishop of Constantinople. He was particularly scathing about the idea that God was wrapped in swaddling clothes and later fastened to a cross, which he dismissed as vile heathen nonsense. Nestorius had an inflated opinion of himself, which did not make him universally popular but probably served him well in securing the Constantinople post in 428 CE. He was responsible for picking up the Christology debate where Arius had been forced to let it go. With no time for paganism or heresy, he resented those who presumed to call the Virgin Mary *Theotokos*. He had been immensely offended by a preacher named Proclus who, at about this time, had delivered a particularly out-spoken sermon in praise of Mary as the *Theotokos*.

The Church of Antioch was keen to promote the human nature of Christ and, immediately after his investiture, Nestorius began a ferocious onslaught against what he saw as blatant heresy. Convinced that *Christotokos* was the only proper title for Mary, and that *Theotokos* generated even worse confusion about the divinity and humanity of Christ, Nestorius wrote to his patron, Pope Celestine. He roundly criticised the Alexandrian Church under its ruling bishop, Cyril, by then the undisputed policy-maker for the western arm of Christendom, who was openly referring to Mary as the 'Mother of God'.

Predictably, some formidable heavyweights were ranged on the side of Cyril, including the bishops Juvenal of Jerusalem and Memnon of Ephesus. They persuaded Pope Celestine that Nestorius must either be made to retract or face excommunication. The Antiochian bishops of the eastern bloc treated this assault on their self-appointed spokesman as an outrage and the threats against Nestorius were energetically resisted. With tempers frayed the *Theotokos* issue gained in intensity and, about a hundred years after Arius had thumped out his pulpit rhetoric, another general council was convened, on this occasion in a small dusty seaside town named Ephesus, clinging to the shores of the Aegean.

What took place in Ephesus in the summer of 431 CE would place Mary in a new light in the Roman Catholic Church. In authorising the council, in an attempt to cool the rapidly rising temperature of debate and believing Cyril to be the main culprit in stirring up dissent, the Emperor Theodosius II went over the head of Pope Celestine. Ephesus was probably chosen by Theodosius because it was thought to be a safe venue in which Nestorius might promote and win his argument. That part of the eastern Mediterranean was firmly under the influence of the eastern wing of the Church, based in Constantinople, and the eastern bishops were strongly opposed to promoting Mary to what was tantamount to the status of a goddess. Ephesus was also a suitable venue because, by the fifth century, tradition had linked the town with Mary who, it was said, had elected to live there with John the Divine. Its citizens had built a basilica in her honour, and it was in this church on a June day, almost four hundred years after the event in Bethlehem which was destined to launch her from obscurity, that two opposed camps of bishops sat down to debate Mary's future. There was, however, a further reason why Ephesus was a significant setting in which to gather two hundred clerics for a debate about the elevation of Mary to the status of *Theotokos*. For centuries it had been the cult centre of another fabled *diva*, the Greek mother goddess, Artemis. Although mistress of the chase, she was better known in Asia as the bringer of fertility and fecundity. Her statues from Ephesus are sculpted in a style which could have been copied from some of the arcane maternal images of prehistory, a myriad of ripe breasts festooning her body.

The Council of Ephesus turned out to be unlucky for Nestorius. Pope Celestine made no open objection to the emperor's decision but, behind the scenes, he was supporting Cyril's view that Mary should be accorded the *Theotokos* title. On the shrewd reckoning that his bread would be more generously buttered by doing so, the local bishop, Memnon, also backed Cyril and showed such hostility towards Nestorius that the latter had to be given an armed military guard while in the town.

Cyril of Alexandria was an unpleasant bully whose bigotry and excesses were already well known. He was an avid follower of Origen, the Alexandrian writer, and pursued a healthy interest in Greek philosophy. Some historians have drawn him as an individual deeply intolerant of pagans but it may be more accurate to say that he was intolerant of dissent against his own views. It is interesting that he displayed particular animosity towards orthodox Judaism which was no more keen than Nestorius to turn Mary into a goddess. In 415 CE Cyril appears to have authorised the lynching of Hypatia, the Alexandrian woman whose only crimes seem to have been that she was a Neoplatonist philosopher, a pagan teacher and a woman!

The conduct of the Council of Ephesus became particularly shabby. Knowing that many of the bishops who would support Nestorius had been delayed *en route*, the Alexandrian contingent convened the crucial vote ahead of schedule and pushed through a motion in favour of 'excluding Nestorius from the episcopal dignity as well as the whole priestly college'. In effect, they elected to take away his bishopric and make him *persona non grata* among fellow clerics. They cemented this with a raft of anathema favouring the pro-*Theotokos* lobby but their advantage turned out to be short-lived. When the irregular circumstances were reported back to Theodosius, he issued an imperial bull condemning the proceedings. A week later, after the arrival of Nestorius' supporters led by John of Antioch, a second council meeting excommunicated Cyril and Memnon for their unprincipled conduct. Crucially, though, the meeting failed to support Nestorius and, in the end, Cyril's argument was endorsed by Pope Celestine. In a move of immense importance for the future perception of Mary, the *Theotokos* title was written into the official doctrine of both East and West.

✦

TWELVE

Queen of Heaven

After the Ephesus Council of 431 CE feelings ran so high that Cyril and Memnon were thrown into gaol to cool off on the orders of Theodosius II while Nestorius returned to his monastery in Antioch to live out his retirement in seclusion. Two years later, in 433 CE, John of Antioch reached the conclusion that Nestorius' argument was a good one. He chose to remain silent, however, and agreed only to a compromised definition of *Theotokos* which had been suggested by Theodoret, a leading Syrian theologian who held the bishop's seat in Cyprus and who died in 466 CE. The explanation put forward by Theodoret was largely a 'fudge', declaring the Christ to be of one substance and two natures, but it satisfied the theologians of Antioch and became known as the *Formulary of Union*. Cyril put his signature to the document.

> Perfect God and perfect man consisting of rational soul and body, of one substance with the Father in his Godhead, of one substance with us in his Manhood, so that there is a union of two natures; on which ground we confess Christ to be one and Mary to be the mother of God.

An uneasy truce grumbled on for another sixteen years but the controversy refused to go away and, in 451 CE, Theodosius convened a second meeting, this time in a town on the Bosphorus. Held under the papacy of Leo and called the Council of Chalcedon, it bestowed another title on Mary, that of *Aeiparthenos*, or 'Ever-Virgin', ratifying the argument that during her life Mary never engaged in sexual activities. It was not until 649 CE, during the First Lateran Council held under the chairmanship of Pope Martin I, that *Aeiparthenos* was incorporated into the dogma of Catholicism but the issue forced Theodoret, unequivocally, to condemn Nestorius.

> Anathema to Nestorius and to whoever does not call the Virgin Mary *theotokos* and to anyone who divides the only-begotten Son into two sons. I myself also have subscribed to the definition of faith and to the letter of the very reverend archbishop Leo; this is my opinion. And after all that you may be saved!
>
> [*Graec. affect. curat.*]

Of course, not everyone within the Christian camp agreed with this process of apotheosis. Bishop Epiphanius had written in one of his anti-heretical diatribes of those who, 'in their folly, wishing to exalt the Ever-Blessed Virgin, have put her in the place of God'. [*Panarion* 78.23]

Mary's rise to fame accelerated in the fifth century. The argument over Christ's status must have been extremely useful to those such as Cyril, intent on giving Mary status akin to that of a divinity. They could justify the change of title from *Christotokos* to *Theotokos* and avoid leaving themselves open to the criticism that they were promoting pagan arguments.

It was a good public relations exercise to parade Mary as the *Theotokos* because this sent back an uncompromising message to various sects, including the Docetics, the Manichaeans, Marcionites and others, all of whom claimed that Christ had never been human and that his 'mother' was, therefore, an irrelevance. Unfortunately the pro-*Theotokos* 'tub-thumpers' often seem to have resorted to crude ideological bribery such as that preached by St Gregory of Nazianzus in the mid-fourth century: 'Anyone who does not accept holy Mary as the *Theotokos* is without the godhead'.

What emerged was a confusing mix of ideology with, in Christian terms, a thoroughly doubtful pedigree. The assertion that Mary had conceived immaculately by a god was a theme of pagan origin, yet it was adopted by Christian spokesmen such as Jerome, Origen, Ambrose and Augustine as the basis of a wholly unfounded argument that Mary permanently shunned sexual relations. Never stated in the canonical narratives, *Aeiparthenos* was virtually discounted by St Paul and other first-century Christians and was positively contradicted in various apocryphal texts. Mary's newly acquired title *Theotokos* had no less of a pagan ring to it and Nestorius is alleged to have made the plea at Ephesus, 'Do not make Mary a goddess!' Yet the *Theotokos* motion was forced through. It may have been a fair defence on the part of its backers that giving Mary the title 'Mother of God' did not turn her into a goddess. Nevertheless, within a comparatively short space of time, it was being used as justification for showering her with the kind of adoration that would otherwise have been reserved for a deity.

The bestowing of the *Theotokos* title was merely a starting point in the transformation of Mary. Having elevated her from housewife to Mother of God the power brokers, led by men such as Cyril of Alexandria with the backing of the imperial Roman court, set about promoting an ever more astonishing public image. The earthly mother of Jesus was about to be 'packaged' as the star of an apocryphal mystery play with a new persona that both transcended and distorted the realities of her life. In twentieth-century terms, it was akin to that generated for a 'goddess' of the cinema screen; in the religious climate of the fifth century, it must have conveyed much of the ideal of a 'sanitised' *diva*.

The process was due, to a large extent, to the manner in which the general popularity of Christianity was spreading. The movement had started to attract influential members of the community, particularly in the major towns and cities, who saw the way the spiritual tide was turning. From about 391 CE the Emperor Theodosius had begun to issue a series of punitive edicts against paganism, in effect making Christianity the exclusive religion of empire.

The power brokers and the more affluent elements of society began joining the conversion 'bandwagon', and the process was set to gain momentum. Money meant that the Church was able to dominate the media. Christian missionaries could afford to employ calligraphers to spread the ideology. Two thousand years ago, anyone who wished to promote political or religious ideas needed the services of these specialists in the skills of handwriting, but calligraphers, generally slaves sold in the markets, were in chronically short supply and their talents therefore represented an expensive commodity. Once the Christian establishment discovered that 'money talked', the available talent was quickly snapped up and, conversely, the chance of anyone managing to put over the pagan version of events was diminished. This imbalance on the public relations front not only helped to eliminate the dissemination of pure pagan ideas but it also reduced the scope for non-orthodox Christian thoughts, those deemed to reveal heretical leanings.

Control of the media enabled the supposedly contentious elements in the lives of Jesus, Mary and the apostles to be altered or removed altogether and replaced with profiles considered by the Church Fathers to be more in line with current thinking. In the case of Mary, her biography, from the beginning of the fifth century, was moving further and further away from anything to be found in the earliest Christian texts.

The machinations of the ecumenical councils of Ephesus and Chalcedon make it reasonably clear that, away from the romances and aspirations which changed perceptions of Mary at 'street level', the more formal Marian story was being controlled within certain agreed, if not universally supported, guidelines. These amounted, more or less, to that which the Catholic Church recognises today. Mary's Galilean background and its apostasy, the women of Matthew's genealogy, accusations of adultery, Jesus' birth in a pagan sanctuary, allegations of incest, retirement to a town dominated by a goddess cult, all these faded from view. By the fifth century Mary was paraded as the embodiment of chastity and more or less all the original elements of her life that suggested pagan leanings had either been suppressed or were being ignored. Even the Feast of the Presentation, marking her upbringing in the Temple, was replaced with the Feast of the Purification, celebrating her visit to the temple as a mother after the birth of Jesus. This suggests that the orthodox camp, epitomised by the old Antioch lobby, exerted pressure on Christians who were perhaps closer to the Alexandrian view in order to eliminate one of the most awkward aspects of Mary's life, linking her with the mother goddess. The existence and belief of the pro-pagan Marian devotees has now been largely excised from the record though it is still detectable through the writings of heretic-hunters like Irenaeus, Origen and Epiphanius.

Distinct pagan traces can also be found in the art of the period. Art was one of the most important propaganda tools at a time when a large proportion of the population was illiterate, unable to understand the Latin and Greek in which much of the theological discussion was written. From about the end of the second century, painting and sculpture has left us with a mirror of the same confusing elements that we find in the texts. Christian scholars have tried to defend these as legitimate borrowing in order to express the aspirations of the new religion, yet early frescoes and mosaics depicting Mary reveal imagery for which the explanation is not convincing. The formal artistic impression has been, predictably, that of a chaste and virginal maiden. Mary is drawn, often in the context of the Nativity or the Adoration of the Magi, wearing a typical Jewish head-dress and an all-enveloping, rather severe robe which falls to her feet in soft discreet folds. We are left without so much as a hint of breast, unless she is suckling, or a prettily turned ankle. An eighth-century fresco, *Three miraculous mothers of the New Covenant* in S. Maria Antiqua, Rome, provides a good illustration of this from a somewhat later period.

Such austere and chaste portraits do not, however, stand alone. The faded decorations of some of the early churches in Rome and elsewhere in the Mediterranean region include details that expose the ideological battle over Mary's persona among painters and sculptors. These works represent the remnants of a once popular artistic vogue that was nearly obliterated in the purges of all religious images during the eighth and ninth centuries. As with so much concerning the real Mary, we are left to pick up scattered pieces that Church politics were not wholly successful in obliterating.

The Roman catacomb of a Christian devotee named Priscilla, dating from the late second or early third century, contains one of the earliest surviving representations of Mary and the infant Jesus and, while it may appear no more than a crude cartoon, it includes a peculiar feature. Most early Christian artists drew Mary with her hair, when not covered, either short and close to the head or piled into a chignon topped by a crown. The modelling of the hair in the catacomb mural, however, is not unlike the Greek letter *omega* with its lower ends curling out, in defiance of the fashion of the day. We can discover the same hairstyle in a sixth-century ivory diptych from Constantinople, now in the Ehemals Staatliche Museen, Berlin, where Mary and Christ are enthroned together.

In much of the ancient pagan world the *omega* design, associated with fertility and the uterus, was loaded with a cryptic meaning that relied, ironically, on a misunderstanding of the female anatomy. Gynaecological knowledge of the time was extremely sketchy, largely reliant on peering into animal carcasses whose internal workings were assumed to be much like those of people. If, however, the uterus of a hoofed domestic animal such as a cow is cut in half the profile, unlike that of the human uterus, is like an *omega*. A gold pendant, found at the site of the ancient Canaanite capital of Ugarit and dated to about 1500 BCE, now in the Paris Louvre, shows the Syrian goddess Astarte wearing her hair in almost identical style. Many of the pagan *divas* were drawn wearing these uterine head-dresses to symbolise their fertility and sometimes the uterus was inverted to become a pair of 'horns' containing a sun disc. The Egyptian goddess, Isis, is frequently depicted wearing this form of headgear. The *omega* design is also believed to be the inspiration for the Egyptian *SA* hieroglyphic, associated with fertility and birth.

Inclusion of *omega* symbolism was not the only deference to pure pagan ideology in early Christian art associated with Mary. From about the fourth century it became fashionable to depict a trio of *maryams* visiting the sepulchre of Jesus; arguably this was copied from the theme of three mother goddesses, such as the 'Matres' popularised by the Romans. One of the best examples is found on an ivory carved panel from Rome, dating to the late fourth or early fifth century (now in the Bayerisches National-almuseum, Munich). Drawn in Hellenistic style, it depicts the three Marys in more or less identical dress lined up before the tomb as Christ clambers up a cloud stairway to heaven. The new Marian mythology, although made to seem of respectable Judaeo-Christian origin, was of solidly pagan nature in its bare bones.

Just as in Mesopotamian mythology the fertility goddess Ishtar stood against her *alter ego*, Ereshkigal, queen of the underworld, Mary was promoted as the antithesis of Eve and as the immaculate virgin who also stood to reverse her counterpart's bequest of death. Ishtar, the apotheosis of life, had triumphed over death through the intervention of the celestial pantheon. Virginity, in the Christian argument, was the key to similar success. St Augustine confirmed that Mary was 'A Virgin conceiving, a Virgin bearing, a Virgin pregnant, a Virgin bringing forth, a Virgin Perpetual' [*Sermons* 186.1]. The bizarre claim that both Mary and her mother, Anna, had been eternal virgins was now accepted by the leading Christian policy-makers.

The claim that Mary was a lifelong celibate who had experienced immaculate conception and virgin birth removed her, at a stroke, from the cycle of sex, sin and death and elevated her to a unique position. Her triumph as the paradigm of virtue had the effect of distancing her from the majority of child-bearing humanity. It was also an example that other women were exhorted to strive for. The Church Fathers could urge little else on their female flock without undermining the fundamental and exclusive Christian dogma connecting sex with sin and death. Women, whose special role was childbirth, were responsible for all three of these problems, according to such stalwarts as St Augustine. Overlooking the fact that the argument was not to be found among the teachings of the Old Testament, Augustine clamoured against all sexuality, trumpeting that sex was the original fatal flaw perpetuated through mortal womanhood, and that abstention was the only sure defence.

> By divine right continence is preferred to wedded life, and pious virginity to marriage. [*On Holy Virginity* 1.1]

Any suggestion that Mary had taken part in fleshly intercourse was firmly suppressed and once agreement was in place about the prerequisite of her celibacy, what followed was little short of astonishing.

The next significant move was to make Mary the partner in a celestial 'marriage' to her son. Yet the imagery of a sacred marriage was strictly pagan. It came from Mesopotamia where the goddess and her demigod spouse were cast as mother and son, divine bride and lover. The Old Testament prophets had borrowed the theme of a royal partnership and made it acceptable first by removing the sexual component and then by reversing the dominance between goddess and consort. This conformed to the principle that the God of Israel was male though, curiously, it implied that he was not a single entity. Parts of the Book of Isaiah are preoccupied with the spiritual allegory of a precarious and often irate marital relationship between Yahweh, the vengeful god, and Jerusalem, his errant bride, whose people commit wanton adultery before foreign idols.

> For as a young man marrieth a virgin, so shall thy sons marry thee: and as the bridegroom rejoiceth over the bride, so shall thy God rejoice over thee. [Isa. 62.5]

More revealing for a society whose mythology subscribed to a celibate male presence in the heavens is the following passage from the Book of Proverbs. It indicates that God possessed a partner from cosmic beginnings. The partner is generally taken to be female (in purely Christian terms it has been interpreted as Sophia or wisdom) and some of the description, 'I was daily his delight ... and my delights were with the sons of men', gives the relationship a distinctly sexual quality.

> I was set up from everlasting, from the beginning, or ever the earth was. When there were no depths, I was brought forth; when there were no fountains abounding with water. Before the mountains were settled, before the hills was I brought forth: While as yet he had not made the earth, nor the fields, nor the highest part of the dust of the world. When he prepared the heavens, I was there; when he set a compass upon the face of the depth: When he established the clouds above: when he strengthened the fountains of the deep: When he gave to the sea his decree, that the waters shall not pass his commandment: when he appointed the foundations of the earth: Then I was by him, as one brought up with him: and I was daily his delight, rejoicing always before him; Rejoicing in the habitable part of his earth; and my delights were with the sons of men. [Prov. 8.23ff.]

When we trace the idea of a celestial marriage forward to the Christian era we discover that the emphasis has changed again – with evangelists like John the Divine substituting the 'New Jerusalem' for the bride who, far from being fickle and backsliding, has been transformed into the pure and innocent virgin.

> Let us be glad and rejoice, and give honour to him: for the marriage of the Lamb is come, and his wife hath made herself ready ... And I John saw the holy city, new Jerusalem, coming down from God out of heaven, prepared as a bride adorned for her husband.
> [Rev. 19.7, 21.2]

And there came unto me one of the seven angels which had the seven vials full of the seven last plagues, and talked with me, saying, Come hither, I will shew thee the bride, the Lamb's wife. And he carried me away in the spirit to a great and high mountain, and shewed me that great city, the holy Jerusalem, descending out of heaven from God. [Rev. 21.9–10]

In his letter to the Ephesians, Paul, never a strong campaigner for female emancipation, compares the wife and the Church.

For the husband is the head of the wife, even as Christ is the head of the church: and he is the saviour of the body. Therefore as the church is subject unto Christ, so let the wives be to their own husbands in every thing. [Eph. 5.23–24]

From this Christianised idea of the relationship between celestial partners it was a comparatively easy step to identify Mary with the Church and, therefore, to place her in a spiritual marriage with God. Mary became the bride of Jesus, her divine son, and her husband, Joseph, was deemed an irrelevance.

The claim of bride and bridegroom was made by many of the early commentators, who applied it not only to Mary, but to any woman who adopted a life of devotion to Christ. In perhaps the most famous of St Jerome's letters, written to a nun named Eustochium in 384 CE, he emphasised the bridal imagery.

Why need the doors of your heart be closed to the Bridegroom? Let them be open to Christ but closed to the devil according to the saying, If the spirit of him who hath power rise up against thee, leave not thy place.

If any of your handmaids share your vocation, do not lift up yourself against them or pride yourself because you are their mistress. You have all chosen one Bridegroom, you all sing the same psalms; together you receive the Body of Christ. [Jerome, *Letters*, 26, 29]

The Church endorsed this portrait of Mary engaged in sublime and spiritual love, but seems to have done little to prevent a more physical interpretation from being introduced. Within a short space of time, as we shall see, the art world was incorporating symbolism into pictures of Jesus and Mary, suggesting the sexual intimacy enjoyed by a husband and his spouse. Mary, the mother, was paraded as the incestuous bride of the son. Why did the Church Fathers voluntarily introduce, and then support, contentious elements that risked stirring up controversy? We should not forget such a passage as that from the *Genna Marias*, cited by Epiphanius. It implied that Jesus committed a ritualised act of incest with his mother, witnessed by Mary of Magdala, 'taking her aside on the mountain [Mount of Olives], praying, producing a woman from his side, beginning to have intercourse with her, and then partaking of his emission.' The conclusion must be that pressure was exerted by those determined to maintain pagan principles in Mary's make-up.

One of the fall-backs of both camps in support of the bridal partnership between Mary and Jesus was undoubtedly the *Canticum canticorum* or Song of Solomon. The linking of certain blatantly sexual passages to Mary was achieved because, notwithstanding the nature of the subject matter, the fact that the Song was included in the Jewish canon provided it with sound credentials: it was time-honoured poetry. Great men of the past had found it no more offensive than an allegory on spiritual love and, composed as a duet with the emphasis on the female partner, it is one of the few texts of the Old Testament where a sense of male dominance does not prevail. The fact that, in the first century CE, some Jewish scholars had begun to question its suitability as part of the Jewish canon was conveniently overlooked.

From an orthodox Christian viewpoint, the words of the Song came to represent a sublime partnership between Yahweh and Israel that had been transferred to Christ and the Virgin and was being emulated by Christian followers in their discipline of piety and chastity. In about 200 CE, Hippolytus, one of the more obscure of the early Christian writers in Rome, had insisted that the Song described the love between Christ and the Church. This view was endorsed by Origen who had recognised its sexual nature but felt that, in a higher sense, it spoke of a pure relationship. St Jerome drew on the Song extensively when writing to Eustochium, apparently content to ignore the blatantly sexual meaning in passages he cited.

> When sleep overtakes you He [the bridegroom] will come behind and put His hand through the hole of the door, and your heart shall be moved for Him; and you will awake and rise up and say, I am sick of love. Then He will reply, A garden enclosed is my sister, my spouse; a spring shut up, a fountain sealed.   [Jerome, *Letters*, 25]

The passage, 'A garden enclosed is my sister, my spouse; a spring shut up, a fountain sealed', paraded as evidence of the age-old sacredness of virginity, is still used in churches to this day. Those who accept the passage unfortunately ignore the fact that the woman was actually awaiting the arrival of her lover. He journeyed from the north, flowing as life-giving waters from the hills to the parched Mesopotamian plain, and a few moments later she cried passionately, 'Let my beloved come into his garden, and eat his pleasant fruits.' If the woman of the Song could claim virginity at the outset she was certainly set to lose it!

The use of the Song was not wholly approved by Christians. Towards the end of the fourth century, Theodore of Mopsuestia stood against the tide of orthodox opinion by claiming that it *did* constitute erotic material and his contemporary, the Roman monk Jovinian, adopted a similar view when attacking the superiority of celibacy. Such spokesmen were, however, in a minority and were generally condemned as heretics. Most others insisted on the exemplary purity of the Song. To draw an analogy, it was as if someone seeking impunity for airing a theme likely to cause public offence, in medieval times, had used salacious material from Chaucer's *Canterbury Tales*, claiming, 'These are not my words. I have only copied innocently from a classical masterpiece. Do my critics presume to criticise Chaucer?'

In order to establish properly Mary's position as a heavenly bride, another piece of fiction had to be written. The tradition was already in place that Christ had been carried incarnate into heaven and that if his mother was to be his consort then she should, logically, be beside him in similar form. There was talk about Carnal Assumption, the fantastic idea that Mary had not died but had left the earth, bodily, by some kind of miracle emulating that of Christ's Resurrection. It was easy to speculate about what exactly had happened to her mortal remains because there was no body, no grave, and a complete absence of verifiable relics. As far as the canonical gospels were concerned, the event had gone without notice and the various apocryphal accounts of the death were long-winded, disjointed and peppered with crude wizardry. In the Latin translation of a Greek manuscript named after a second-century Bishop of Sardis, the *Pseudo-Melito*, the apostles were whisked off to Mary's deathbed by magic.

> And lo, suddenly, by the commandment of God, all the apostles were lifted on a cloud and taken away from the places where they were preaching and set down before the door of the house where Mary dwelt. [*Pseudo-Melito* 5, NTA]

The fairy-tale elements that embodied the Dormition (Falling Asleep) and the Carnal Assumption began to take shape in the third century in the eastern wing of Christendom. One of the earliest fragmentary accounts, the *Obsequies of the Holy Virgin*, written anonymously in Syriac some time between the beginning of the third and the middle of the fourth century and found in the mid-nineteenth century, records a conversation that allegedly took place in front of Mary's tomb. A group of disciples, including Paul, discussing the policy to be adopted for preaching the Christian message were confronted by an apparition of Jesus who summoned the archangel Michael, ordering him to carry Mary's corpse to heaven. [Syriac narrative fragment, version E.ii, (Wright, 1865, p. 42)]

The Greek text known as the *Assumption of the Virgin*, attributed to John the Evangelist, provides other details and is significant in several respects. It states that the period between Mary's funeral and the discovery of an empty tomb was three days, the same passage of time as that recorded for the Resurrection of Christ. The time factor also carries strong echoes of the old pagan traditions of Inana and Ishtar who languished in the underworld for three days before bodily resurrection.

> The apostles carried the bed and laid her precious and holy body in Gethsemane in a new tomb. And lo, an odour of sweet savour came out of the holy sepulchre of our lady the mother of God: and until three days were past the voices of invisible angels were heard glorifying Christ our God who was born of her. And when the third day was fulfilled the voices were no more heard, and thereafter we all perceived that her spotless and precious body was translated into paradise.
> [*Assumption* 48, ANT]

The Greek text is one of several referring to the assault on Mary's corpse by the Jews, but this version suggests that it was a premeditated matter and that even Mary knew of it in advance of her death.

> The holy mother of God answered and said to me, The Jews have sworn that when my end comes they will burn my body.
> [*Assumption* 10, ANT]

The same text exposes as a fallacy the strenuous denial made by the Roman Catholic Church that Mary is not the object of worship. In Christian terms, worship is a form of adoration specifically reserved for a deity, and here we find unequivocal confirmation of the worship of Mary by the apostles.

And we approached the mother of our Lord and God and worshipped her.

We beheld ... all the choirs of the saints worshipping the precious
body of the mother of the Lord.   [*Assumption* 15 and 49, ANT]

Pseudo-Melito amplifies the incident of the Assumption in picturesque detail.

And the Lord said, Rise up my love and my kinswoman; you who
did not suffer corruption by the union of the flesh shall not suffer
dissolution of the body in the sepulchre. And immediately Mary
rose up from the grave and blessed the Lord and fell at the Lord's
feet, saying, I am not able to render you worthy thanks, O Lord,
for your innumerable benefits which you have vouchsafed to grant
to me, your handmaid ... and the Lord kissed her and departed,
and delivered her to the angels to bear her into Paradise.
                            [*Pseudo-Melito* 17.1ff., ANT]

By the seventh century the various strands of myth associated
with Mary's death became accepted as the basis of a more solid
historical tradition and this was formalised into the *Transitus*, the
passing from earth to heaven and from life to death. In about
600 CE the Feast of the Dormition, celebrated on 15 August, was
introduced into the religious calendar by the Byzantine Roman
Emperor, Maurice, and we find the first evidence of its celebration
in the West in Gaul less than fifty years later. By the eighth century,
under Pope Nicholas I, the celebration of Mary's death and bodily
removal to heaven was being accorded the same level of importance in the Church's festival round as the Incarnation and Resurrection of Christ. The name seems to have been changed
formally to the Feast of the Assumption some time during the
ninth century when, for the first time, it appears in liturgical
calendars.

Once the myths of Mary's carnal assumption and her marriage

to Christ had been officially recognised, the way was open for the third pagan element to be incorporated into the Roman Catholic dogma of Mary, that of *Regina coeli*, the Queen of Heaven. The accolades Mother of God and Bride of Christ were contentious, but it must have been extraordinarily difficult for some of the orthodox Christian Fathers to tolerate the name 'Queen of Heaven' because it was infamous. The Old Testament writer Jeremiah had used it openly when referring to Ishtar, the great fertility goddess of Babylon.

The children gather wood, and the fathers kindle the fire, and the women knead their dough, to make cakes to the queen of heaven, and to pour out drink offerings to other gods, that they may provoke me to anger. [Jer. 7.18]

We have vowed to burn incense to the queen of heaven, and to pour out drink offerings unto her. [Jer. 44.25]

Those faithful to the Marian cult but who harboured pagan sympathies would undoubtedly have found the accolade being bestowed on their *diva* attractive. Less easy to understand, however, is why the orthodox forces in the early Church consented to its adoption.

Early Christian art provides the most convincing record of Mary's rise to celestial royalty and indicates that it was a gradual affair. At first she tends to have been drawn modestly as an earthly mother with her child while the images of Christ, often crafted to a high standard, sometimes made him look like a Roman emperor. So, for example, in 306 CE Constantine the Great commissioned and set up in the basilica of San Giovanni in Laterano a pair of life-sized images of Christ *imperator*, each modelled in solid silver. But as Mary gained in popularity, a subtle shift of emphasis began to take place: Christ tended to be downgraded and his icons progressively eclipsed by those of his ascendant mother. This is not to say that artists ceased to draw Christ the King but that messages began to emerge from Marian portraits speaking of regal status.

Towards the mid-fifth century, during the building of the great Roman church of S. Maria Maggiore under the *aegis* of Pope Sixtus III, various affluent sponsors funded the creation of mosaics depicting an assortment of biblical scenes and these were installed on the side walls and the triumphal arch. Some, recording the Nativity at Bethlehem, show Mary in the role of a mother who is clearly subordinate to Christ. But one group of portraits, commissioned by an unknown benefactor, is now believed to mark the watershed between Mary the commoner and Mary the queen. Tragically, these works have now worn away beyond trace but we know from historical commentaries that Mary was dressed as a Roman empress or *augusta* seated before a line of martyrs who offered her their crowns.

Ultimately Mary was to be portrayed as a truly celestial queen but first she was drawn as an *earthly* sovereign before whom pontiffs and emperors alike bent the knee. The reasons probably had more to do with politics than pagan ideals. During the reign of the Emperor Diocletian, which began in 284 CE, moves were afoot to split the Roman world into two geographically distinct wings. The West, effectively Europe, was to be governed from Rome and all to the east of the Aegean controlled from Nicomedia, lying at the eastern tip of the Sea of Marmara in Anatolia. In order to facilitate the division, Constantius and Galerius were appointed in 293 CE as co-Caesars in the West and East. The formal partitioning took place in Milan in 313 CE, at a meeting between the emperors Constantine the Great and his eastern counterpart, Licinius.

The separation under two heads of government was to mark the beginning of the end for the Roman Empire. The scene was set for an era of chronic and, at times, bitter rivalry between the two wings and, in the following year, hostilities broke out in which Licinius was defeated. Constantine decided to move his seat away from Rome. On the site of the small town of Byzantium, a little to the north of Nicomedia, he built a new capital city of the East which he named Constantinople. An uneasy truce continued until 455 CE when the Vandals sacked Rome, the Lombard kings established themselves in northern Italy and the seat of secular power was transferred permanently to Constantinople from whence the decay of Roman might was overseen by the Byzantine emperors.

Long before this, however, the wings had tended to separate culturally, with the effect that while Latin was spoken in Rome, Nicomedia spoke Greek. The Christian Church became divided along similar lines and eventually strong rivalry developed between East and West for moral and ethical supremacy. The doctrine promoted in the East became Greek Orthodoxy while that of the West became Roman Catholicism. Mary was destined to be venerated almost exclusively as the *Theotokos* in the East while in the Roman Catholic West the emphasis rested equally on her status as *Theotokos* and her permanent virginity. In the West, Mary became recognised as a queen because the Church of Rome decided that by presenting her in regal clothes she would be identified as a symbol of its own secular capacity. We should remember that the Roman Church was not only concerned with the spiritual welfare of its flock, it also wielded huge political power. Giving Mary a temporal regality was probably a shrewd idea in a period when Rome felt increasingly vulnerable, both to attack by the Lombards and to losing its status in favour of the Eastern Church. The royal Marian vogue was not universally favoured. Perhaps not surprisingly, the Byzantine Patriarchs objected on the grounds that investing the *Theotokos* in the trappings of earthly power risked blurring her supernatural position. For the time being, however, the policy seemed unstoppable and artists went on venerating Mary as an earthly queen. This was the start of an artistic journey which, within a hundred years and once the Assumption had been officially recognised, depicted Mary in her new *celestial* status.

One of the first paintings revealing the full royal attire can be found in the Roman church of S. Maria Antiqua. Drawn early in the sixth century, it shows the infant Jesus on Mary's knee and she is decked out in the opulent regalia of the Byzantine court. She gazes, imperious and expressionless, wearing a royal robe, a diadem and a weight of jewels. Her outfit is already in sharp and shocking contrast with the modesty of dress and ornament demanded by the Church for ordinary women.

Artistic representation of Mary as Queen of Heaven was to come within two hundred years. By the turn of the eighth century Pope John VII commissioned a huge, ornate painting for the basilica of S. Maria in Trastevere, Rome. In one of the most famous and politically extreme depictions of Mary, she is drawn as a larger-than-life figure, crowned *Regina coeli* and surrounded by adoring angels. Dazzlingly bejewelled and wearing a sumptuous diadem, she sits on a purple throne with her feet on a royal footstool. John, who refers to himself as the servant of the Mother of God, is shown kneeling before her in abject humility.

Even works that show Mary in more modest surroundings can be revealing. In the tiny church of Panagia Angeloktistos in southern Cyprus there is a seventh-century mosaic of the Virgin and Child in which the right hands of both are extended forward and faint traces of pigment reveal that these were once highlighted in gold. The gesture was, traditionally, one of authority by an empress but it is also one of salvation by a god or goddess.

The elevation to royal status was a contributory factor in setting off what became known as the iconoclastic controversy. From the sixth century onwards a new style of sculpting and carving images of Jesus, Mary and the apostles in the round took over from two-dimensional mosaics and paintings. Judging from the number of these early Christian statues that turns up in excavations, they became fairly common and were regularly being commissioned both for churches and for private houses. Soon, these Christian figures in plaster and stone were reported to be the subject of miraculous activities. This was but another turn of events that smacked openly of pagan idolatry in which claims of images that sweated, smiled, wept, moved or rose a little distance from their bases had long been recognised.

The counterblast to pagan trends in Christian art came through a policy of idol-smashing instigated by the Byzantine Emperor Leo III, otherwise known as Leo the Isaurian. It began officially in 725 CE and it served to deepen the rift between East and West. Iconoclasm was not new but, hitherto, it was focused on the pagan, and was conducted with considerable energy and zeal by Constantine, who considered the breaking up of statues of gods and goddesses to be the absolute duty of dedicated Christians. Writing during the reign of Constantine, Eusebius reported that 'friends of the emperor' had engaged in a spate of derogatory attacks on pagan images.

> They ordered the priests themselves, amidst general laughter and scorn, to bring their gods from their dark recesses to the light of day: they then stripped them of their ornaments, and exhibited to the gaze of all the unsightly reality which had been hidden beneath a painted exterior. Lastly, whatever part of the material appeared valuable they scraped off and melted in the fire to prove its worth, after which they secured and set apart whatever they judged needful for their purpose, leaving to the superstitious worshippers that which was altogether useless, as a memorial of their shame.
>
> [*Life of Constantine* 3.54]

Anti-pagan iconoclasm had reached something of a climax when, towards the end of the fourth century, a Christian mob attacked the Temple of Sarapis, a major centre of pagan worship in Alexandria, smashing the image of the god, Sarapis, and destroying the building.

The Church was guilty of double standards when it came to idolatry. Somewhat hypocritically, Christian intellectuals ridiculed the idea of the boundlessness of a pagan deity confined within idols of stone and wood, and they were even more scathing about the adoration that was lavished on these icons. Yet, from the third century, they had been ordering the demolition of pagan images with one voice but encouraging the crafting of Christian icons with another. Devotees were beginning to behave in an adoring fashion towards sculptures and carvings of Jesus, Mary and the apostles. The shrines of saints were becoming crammed with works of art. In the words of Robin Lane Fox in *Pagans and Christians*, 'Like a pagan sacrifice, the Christian liturgy was drawing a heavenly presence to its offerings.' Christian worshippers were also conducting rituals in front of these images of a kind that the pagan would have found quite familiar. These included relying on the images for oracular advice. An indication of the concern felt by more orthodox Church Fathers over this practice is to be found in a decision made by the Council of Antioch in 379 CE outlawing Christians who practised divination.

Leo the Isaurian's edict against the adoration of icons marked the first occasion that the Church had applied self-recrimination over such worship, suggesting that there was a backlash against those keen on giving Jesus and Mary the trappings of pagan deities. The iconoclastic controversy took on violent overtones when, in 727 CE, an image of Christ was forcibly removed from its position over the entrance to the Sacred Palace in Constantinople on the orders of Pope Leo. This act was viewed as little short of imperial sacrilege and it triggered a violent protest, mainly among dissenting women who responded by organising a street riot.

Constantine V (741–775), Leo III's son and heir, became even more determined to stamp out the cult of icons. He was responsible for instigating a synod of bishops in 745 CE, the Seventh General Council of Constantinople, that decreed officially against all Christian images and claimed those who worshipped before them to be heretics whose crime was punishable by death. The decree made an interesting distinction between a direct representation of Christ and his symbolic presence as the Eucharist.

The only lawful representation of Christ is the Holy Eucharist.
Images of saints are equally to be abhorred; it is blasphemous to
represent by dead wood or stone those who live with God.

[Proceedings of the Seventh General Council]

Large numbers of Christians rebelled and the immediate consequence was a violent purge, Christian attacking Christian, often to
the death. The persecution continued under Leo IV (775–780 CE).

After seventy years of iconoclasm Leo IV's wife the Empress
Irene, who appears to have been marginally less puritanical, provided a respite. Fresh controversy arose under Leo V in 815 CE,
after which iconophiles again tended to lose their eyes, tongues,
limbs and lives. The process of icon-bashing lasted for about a
hundred years and was finally quelled by the Empress Theodora
who restored freedom of art and worship through a decree known
as the Triumph of Orthodoxy in 843 CE. Ironically, although the
intention of iconoclasm had been to discourage the adoration of
Christian images and relics, the effect of suppression was to give
a shot in the arm to the Marian cult in the West where people
came to value icons to the point of fanaticism. It also meant that
Marian devotees from the East fled to Europe in large numbers
and the Roman papacy was glad to take the opportunity of political
gain. It anticipated the advantage in an open stand of defiance
against the authority of Constantinople, knowing that it had the
solid backing of a public who, by and large, did not share the
eastern mood. Pope Gregory III cocked a deliberate snook at
the imperial court by decking out icons in Rome with the most
luxuriant trappings that mind and matter could offer. He commissioned an icon of Mary for his personal chapel, the Grotte
Vaticane, which was crowned with a gold-encrusted diadem and
necklace and with earrings smothered in precious stones.

Yet disquiet showed itself even in Rome where, for some, the
adornment of Mary with ever-increasing opulence was nonsense.
Arguably these were the first rumblings of the religious fireball of
sixteenth-century Protestantism, but the Reformers' time had not

yet come and successive popes punished dissenters by having them flogged and bundled off into ignominious exile.

Looking at the broad view of the Marian tradition from the fifth century onwards, aside from the controversy concerning icons its most extraordinary aspect is that the distortions surrounding Mary became accepted as part of the 'absolute truth' of Christianity. People in both East and West were persuaded to forget that they were confronting folklore and to recognise it as fact. The spread of legends and the transferral to Mary of popular myths became spiced still further with such matters as civic rivalry over houses where she was claimed to have lived, and the sighting of Marian apparitions. Some of these were reported by highly respected sources. One of the first visitations was experienced by St Gregory Thaumaturgus, a bishop of Neocaesarea who died towards the end of the third century. By the fifth century, another aspect of the growing Marian frenzy was the discovery of relics attributed to Mary.

According to the early-sixth-century historian Theodore Anagnostes, whose work survives only in excerpts dating from the fourteenth century, the Empress Eudocia, wife of the Emperor Theodosius II, made a pilgrimage to Jerusalem in 438 CE. From here she sent back one of the first recorded Marian relics to her sister-in-law, the Empress Pulcheria. It is a portrait of the Immaculata and the infant Jesus, allegedly painted by St Luke and known as the *Theotokos Hodegetria* (Mother of God, Guide of Travellers). The portrait became an object of great veneration in Constantinople where Pulcheria installed it in a church, the Panagia of Blachernae, built specially within the imperial palace. The picture now rests in the Pantheon in Rome. The historian Edward Gibbon described the event in *Decline and Fall of the Roman Empire*.

In the Holy Land her alms and pious foundations exceeded the munificence of the great Helena; and though the public treasure might be impoverished by this excessive liberality, she [Eudocia]

enjoyed the conscious satisfaction of returning to Constantinople
with the chains of St Peter, the right arm of St Stephen, and the
undoubted picture of the Virgin, painted by St Luke.

[Gibbon, 1910 32]

A legend relating to Pulcheria describes how, in 451 CE, the
Patriarch of Jerusalem sent Mary's funeral shroud to her. It had
miraculously resisted decomposition and was deposited by the
Empress in Blachernae church. From the 620s CE the event was
commemorated in the Feast of Deposition.

A different aspect of Mary's fictional credentials that continued
to grow was that of the intercessor. Christians inherited the
Hebrew God, Yahweh (during the Renaissance, fourteenth-
century Christian Fathers would devise the name Jehovah by
combining the consonants of Yahweh with the vowels of Adonai
or 'Lord'), but this deity was invisible and out of touch. Increasingly, Jesus Christ was being seen less as the gentle friend to all
and more as the vengeful colossus. At the time of the Council
of Chalcedon in 451 CE, formidable churchmen like the ascetic
Patriarch of Constantinople, John Chrysostom, were serving up a
constant pulpit diet of hardship, woe and recrimination. The
Christian altar was becoming, as Chrysostom put it, 'a place of
terror and shuddering', with its ministers serving as the agents of
doom. Who was to act as the mediator between humanity and the
uncompromising Trinity of Father, Son and Holy Ghost? In this
oppressive atmosphere, Mary, in her special position of favour and
with all that her chastity stood for, became the matronly figure
who held humanity back from free-falling to everlasting dam-
nation. She was the popular guardian standing up to the priesthood, determined to impress on ordinary people the dangers of
sex and the agony of hell, a Jungian universal mother on whose
comforting breast all men could lay their heads. A scrap of papyrus,
discovered in 1938, thought to be dated as early as the third
century but certainly no later than the eighth, is evidence of the
antiquity of supplication to Mary the intercessor. It is the basis of

an ancient Roman Catholic prayer, the *Sub tuum praesidium*.

> We fly to your patronage, O holy Mother of God; despise not our
> petitions in our necessities, but deliver us always from all dangers,
> O glorious and blessed virgin.

Much of Mary's extraordinary transformation from simple
Jewish mother to Christian superwoman is, I believe, summed up
in one striking portrait of Mary and Christ to be found high in
the roof of the church of S. Maria in Trastevere, Rome. Worked
as a mosaic, it was completed in 1140 CE, having been commissioned by the twelfth-century pope Innocent II, who had
himself included in the picture as a bystander carrying a model of
the church. The scene is created in typical Byzantine style. The
figures are stiffly posed, their faces lacking expression, dark eyes
staring down without emotion into the space of the church's apse.
Mary and Jesus are drawn side by side as monarch and queen,
seated on a double throne. He wears a plain, gathered robe, she is
weighed down with a jewelled crown and an intricately embroidered dress.

Leaving aside for the time being the comparative opulence of
Mary's outfit beside that of Christ, other details in the composition
of this portrait beg explanation. Mary displays to the world a
parchment scroll known as a phylactery and inscribed with a
passage of scripture: 'His left hand should be under my head, and
his right hand should embrace me.' The text comes from one of
the most blatant sexual descriptions of the intercourse between
the mysterious woman and her lover in the *Canticum canticorum*.

> O that thou wert as my brother, that sucked the breasts of my
> mother! when I should find thee without, I would kiss thee; yea, I
> should not be despised. I would lead thee, and would bring thee
> into my mother's house, who would instruct me: I would cause thee
> to drink of spiced wine of the juice of my pomegranate. His left
> hand should be under my head, and his right hand should embrace

me. I charge you, O daughters of Jerusalem, that ye stir not up,
nor awake my love, until he please.   [Song of Sol. 8.1–3]

The pomegranate is one of the oldest symbols of fertility and has
often been seen as a euphemism for a woman's sexual organs.
Mother goddesses such as Hera, the wife of Zeus, sometimes held
pomegranates as their symbolic attributes. The position described
for the hands mirrors exactly some of the clay models of Sacred
Marriage rites discovered in Mesopotamia.

The same position is copied, at least in part, in the mosaic in S.
Maria in Trastevere, in which Christ's right arm embraces his
mother. He also holds a phylactery that reads, 'Come my chosen
one, I shall place thee on my throne.' The words come from a
chant or antiphon originally published in the eighth century, the
Liber Pontificalis of Pope Gregory the Great, sung at the Feast of
the Assumption. The text, elevating Mary to queenship with her
son, is hardly less contentious than that displayed by Jesus' mother.
In spite of the ecclesiastical emphasis on her chastity and permanent virginity, the immaculate wife of Joseph has become transformed in the Trastevere picture into the sexually charged bridal
queen. The artist seems to be saying, 'Don't be fooled by appearances. Look carefully and you will discover the real Mary!'

By the dawn of the sixth century little stood in the way of the
elevation of Mary into a cult which, by the thirteenth, would rival
the most fervent goddess worship known in the ancient world.
The elements that made up Mary's official biography – the outer
layers of paint that cover the authentic portrait – remain a considerable deception on the part of early Christian policy-makers.
It is particularly interesting that several of the key aspects of
fabrication became recognised by the Roman Catholic Church in
response to pressure from minority groups. The myth of permanent virginity and Immaculate Conception was supported only
by the Docetics. The *Theotokos* dogma was less than popular with
most of those attending the Council of Ephesus in 431 CE and
only reached the Christian statute-books due to underhand

machinations, aided by the incumbent of the papacy. Yet Marian spokesmen were soon confidently making even more extreme claims. Early in the eighth century St Germanos called himself 'a slave of Mary' and announced of her: 'God obeys you through and in all things, as his true mother.'

Suddenly doors were opening on possibilities that had been unthinkable when they were part of the bedrock of pagan belief. Christianity, modelled on the idea of an exclusive male god, had found a way to worship a goddess in all her wondrous alien colours. It is from this curious foundation of pagan and Christian ideology that we move forward to discover how the Mother of Christ fared in the religious turmoil of Europe during the Middle Ages.

THIRTEEN

The Medieval Mary

During the Middle Ages – which began with the collapse of the Roman Empire in the west in the fifth century and ended with the European Renaissance in the fifteenth century – Mariolatry continued to be developed by the Roman Catholic Church in ways that owed little fidelity to the biblical account of Mary. Most of these carried her pagan elements forward, and yet time was probably making their true origins less and less obvious.

The dogma of the Immaculate Conception remained at the forefront of Marian orthodoxy. This was not about the divine impregnation of Mary, but of her mother, Anna, since it was important to the orthodox establishment that Mary had been free of sin since before her birth. Mary's allegedly permanent state of grace was occasionally challenged by dissenting voices, but nothing prevented it from remaining in the limelight. Theologians of the calibre of John Duns Scotus (1266–1308 CE), a Scot otherwise known as 'Dr Marianus' who effectively developed the medieval concept of the Immaculate Conception, asserted forcefully that Mary had been freed from original sin in order to become the *Theotokos*. Other churchmen, including St Thomas Aquinas, one of the great thirteenth-century philosophers of the Dominican order of friars, denied the argument. In his writings Aquinas argued, 'Mary must have been conceived in original sin, for her conception was the work of sexual union ... now sexual union, which after the sin of our first ancestor cannot take place without sinful pleasure, introduced original sin into the child.'

Increasingly, however, the Immaculate Conception became a

weapon in the arsenal of men intent on imposing rules of celibacy among the clergy and the monastic orders. Medieval bishops laid the same emphasis on the 'virginity factor' as had their predecessors in earlier Christian centuries. They were adamant that Mary's marriage to Joseph was never consummated and that the 'Lord's Brethren', the *Christadelphoi*, were either adopted children or the children of Joseph by a previous marriage. Little attention was paid to poor Joseph, whose elderly role in Mary's life was not observed by so much as a modest feast-day in the western Church during the Middle Ages. Attention was focused not only on Mary's lifelong celibacy but, by this time, on the permanent or *in partu* intactness of her hymen even after the birth of a child.

By the second half of the fourteenth century, the argument was still raging strongly, fuelled by such notables of piety as the influential Catherine of Siena (1347–1380) who alleged that Mary had come to her in a vision and declared that she was not immaculate. Although Catherine of Siena was made a saint, any slur on the Immaculata raised hackles sharply. Pope Sixtus IV (reigned 1471–84) revoked her canonisation a few years later and, in a papal bull, condemned anyone who stood against the Immaculate Conception. This was placed on the annual devotional calendar in 1476 when the pope officially approved a feast to mark the occasion. In 1496 the Sorbonne, one of the oldest parts of the University of Paris founded by Robert de Sorbonne in about 1257, approved a statute that made it obligatory to defend the concept of the Immaculate Conception.

The image of lifelong celibacy that became attached to Mary was one that the Roman Catholic clergy themselves were expected to follow rigidly. The third canon of the Council of Nicaea (325 CE) is unequivocal.

> The great council absolutely forbids any bishop, priest, deacon, or any other member of the clergy to have a woman living with him, unless she is a mother, a sister, an aunt, or any other woman completely above suspicion.   [Huillier, 1996, p. 34]

Yet this apostolic decree, supposedly the bedrock of Catholic dogma, became something of a joke. It resulted in considerable hypocrisy that extended to the very top of the ecclesiastical ladder because successive medieval incumbents of the papacy hardly set the best example. Clement VI (reigned 1342–52) was only the first of many popes to be criticised by his contemporaries over sexual licence. The antipope John XXIII (reigned 1410–15) was truly promiscuous. According to innuendo, he had seduced more than two hundred women during his time as a legate to Romagna and Bologna. Among others notorious for their licentious life-styles, Alexander VI (reigned 1492–1503) was an unashamed lib-ertine who took a veritable string of mistresses from the time that he was appointed a cardinal in 1457. One of the best known of these women was an aristocrat named Vanozza Cantanei who bore him three sons and a daughter. Julius II (reigned 1503–13) fathered three daughters while serving as a cardinal. Paul III (reigned 1534–49) enjoyed mistresses from among the Roman social élite, one of whom mothered three sons and a daughter. His sister Giulia was also a mistress to Alexander VI.

To a cynical populace, such scandals probably represented little more or less than secular dalliances. Of greater concern may have been the conduct within certain sectarian Christian groups, including the monastic institutions. Throughout the so-called Dark Ages of the seventh and eighth centuries when learning was at its lowest ebb, particularly in Europe, the monasteries kept scholarship alive. Their monks, who vigorously backed the papal supremacy in Rome, stood out as models of pious discipline and, with papal approval, became enormously rich. The building and endowment of such bulwarks of faith was seen as one sure way by which the wealthy could secure their passports to paradise. A simple philosophy assumed that the larger the cash premium to God's account, the greater the dividend to be eventually handed back. Money brought influence for the monasteries but it also achieved more material rewards. The monasteries were among the most important centres of culture: they were the 'factories' of liturgy, art and music. Out of seemingly bottomless coffers topped up by pious benefactors the monks were able to promote painting, prayer, music and architecture, intended to encourage Christian fervour in general and Mariolatry in particular.

By the end of the first five hundred years of Christendom the orders of monks and nuns had acquired enormous influence and they effectively 'Marianised' Christianity. The great monastic institutions became Mary's medieval champions jousting for their celestial lady, their immaculate Virgin, with zeal and armed with the weapon of celibacy which orthodoxy claimed for her. Or did they? Cosy convention has left us with a picture that is not entirely authentic. In spite of their laudable beginnings, the high standing of the monastic orders did not always remain as it may appear from a casual reading of Christian history. Monasteries were also to become the focus of scandalous accusation, much of it concerning excesses of a sexual nature. The monks, and later the quasi-religious orders of military knights, the Templars, gained a reputation for risqué behaviour and, ironically, these religious orders were responsible for keeping alive much of the pagan in Mariolatry. The powerful organisation of the Templars, licensed by Pope Honorius II in 1128 with a principal role of fighting the infidel, was accused of heresy in 1307 and forcibly eliminated between 1312 and 1314. The charges against the Templars included holding secret meetings at which numerous indecencies were practised, participating in a ceremony that included defiling the cross and worshipping a bearded head named Baphomet.

It was the monasteries, however, that held the real influence in the medieval centuries and to understand their impact, in both secular and non-secular worlds, we need to take a closer look at them. Monks of one sort or another had been around for some considerable time before the Christian era. The Essenes of Qumran are typical of the kind of austere sectarian order from which, far away from secular bustle, the germ of monastic life gained inspiration and took root. Monasteries had not started out with the kind of money and power that was later used to boost

Mary's image. During the third and fourth centuries, persecuted Christians fled to the deserts of Egypt to serve their God in safety, solitude and self-denial. These were men who followed the maxim that material wealth was another name for spiritual decay. They also subscribed fervently to the philosophy of the Church Fathers: that sex could be held accountable for just about every evil that had descended on humankind since the Fall. The results of their monastic zeal and determination did not become clear until the close of the ninth century, but much of the kudos and adoration in which Mary the ultimate celibate became held, effectively began with these communities of ascetics.

The first Christian monk was probably an Egyptian hermit, St Antony (270–356 CE), and by the reign of Constantine the Great (306–37 CE), there were large numbers of reclusive men in Egypt who had come together in loosely bound colonies known as *laurai*. Effectively hermits, they had abandoned their wives and families because they believed that seclusion linked with celibacy was essential to their contemplative lifestyle. One of Antony's disciples, St Pachomius, then began organising individual monks into groups known as *manorai*. But it was in the East, under the aegis of St Basil during the fourth century, that the process of founding monasteries run by hierarchies of officialdom really began. It was under a strict code of conduct based on asceticism, which became known as the *Rules of St Basil*, that an irrevocable split opened between eastern and western monasticism, the so-called Great Schism. This is not to be confused with the Great Schism of the papacy that began in 1305 under pressure from the French and resulted in the papal court moving to Avignon for seventy years. In effect, the East opted for Basil's extreme conservatism and more or less stagnated in the austere and isolated way of life first laid down by St Antony while communities in the West, with a stronger history of liberalisation, were poised to adopt a more progressive attitude.

Monasticism probably came to the West in about 340 CE when St Athanasius, Antony's Greek biographer, visited Rome from

Athens. He promoted the same programme of austerity which St Antony had adopted in Egypt and, from Italy, his message spread rapidly to Gaul and the old Celtic regions. But Athanasius' style of ascetism was not to last and the flavour of monasticism in the West changed for ever in the sixth century. The man responsible for liberalisation was St Benedict of Nursia (480–54 CE) who drew up legislation that effectively took the eastern model and adapted it to meet western needs. Monastic life under Benedict was altogether more relaxed: he gave his monks the liberty of drinking wine, eating well and getting a reasonable amount of sleep, indulgences frowned upon under the severe rules of the East. The liberalisation was a strong feature of what became known as *St Benedict's Rule*. By the eleventh century, the monastic orders in the West had gone significantly beyond a routine of prayer and bodily mortification. In the twelfth century, the Order of St John came into being to care for the sick in a Jerusalem newly liberated from the infidel by the Crusaders. It was this foundation which gave rise to the celebrated military cult of Knights Templar.

There is a significant difference between monks and priests. Some monks were ordained in order to administer the sacraments to members of their communities, but the man who chose a monastic existence was, and still is, a lay person who decides more or less to abandon secular contact. Priests, on the other hand, who are ordained and employed by the bishops, remain very much a part of the material world. In the West, the priesthood is also responsible for administering to women who have entered religious retreats.

During the medieval centuries, women took up the contemplative life for emphatically different reasons than men. Any girl who had grown past her early teens and was still unmarried became something of an awkward social liability to her family. Unless hurried into wedlock, she was potentially a predator on the souls of God-fearing men. Widows were also suspected of iniquity and were expected to remarry as soon after burying a spouse as decently possible. The position of any single woman past puberty was therefore unenviable and the solution, for affluent families, was to provide endowment to a nunnery. On the other hand, a large proportion of the women who entered religious establishments are said to have done so out of sheer disgust at the thought of sexual contact with men. The revulsion had been drummed into them by an avalanche of popular romantic literature that extolled celibacy and, at the same time, created horror stories about the extreme sinfulness of marital sex and childbirth.

Nuns had a strong part to play in the shaping of monastic Mariolatry. We know that women had been entering religious orders from at least the fourth century when the monastic sororities started to become powerful in their own right. In this respect a strange situation arose that would seem at odds with the male supremacy in the rest of the ecclesiastical establishment. Often the orders of nuns were attached to religious retreats for men as double monasteries and it was a woman, the great lady abbess, who tended to dominate all. From the outset, however, many male clerics saw nuns as a serious threat to their own chastity and nuns earned considerably less approval than their male counterparts. The presence of women began to cast doubt on the celibacy claimed for monasticism and as the medieval period got under way the nunneries, for several reasons, suffered a decline. When a new and highly influential religious organisation, an offshoot of the Benedictines known as the Congregation of Cluny, founded dozens of monasteries in the tenth and eleventh centuries, only one was for women – the wives of men who had become Cluny monks! In the twelfth century, however, the nunneries were bucking the trend. By about 1100 CE women were flocking to join religious retreats, largely inspired by the evangelism of two French preachers, St Norbert and Robert of Arbrissel, both of whom gathered sizeable followings. For a time Norbert even managed to revive the institution of double monasteries although the once all-powerful abbess no longer held sway over her mixed-sex flock.

Though rarely explicit, evidence of sexual activity within the monasteries is implicit in the adverse comments of critics and in ecclesiastical edicts. An official rejection of fleshly desires on the part of the priesthood, the monastic communities and, later, the religious orders of knights, justified imposing strict rules of sexual abstinence. A monk or nun found indulging in sexual activities risked excommunication for up to fifteen years. Celibacy had become regarded as an attribute of the contemplative vocation and as early as 387 CE, Pope Siricius had strengthened the canons of the Council of Nicaea by making celibacy, though not virginity, an absolute necessity for anyone considering joining holy orders.

The ruling was, however, received with less than wholehearted enthusiasm. Opponents, including the notably outspoken Jovinian, led the opposition. The little that is known about him is derived principally from a hostile work of Jerome's called *Adversus Jovinianum*. Once an advocate of strict celibacy and asceticism, Jovinian subsequently pursued anti-ascetical tendencies. He came to Rome pointing out that the gospels nowhere claimed Mary's sexual abstinence or her perpetual virginity and arguing that celibacy, fasting and an assortment of other 'good works' were a waste of time. He put forward the suggestion that monks and nuns should give up abstinence and get married. Pope Siricius was not amused. In 390 CE the pope convened a synod which rubber-stamped the decretal of celibacy and, at the same time, excommunicated Jovinian and any of his supporters who could be identified. Siricius then sent a deputation of priests to his contemporary and henchman Ambrose, Bishop of Milan, with instructions to eliminate any so-called heretics he could locate before they had the chance to experiment with connubial bliss.

Siricius' edict was by no means the end of the story. In the eighth century, at the time of the iconoclastic movement in the East, Constantine V concluded not only that Marianism and celibacy were inseparable but that they were less than desirable. He demanded that monks and nuns should be married off, forcibly if need be, and this draconian state of affairs persisted until the Festival of Orthodoxy in the mid-ninth century overturned the ruling under the authority of the Empress Theodora.

Constantine was the first of several influential men in medieval times to hold views disputing the value of celibacy among the clergy. In the West, in the second half of the twelfth century, Pope Alexander III (reigned 1159–81) tried to restore marriage among the church and monastic communities. Alexander's reasoning is more clearly identified. He was anxious to put an end to the growing scandal of sexual impropriety among the priesthood and the Knights Templar. At this time the Roman papacy was faced with steadily worsening problems, not least of which were accusations about misbehaviour among the clergy from reformist movements such as the Albigenses in twelfth-century Lombardy. With the Cathars, a sect that spread to Western Europe from Bulgaria in the eleventh century and prospered in France until wiped out by the Inquisition, they were opposed to marriage and procreation. The chorus was joined by the Waldenses, founded in 1176 CE by Peter Waldo, a wealthy merchant of Lyons, who took simple illiterates as his itinerant preachers and stood robustly against the principle of ordained clergy. All three sects, although firmly labelled as heretical, were making loud and unwelcome noises about corruption and the decline of good apostolic standards. It seems from these accusations that the outward displays of purity and ascetic behaviour in the ecclesiastical establishment were being matched behind the scenes with activities as questionable as any of the old pagan rituals. Monks were said to be enjoying concubines who were only barely concealed from their critics and celibacy amongst the military orders was something of a standing joke. Such was the power of the monasteries and the other clerical orders by the twelfth century, however, that Alexander III's move was quashed and liberal romping behind cloister walls was set to continue more or less unabated through the rest of the Middle Ages.

Was the sexual laxity of monks and nuns a purely gratuitous indulgence between individuals who found themselves unable to resist normal biological urges or did it contain, at least on some occasions, a more esoteric element? Were the time-honoured conflicts between those who wished Mary to be remembered and adored as the pure and chaste spiritual figurehead, and those who were determined to keep her as a sexually-charged mother goddess, carried through into the medieval period? We do not know whether a parallel existed between monks indulging in sex and their attitude towards Mary; in other words, whether their sexual activity may not also have been a 'ritual of faith'. In the absence of any surviving investigative study, such as Epiphanius' *Panarion*, we can only hope to pick up hints.

The more misogynistic element of the Church clearly abhorred a vision of powerful sororities springing up across Europe but critical attitudes towards nuns were not due to anti-feminist sentiments alone. There was genuine concern in the world at large that the admission of women to monasteries encouraged corruption and sexual licence. The nature of the opprobrium had a familiar ring when one abbot, Conrad of Marchtal, preached:

> We and our whole community of canons, recognising that the wickedness of women is greater than all the other wickedness of the world, and that there is no anger like that of women, and that the poison of asps and dragons is more curable and less dangerous to men than the familiarity of women, have unanimously decreed for the safety of our souls, no less than for that of our bodies and goods, that we will on no account receive any more sisters to the increase of our perdition, but will avoid them like poisonous animals.   [*Annales Praemonstratensis*, ii, 147 (after Erens)]

To get to the heart of the matter, we need to cast back to the writings of the great heretic hunters such as Epiphanius. In his *Panarion*, he catalogued a large number of Christian sects, including Collyridians, Marcosians, Origenists, Samaritans, Valesians, Ossaeans and others which he claimed were guilty of heresy and practices that were often strikingly pagan, involving ritualised sex. One of the problems for the ecclesiastical establishment in dealing with such communities was that their activities were often surreptitious and disguised as orthodox. Epiphanius detailed the activities of the Quintilianist sect.

> In many places [they] deceitfully celebrate a very great festival on the very night of the Epiphany, to deceive the idolaters who believe them into hoping in the imposture and not seeking the truth ... [they] stay up all night singing hymns to the idol. Torch bearers descend into an underground shrine after cockcrow and bring up a wooden image seated naked on a litter [with] a sign of the cross inlaid with gold on its forehead, two other such signs, one on each hand, and two other signs [one] actually on each of its two knees. And they carry the image itself seven times round the innermost shrine with music, hold a feast, and take it back to its place underground. And when you ask them what this mystery means they reply that today at this hour, Kore, that is the virgin, gave birth to Aeo.   [*Panarion* 22.8]

In Greek mythology Kore was the virginal daughter of the great mother goddess Demeter, the counterpart of the fertility goddess Kybele, and Quintilianists had clearly merged pagan goddess worship into that of Mary. Epiphanius did not mention Mary in connection with specific sectarian activities, but some of his intention was to expose the kind of unorthodox devotion being practised in her name behind closed doors.

> It is time for the error of those who have gone astray to cease. Mary is not God and does not have her body from heaven but by human conception. And no one should make offerings in her name, for he is destroying his own soul. But neither, in turn, should he be insolent and offer insults to the Holy Virgin.   [*Panarion* 78]

Most, if not all, of the supposedly orthodox monastic institutions were also openly moving towards worship of Mary with such supplications as the fourth-century prayer, the *Sub Tuum Praesidium*. If a sectarian group like the Quintilianists could pursue

pagan activities while ostensibly following good Christian practice, so could one parading as a monastic institution. Such groups
may not consciously have seen themselves as pagan but they were,
none the less, keeping up ceremonies in Mary's name behind
closed doors that were pagan in spirit and origin. For some, the
ritual was incomplete without a sexual element. There is evidence
that pagan ritual was probably alive and well in Roman society
as late as 1468 when Pope Paul II (reigned 1464–71) took the
unprecedented step of closing down the prestigious Roman
Academy because its members were accused of engaging in pagan
rituals and ideas.

The dogma of the Immaculate Conception and the eternal bliss
won by triumph of spirit over flesh was in the forefront of the
Roman Catholic arsenal that supposedly kept its flock in order
and away from paganism. To counter scepticism about Mary's
biologically impossible *aeiparthenos*, or permanent virginity, it was
necessary to impress on the faithful the circumstances in which
she had been honoured with the unique role of virgin mother, the
Handmaid of the Lord. So the Annunciation, the visit to Mary by
the archangel Gabriel when he informed her that God was about
to impregnate her by the power of his divine will, was pushed to
the very forefront of Mariolatry.

The Immaculate Conception was not, however, the only device
in the arsenal of the Marianists. They also came to recognise the
publicity value of the experiences of visionaries. A popular method
by which Marian fiction has become endorsed as part of an infallible Catholic truth has been through the promotion of the miraculous experiences of visionaries. These people, often young,
impressionable girls from poor and illiterate families, who have
received spectral visitations from Mary, frequently in times of
trouble, have been exploited by the Church in its defence of some
of the more far-fetched inventions about the mother of Christ.
Mary, it is claimed, has been showing herself to selected recipients
among the faithful since about the third century and, more or
less straight away, hers was advertised as the 'revealing voice of

orthodoxy'. Through times when superstition held sway among large sections of the population, her alleged utterances proved an effective weapon against often conflicting theological arguments. These, irrespective of whether or not the Church had supported them in the past, were now deemed to be heretical by the ecclesiastical power brokers. The Church followed the principle that if Mary had given 'the nod' to some or other piece of doctrine, then it had to be right. This was a crude but effective strategy since credibility was impossible to prove or disprove. All that the Church had to do was to select those visionary experiences which suited its purpose and assert them to be valid, while deriding others as the inventions of simple minds.

The earliest claim for a Marian vision had come from the eastern Church as far back in time as the anti-Christian persecutions by the emperors Decius and Valerian. St Gregory Thaumaturgus, the Bishop of Neocaesarea, otherwise known as 'Gregory the Wonderworker', who died in about 270 CE, witnessed a heavenly apparition of the Virgin accompanied by John the Divine. The next visionary seems to have been St Martin de Tours, a rampant misogynist who died in 397 CE and who had founded monasticism in Gaul with the impassioned rallying cry that, 'Marriage is pardonable, virginity glorious'. These are, however, oral traditions that cannot be verified through documented evidence.

Marian apparitions became more frequent from the start of the medieval period and those accepted as 'genuine' were usually of a kind that conveniently reinforced one or more of the four binding principles of Mary's fabled life-story: Immaculate Conception, Divine Motherhood, Perpetual Virginity and Bodily Assumption.

During the thirteenth century, Helsin, Abbot of Ramsey in England, claimed to have seen Mary appear during a stormy sea voyage and was promised that he would be saved from a watery grave if he devoted his life to the defence of the Immaculate Conception. This miraculous event was then used by St Bonaventure, the thirteenth Minister-General of the Franciscan order, in further efforts to press home the credibility of the doctrine.

Sometimes the miraculous visions affected the way in which the basic principles of Mariolatry were depicted. A German nun named Elisabeth of Schonau who died in 1164 CE claimed to have had many intimate conversations with the Virgin but also to have actually seen her rising bodily into heaven. She related her experience of this event to other nuns and to her brother, the Abbot of Schonau, who prudently wrote it down for posterity. Early copies of the original manuscript achieved wide circulation in France and Germany and had a strong influence on the visual concept of the Assumption. Marian appearances were also convenient for establishing new traditions. One of the better known of these had been made to the Prior-General of the Carmelite Order, Simon Stock, who died in 1265 CE. The Virgin handed Stock the brown scapular, the cloth aprons strung together over the shoulders which became the most important part of the Carmelite order's habit, and informed him, 'This shall be the privilege for thee and all Carmelites: whosoever dies in this shall not suffer eternal fire.'

Some of the details provided by Marian apparitions verged on the bizarre but, again, had a practical value in furthering Catholic dogma. Records maintained at the Catholic shrine of Little Nazareth at Walsingham in Norfolk indicate that some time during the year 1061, a lady in the manor of Walsingham, Richeldis de Faverches, claimed to have received the exact architectural details of the house in which the Annunciation took place. This vision had been given to her so that a replica could be built. The mockup, built in about 1130 and including a miraculous statue, became a popular stopping point for pilgrims. It received royal patronage from Henry III in 1226 but was torn down in 1538 during Henry VIII's dissolution of the monasteries.

During the medieval period, moves continued by the Roman Catholic Church to eradicate awkward details of the Marian biography. In the eighth century the Feast of the Presentation, held on 21 November in the old Byzantine calendar to mark the beginning of Mary's contentious upbringing by the Temple priests, was omitted from an official eastern diary of events known as the

Menology of Constantinople. It reappeared in liturgical documents published during the eleventh century and eventually reached the West, under Pope Gregory XI, late in the fourteenth century. But it remained something of an embarrassment and was missing from many calendars by the end of the Middle Ages. It was gradually sidelined in favour of the Feast of the Purification, or Candlemas, held annually on 2 February when, according to Luke, Mary went to the Temple, not as a toddler but to present the infant Christ as part of her rite of cleansing after childbirth. Yet a rite of purification is no less illogical in Christian terms since Mary allegedly gave birth to Jesus free from sin. Candlemas is also daubed with distinctly pagan colour and, as we shall discover, it has elements borrowed from more ancient fertility invocations marking the dead of winter when food supplies were usually running low.

The level of Marian adoration rose steadily and, as it did so, Mary's treatment became increasingly indistinguishable from that of a goddess. An important step came towards the end of the thirteenth century when, not satisfied with the title *Theotokos*, St Thomas Aquinas asserted that Mary was worthy of some special form of worship. The Catholic Church permits the conferral of varying degrees of honour to its celebrities at levels which were probably first laid down by St Augustine. Since God is officially the only figure in Christian theology entitled to be worshipped, this act is uniquely termed *latria* or 'adoration'. The honouring and praise of saints is known as *dulia* or 'reverence'. Augustine shrewdly insisted that the distinction between Mary and God was absolute and the Church agreed to the invocation of Mary as a saint but not to her worship in the style of deity. Mary's devotees could call her Queen of Heaven with impunity, but they were on no account to offer her worship in the sense of *latria*. Yet this conflicts with the text of the *Assumption of the Virgin*, attributed to St John the evangelist, which claimed that the apostles worshipped Mary.

There were genuine worries as to how far Marian adoration could be allowed to go. Nestorius' impassioned plea at the Council of Ephesus had not been the only admonition against treating her as a goddess. Epiphanius himself had warned, 'Let the Father, the Son and the Holy Spirit be worshipped, but let no one worship Mary.' [*Panarion* 78.23; 79.1 and 7] Thomas Aquinas attempted to reconcile the problem by proposing a new level between *dulia* and *latria*: Mary should receive *hyperdulia*, a degree of adoration greater than that accorded to any other creature, barring God himself, because she alone was privileged to be Mother of God. In all but name, Augustine's ruling was to be ignored. A Franciscan monk named St Bernadine of Siena, who died in 1444 CE, declared ecstatically that, 'Only the Blessed Virgin Mary has done more for God, or just as much, as God has done for all mankind.'

In the context of these excesses it is not altogether surprising that objections arose. In the last years of the fourteenth century a German organisation known as the Brethren of the Cross rejected many of the Roman Catholic tenets which had become familiar: clerical celibacy, worship of images, absolution and all the other components of Marianism. In England John Wycliffe (*c.* 1329–84), whose followers, the Lollards, were the forerunners of English Protestantism, took a similar line. In their treatise of 1394 CE, *Conclusions*, the Lollards made reference to Mary as 'The Witch of Walsingham'. A century and a half later, in his major work *Institutes*, the French Protestant Reformer John Calvin (1509–64) described the Marian cult as an 'execrable blasphemy'.

For the majority of the medieval Christians, still loyal to the strictures of the Holy Roman Church, Mary had risen beyond the role of the saintly mother of Christ and was fast becoming all things to all people. At first she had been simply the shining light for men who believed passionately in rejection of the flesh, for whom she stood as an ideal role model. But they soon discovered that she could also bring a spirit of softness and womanly compassion into their austere male lives.

It is arguable that, in part, Mary became the object of a cult because she radiated the same maternal quality that has attracted suffering humanity down the ages. In terms of psychoanalysis she became the latest embodiment of the *anima* which in recent times, alongside the masculine *animus*, Carl Jung has argued to be the archetype of femaleness imprinted into the collective subconscious of each and every human being from their first stirring in the womb. There was, of course, a bitter irony in this since the ordinary women making up the rest of the human race were being denigrated by the Roman Catholic Church as inferior beings. Once Mary became the embodiment of our collective *anima*, it was not difficult for her to become the more approachable alternative to her divine son. Jung identified this archetypal image of a woman as possessing a timeless quality: young-looking but with the suggestion of much experience, wise but not to the extent of being intimidating, close to nature and charged with emotion. The image is seductive. It is, Jung argued, projected not only on to pagan goddesses but on to the Virgin herself.

For many people, used to digesting the grim prospect of fire and brimstone promised by such as John Chrysostom, Patriarch of Constantinople, Christ had been turned from 'gentle Jesus, friend of sinners, supporter of the humble and meek' into a formidable and vengeful despot. Mary, on the other hand, stood listening intimately, ready to soothe our brows and, if necessary, intercede with heaven as a transcendental go-between. That she was thought spiritually well positioned to do so is revealed in the words of the standard form of invocation to the Virgin used in the western Church in the later Middle Ages: 'Hail Mary, full of grace, the Lord is with thee, blessed art thou among women and blessed is the fruit of thy womb, Jesus.' Her special liaison with God is also implied in the well-known idyll from the first chapter of Luke, beginning, 'My soul doth magnify the Lord' and which goes on, 'For he hath regarded the low estate of his handmaiden: For behold, from henceforth, all generations shall call me blessed'. These words were to form the great song of Christian praise known as the Magnificat.

The view of Mary as a bridge between God and man gained strength through the Middle Ages and her maternal aura probably explains why, from the Byzantine period onwards, she has been portrayed as the *Deesis*, a term derived from the Greek word meaning intercession. Artists have, by convention, represented the *Deesis* in portraits made up of three panels known as a *triptych*, with Christ occupying the central section. Mary stands to one side and John the Baptist to the other, each pleading on behalf of sinners. Mary was thus clung to for comfort, for safety and for wisdom in ways that Christ was not and one predictable result was that the dividing lines between intercession, adoration and worship became almost impossibly blurred.

The belief in Mary as the intercessor led to the emergence of two new aspects of the pagan mother goddess, those that involved her with war and with death. The Mesopotamian goddess Ishtar was not only the prima donna of love, she was also a war goddess, as was her Canaanite counterpart Anat. This aspect of Ishtar's personality is highlighted in an ancient hymn from the third millennium BCE.

> *Arrayed in battle,*
> *beautiful . . . who handles the utug-weapon,*
> *who washes the tools in the blood of battle.*
> *She opens the door of battle.*
> *The wise one of heaven, Inana.*
> [Sjoberg and Bergmann, 1969]

It may seem incongruous that a figure of mercy and compassion should also preside over war, yet Mary is well documented wearing the armour of righteousness, cloaked in the aura of an avenging Christian *diva*. Even in the Byzantine era several of the Roman emperors set a precedent by removing images of their pagan war goddess, Minerva, who had also, incidentally, been a goddess of peace, from seals and replacing them with Mary and child.

Mary has also been represented as the 'Queen of Hell', a role in which she intercedes on behalf of those sinners who might otherwise take the downward, post-mortem elevator. This image, too, is pagan in origin. The Mesopotamian goddess, Ishtar, visited Ereshkigal, her *alter ego* in the underworld, to champion the cause of life and good in the face of death and evil. The mythology found its way into Roman culture because Minerva was often depicted on sarcophagi as a deity offering new life beyond the grave and, from there, it entered the Christian tradition. Until 1900, in the Forum at the foot of the Roman Palatine Hill, there was a church known as S. Maria Liberatrice. Its more ancient name of S. Maria de Inferno recalled a legend that the entrance to the underworld was close by and that Mary stationed herself there to intercede for those about to die. The Roman Catholic world has thoroughly relished elaborating on the unremitting terror of hell with its flames, the devil and his predatory shop stewards equipped with red eyes, curly tails and toasting forks. But it has built into its doctrine a possible escape clause in that the descending elevator to this ultimate sanction has an emergency exit. This is the medieval concept of purgatory, the place where earthly sins can be expiated during the interval of time before the *Dies Irae*, the Day of Wrath, when all souls will be judged and returned in the flesh. Hence a soul can be posted to purgatory and still manage to catch the ascending lift to paradise.

It is in the juxtaposition of Mary, purgatory and hell that much of the strength of the rosary lies. In 1470 CE a Dominican friar named Alain de la Roche popularised this penitential device with which Mary then became closely associated. The string of one hundred and fifty beads acting as a devotional 'finger guide' was first used as an aid to reciting the Psalter of the Old Testament. The lengthy practice was eventually replaced by chanting the same number of Hail Marys (of considerable advantage to those who needed salvation but could not read or spare the time). It is also no small coincidence that the Ave Maria, one of the oldest and most oft-recited prayers of Catholics the world over, ends with the cry, 'Pray for us sinners, now and at the hour of our death.'

In terms of sheer physical blood, sweat and tears, Mariolatry exploded during the medieval period. In France alone, eighty cathedrals largely devoted to honouring the Madonna were built in the twelfth and thirteenth centuries. The official explanation for the almost hysterical degree of veneration was that it had become necessary to prevent the view of Christ becoming a completely spiritual one. God the Son had become a man and because of this he had to have a mother! So, Mary was depicted in the whole gamut of her romanticised life-story. A profusion of art works illustrated the Annunciation, the Nativity, the Crucifixion, the Assumption, being impregnated with the Son, cradling the infant Son, grieving for the Son, ascending to be with the Son, being crowned *Maria regina coeli* and sharing the bridal throne of the Son. Soon most churches also had a Lady chapel, or at least a Lady altar, dedicated to the Virgin, and most churches had at least one Marian statue.

Much of this burgeoning imagery, however, remained rather cold and impersonal and it was not until the Florentine Renaissance of the late fourteenth century that a more liberal climate allowed a reversal of the distancing process. The response was to make Mary appear far more accessible, ceasing to be the mother of God and becoming simply the mother of an ordinary baby. Mary's humanity in this respect was boosted through a strong move to bring the romance of the Nativity back into people's lives. As early as 1223 CE Francis of Assisi had begun a popular trend in the Italian town of Greccio when he elected to celebrate the Christmas Eve midnight mass in a genuine working stable. This caught the public imagination and although few priests chose to match the extent of his realism, it led to all kinds of fresh romantic inventiveness. The crib became fashionable and models of the Bethlehem stable were soon being dusted off for their seasonal appearance. Priests blessed toy figures at midnight mass and devotees crafted new additions to the scene, including the wise men and the animal menageries standing in the background. In all the enthusiasm and sentimentality, the nature of the place where Mary had actually given birth seems to have been conveniently forgotten. No matter that the *messiah*'s crib was almost certainly a stone cattle trough and his first cries echoed from the walls of a gloomy cave witnessing rites to the fertility god Tammuz. It suited public relations better that the Nativity had taken place in a cosy and innocent barn complete with thatched roof.

At least one more aspect of Mariolatry with pagan roots developed in the medieval period: the veneration of relics. During the thirteenth century, sacred objects came to be associated with Mary as they had been with Christ. There was a problem, however. Because Mary had been assumed bodily into heaven there could be no bones or other physical remains, as was the case with other saints whose bodies were eagerly dismembered upon their deaths and distributed for cash. Mary's relics had to take the form of places where she had allegedly lived and objects which she was claimed to have owned or worn. There were various contenders for claiming the privilege of being Mary's home town, most notably Ephesus and Jerusalem. The situation was complicated by a fifteenth-century legend that, when the Muslim hordes overran the Holy Land in 1291, angels came to Mary's property in Nazareth, lifted the building by its foundations and carried it to Loreto in Spain.

The Church of Constantinople claimed to have acquired Mary's cloak. Another of the most powerfully imbued 'relics', again based wholly on myth, was the blue sash which Mary wore round her hips and, allegedly, dropped at the moment of Assumption. The location of the genuine article is also hotly contested. One garment vying for authenticity rests in the Italian cathedral of Prato and has been the subject of several quaint legends, all of them relying on the slightly erotic connotation of such an intimate item of clothing. Chartres Cathedral, on the other hand, has played host to a chemise that Mary allegedly wore at the moment of Jesus' conception. As garments empowered with fertility, both are objects of devotion for would-be parents.

Throughout this investigation we can never afford to forget that early Christianity involved not one but two religions which operated in uneasy tandem. One was radical, forged in the heat of a fervent desire to establish a spiritual movement wholly distinct from anything that had gone before; the other was more conservative and equally determined to preserve time-honoured pagan ideals. Within these conflicting ideologies Mary acted as the linchpin. Christianity viewed Mary as the sublime and infinitely pure mother of God incarnate, but it also drew on the much older religion for whose advocates Mary was still the eternal mother and bride, the Queen of Heaven parading under another name. Professing the one and concealing the other, hiding the female dimension of God, the priesthood and the monastic orders carried this dual system forward. Every once in a while through the medieval centuries the anomalies generated by trying to juggle the Christian and the pagan Mary bubble to the surface.

The case against the Mary of Roman Catholic fabrication can now move towards the modern era which effectively began with the Counter-Reformation movement of the sixteenth century, marking the end of the Protestant onslaught against Roman Catholicism in general and Mariolatry in particular. The vehicle on which we shall be travelling this late stage of the journey is art. Ironically it has barely been touched on thus far in the unscrambling of Mary's picture.

FOURTEEN

Icons

From the onset of the sixteenth century the manipulation of Mary's public image continued much as it had during the medieval period. Among the Church hierarchy the period witnessed the ongoing gulf between Roman Catholic dogma and practice, particularly when it came to matters of celibacy. Pope Julius III (reigned 1550–5) behaved, for example, in the same inappropriate manner as some of his fifteenth-century predecessors in the papacy. He enjoyed an extravagant lifestyle, developing a scandalous homosexual infatuation with a fifteen-year-old boy, Innocenzo, taken from the streets of Parma and subsequently made a cardinal.

The Mariolatry pervading Roman Catholicism in the sixteenth century was a major factor in the creation of Protestantism, the movement for Church reform that arose in the West among such notable dissidents as Luther and Calvin. The principal cause of objection by the Reformers was the growing incompatibility between ecclesiastical tradition and the biblical texts. Luther and his allies repudiated the special veneration afforded to the Virgin Mary on the grounds that it had no substance in the books of the New Testament and that it verged on pagan idolatry. Mariolatry, for its part, was to stand increasingly as a bulwark against the Protestants and their adherence to biblical veracity.

If any aspect of Mariolatry inside the Roman Church changed from the end of the medieval period, it was the way in which it was conveyed to the public at large. Hitherto, partly due to practical limitations in disseminating information, the Marian debate had been mainly the concern of the clergy and monastic orders. Until the fifteenth century, when printed books began to circulate, sources of information were largely in the form of diocesan records and private manuscripts. The Church was also encumbered by educational ignorance not only among large masses of ordinary lay people but also among its own clergy. This ignorance and indifference was not helped by the fact that worship went on in churches that were too small to accommodate everyone and many services were conducted in a foreign language, Latin. Sermons were pitched far above the heads of the average illiterate church-goer, and more often than not were composed to satisfy the egos of wealthy patrons. All of this tended to turn Church dogma into virtually meaningless mumbo jumbo.

In the face of inadequacies in pulpit rhetoric, art was to be the principal vehicle for transmitting belief and ideology to the masses. Technological advances such as printed woodcuts became a new and important tool for conveying an effective religious message without relying on words. Although used in China from about the fourth century, the technique was not taken up in Europe until the fourteenth century. It was cheap and lent itself to the production of simple illustrated books. It served as a powerful tool in the hands of ecclesiastical propagandists intent on promoting Mary as a 'superwoman'.

Art possessed an inherent advantage over the spoken word in an age racked by bigotry and terrorised by the Roman Inquisition. Its messages were more ambiguous, less clear-cut, and therefore ideas could be conveyed without the risk of censure that attached to a contentious letter or a pamphlet. Yet religious art possessed its own dangers and was to be the root cause of considerable disagreement within the Church establishment. Indeed, the fact that artistic representation of Christian figures developed at all indicated an about-turn of founding principles.

In the second century Tertullian, the Bishop of Carthage, had voiced the fairly unequivocal opinions of the early Church on the subject of religious icons.

What solemnity of idolatry is without the circumstance of dress and ornament? In it are lasciviousnesses and drunkennesses; since it is, for the most part, for the sake of food, and stomach, and appetite, that these solemnities are frequented. In it is unrighteousness. For what more unrighteous than it, which knows not the Father of righteousness? In it also is vanity, since its whole system is vain. In it is mendacity, for its whole substance is false. Thus it comes to pass, that in idolatry all crimes are detected, and in all crimes idolatry. [*On Idolatry* 1]

Tertullian's concern lay in the fact that idolatry was synonymous with paganism and could be used to boost the pagan elements which permeated early Christianity. The process of adoration through images rekindled worries about improper worship. Notwithstanding Tertullian's admonition, the creation of Christian images quickly become unstoppable.

Among the earliest paintings of Mary were crude portrayals of the Annunciation dating from the second and third centuries. Mary and the angel Gabriel tend to be drawn in these compositions with much the same attributes as Roman deities, illustrating the reasons for the concern of men like Tertullian. They are often modelled in a distinctly pagan style and it is sometimes difficult to see where Christian imagery takes over from earlier themes. Annunciation scenes, intended to reinforce the message of the Immaculate Conception, are to be found in several Roman catacombs, including that of the disciple Priscilla. They mark the beginning of a regular manufacturing process in which artists of the medieval period were encouraged to turn out their interpretations of the Annunciation and other aspects of Mary's fictitious biography with almost conveyor-belt efficiency.

Artistic representation of Mary truly erupted in the Byzantine era, the period after 330 CE when Constantinople (the renamed town of Byzantium) became the new Roman imperial capital, which ended in 1453 when the city fell to the Turks. Popes, influential clerics and other wealthy patrons (including the monasteries) commissioned artists to transform Mary's public image from that of a simple mother to the lofty status of a queen. The painters and sculptors who created icons of Mary gave her many of the attributes that one would expect to find in both a queen and a goddess – titles implying apotheosis, celestial backcloths, adoring angels, regal attributes and trappings of immense wealth. Many of these features can still be seen preserved in the Russian orthodox art of the eighteenth and nineteenth centuries.

Concern grew as the first rumblings were heard of the iconoclast controversy. There were several reasons for Christian iconoclasm, the destruction of religious images, not all of them theological. The Byzantine emperors viewed the adoration of icons as an erosion of their own powers over the Church and decided that the practice had to end. In their condemnation of images they were also taking a calculated swipe at the monasteries, the wealth and influence of which was resented and within whose walls the most intensive Marian devotion took place.

In tandem with political resentment, a strong theological concern continued about image adoration. The non-secular argument against icons had first made itself heard about a hundred years before the iconoclastic movement came into being. It is revealed in some correspondence between Pope Gregory the Great (reigned 590–604 CE) and Serenus, Bishop of Marseilles. Serenus was diametrically opposed to all religious pictures, echoing the views of Tertullian that they amounted to nothing short of idolatry in a faith which was already adversely permeated by superstitious and magical practices. This was essentially the position held by influential members of the eastern Church in Constantinople. Gregory, however, took the more liberal view that holy pictures in particular were useful tools with which to teach the illiterate. His attitude was that it was wrong to destroy icons but that it was equally important not to adore them. In Mary's case, this was a fruitless argument because her burgeoning portraits had already become a focus of adoration, invocation and prayer in the Roman Catholic world.

During the eighth century, icon production came to a halt in Constantinople under the edicts of the Emperor Leo III (reigned 717–41) and churches were stripped of their images. But iconolatry continued in Rome and, if anything, Marian images became even more fiercely supported as spiritual paths for the faithful. It is not hard to see how the magical aura of these painted figures took them across the permissible boundaries of Christian doctrine and into the realm of paganism. They became objects in which Mary *resided*. Of particular concern to those determined to stamp out iconolatry was the kind of portable icon of either Jesus or Mary that possessed magical powers. According to rumour, such images not only moved, bled, wept and groaned but pronounced cures for the sick.

In the early part of the eighth century Germanos, who became Patriarch of Constantinople in 715 CE, resisted iconoclasm but was thrown out of office to be replaced by a pro-iconoclast, Anastasius. Pope Gregory III (reigned 731–41), a defender of Mariolatry and supporter of the monasteries, was also subject to stiff penalties (in his case financial) after he held a synod, on 1 November 731, denouncing iconoclasm and threatening excommunication to anyone found destroying images. But towards the end of the century, which saw riots in the streets of Constantinople led by women infuriated with the destruction of Marian images, more powerful voices were being raised, arguing that there was nothing wrong with either the worship of saints in general, or of Mary in particular. Among these was the Empress Irene, widow of Constantine V, who was joined by Platon, the Abbot of Sakkoudion, and Theodore, the abbot of the monastery of St John of Stoudious. The Seventh General Council of the Church, held in Nicaea in 787 CE, repudiated iconoclasm at least for a time. It was to return with no lessening of intensity but eventually was brought to a halt when, in the ninth century, the Empress Theodora permitted the restoration of images in the Festival of Orthodoxy of 843 CE. She emphasised her position as an iconodule by having coins minted to show Mary conferring power on the papacy by holding crowns over the heads of its incumbents.

Despite the persecution being waged in the East, the western Church had not been slow to recognise the benefits of Mariolatry through art and the ecclesiastical establishment set about exploiting them for all it was worth. It approved of artistic liberalisation and so painters found themselves free to work a host of innovative elements into their portraits of Mary, the royal goddess. Even in the eastern sphere of influence, relaxed attitudes brought about a new golden age of image-making to the Byzantine artists and the plaster surfaces of basilicas became smothered with religious pictures.

While turning Mary into a monarch may have been politically valuable to the Church in the West, it also had the unfortunate effect of making her seem distant from ordinary people. The images of the period do not exactly shine with warmth and personality. There remained a considerable formality about Byzantine art that did not change until the dawn of the European Renaissance. The haughtiness that had accompanied Mary's apotheosis into a remote and disinterested figure, guarded by angelic 'minders', was destined to fade. Under the influence of the western monastic institutions, staffed by men and women hungry for a little tenderness in the unremitting daily round of prayer and denial, her profile would soften, but this did not happen immediately. Eastern Mariolatry had made a strong impact on the growth of similar devotion in Europe where such fervent believers as Ambrose, Bishop of Milan, did much to preach the Greek view of Mary to the Latin Church. So, for a while, her regal aura was also copied in the West.

The Marian faithful clearly appreciated the more relaxed manner in which Mary was presented to them and the practice of pilgrimage to holy shrines of the Virgin (quickly readorned with images) burgeoned once more, accompanied by a roaring trade in relics. In the process, it would appear that the boundary between *hyperdulia* and *latria* evaporated almost to nothing. Today, one has only to walk into any Catholic church and watch a modern worshipper kneeling before a painted plaster statue of the Virgin, gazing rapturously into her face, to understand how easily it happened in an age beset, to an infinitely greater degree, by superstition and magic.

By the dawn of the twelfth century, representation of the Virgin Mother in all her queenly perfection had become almost as commonplace as that of the crucified Lord in both Greek Orthodox and Roman Catholic worlds. We are left in little doubt about who was placed in the more commanding position. A typical wall-painting in the church at Lagoudera, in Cyprus, depicts Mary as a central and dominant figure reposing on a mountain with a Christ child wholly eclipsed by her radiant majesty. Often in Nativity scenes of the period, the Magi are drawn less as wise men calling to worship the baby Jesus than as visiting potentates who bring Mary symbols of sovereignty. Thus, in the basilica of Sant' Apollinare Nuovo at Ravenna, it is clearly Mary who gives a royal audience to foreign monarchs.

In Europe, crowned heads devoted great energy and ingenuity to outdoing one another in gaining Mary's favours and then having their personal efforts immortalised in art. At the abbey of Monreale outside Palermo in Sicily, a superb twelfth-century mosaic has been preserved in which King William II, like an architect touting for recognition, holds out a model of the building to the enthroned Mary. For much of the medieval period the European royal courts vied with one another to make themselves the best outposts of heaven on earth.

One of the most influential figures in the world of European religious art during the Middle Ages was a historian and politician named Suger, who became the Abbot of St-Denis near Paris. He was probably responsible for a Western trend that went a step further than the mere tête-à-têtes between Madonna and monarch which Byzantine artists had offered. The new vogue actually started to blend heavenly divinity with earthly royalty. We have seen how, in the old imperial iconography, Mary was sometimes depicted as a Roman *augusta*. Whereas in early frescoes and mosaics she was not obviously modelled on any particular living individual, the medieval artists frequently identified her with the great queen-regents of Europe. Needless to say, for these works, they were usually working under commission from the earthly half of the merger! It is fascinating to open a Bible prepared for Blanche of Castile and discover that an artist has chosen to illuminate her sitting to the right of her son, Louis IX. This is precisely the pose of intercession found in portraits of Virgin and Christ which decorate almost any French medieval cathedral. Mary, conversely, found herself acquiring features which bore an uncanny resemblance to royal personages, including Blanche, who had their feet firmly anchored on *terra firma*. Since these human regents held power on behalf of their under-age heirs, it also became fair game for artists to merge their images with that of Mary holding the Christ child in her arms.

Suger's interest in regal portraiture evolved into a particular theme known as the 'Triumph of the Virgin'. It probably owes its innovation to an artist commissioned to work in the old medieval cathedral of Notre-Dame where there used to be a stained-glass window showing Christ placing a crown on his mother's head. The romance became so popular that it was repeated throughout the medieval cathedrals and churches of Europe and, when the new Notre-Dame was begun in 1163, the window from the original cathedral was reinstalled by Suger, where it remained until it was destroyed in the eighteenth century. Among the many existing 'coronation' portraits from which to choose, one of the best is in the National Gallery in London. Lorenzo Monaco's *Coronation of the Virgin*, painted in the early 1400s, once formed the centrepiece of a monastery altar. Monaco has drawn a humble but wholly impersonal and unemotional Mary receiving her crown from Christ while angels lift their gaze ecstatically.

With the coming of the Renaissance, the intellectual and cultural rebirth that began in Italy towards the end of the fourteenth century, art started to become accessible and more understandable to the ordinary man and woman. The intellectual movement forming the core of Renaissance culture was humanism. Its scholars rejected the theological bias of the medievalists in art and made their goal the representation of human achievement. In pursuit of this goal, the Renaissance painters were keen to throw off the image of Mary as a cold and remote figure. So often in the past she had been portrayed staring blankly at the world while holding her doll-like and passive infant like a ventriloquist's dummy. The famous *Madonna della Rondine* of Carlo Crivelli, the Venetian painter born in about 1430, is typical of the shift towards a more sentimental style. Crivelli has swathed Mary in a heavily girdled blue cloak. She has a sweet and serene expression on her young face as she cradles a chubby, naked and extremely human baby. Jesus looks keen to wriggle on her lap while the swallow of the title perches cheerily on a balustrade above her head. Another exemplary portrait, from the last decade of the fifteenth century, is that of *Virgin and Child Enthroned* by the Flemish painter Quentin Massys, who was strongly influenced by the Italian Renaissance artists. Aside from two playful angels floating above her head and two more angels strumming instruments, Mary's face has the plump and youthful normality of the girl next door. Almost entirely missing, incidentally, are depictions of Mary as a mother-to-be. The Virgin Immaculata drawn with a swollen belly would not have been appropriate in a culture that, by now, firmly rejected all representation of the normal human process of pregnancy brought about by sexual intercourse.

Mary's humanity as a mother was brought to the fore in a different way when she was portrayed agonising over the death of Jesus. This imagery had begun to develop as early as the sixth century when, in Syria, dirges were first composed by poets, including Romanos Melodos, about Mary's sorrows at the foot of the Cross. The cult of the *Mater dolorosa* took shape in Europe in the twelfth and thirteenth centuries. A fine English ivory panel dating from about 1150 CE depicts Mary receiving the body of Christ from the Cross. The *Mater dolorosa* did not, however, reach its most dramatic expression until the sixteenth century. Housed in Florence's great cathedral, that glorious marble-hewn monument to Roman Catholic faith, is one of many *pietàs*, images of Christ's sorrowing mother, created by Michelangelo Buonarroti (1475–1564). Though less well known than his superb sculpture in St Peter's Basilica, Rome, this one is made memorable by being unfinished and raw. The broken body of Christ is lifted by Joseph of Arimathea and Mary, bent under its weight. Here is the true spirit of the *Mater dolorosa* and it was from this imagery of compassion that Mary's role as mediator and intercessor was to arise.

The theme of the sorrowing mother was also taken up eagerly by composers. The sixteenth century saw the first performance of Palestrina's *Stabat Mater Dolorosa*. Later, Bach was to include in his *St John Passion* an aria with the words, 'O heart, melt in weeping, and pour out thy dolour ... thy Jesus is slain.'

The monastic institutions of the time saw in Mary the compassionate and approachable mother. As patrons of the arts, they hastened to commission works revealing Mary's new-found accessibility and it was the Christian painters and sculptors of the West who were most influential in bringing this to the forefront of public attention. In certain respects, what Mary offered the man or woman in the Christian street, through being humanised by artists like Crivelli and Michelangelo, was the possibility of becoming 'godly' in the earthly life instead of in the world to come.

How strikingly different from the works which set out not only to humanise Mary the Virgin, but also to portray her as a beautiful young woman, were those which depicted Mary of Magdala. The alternative, ungodly decay, shocking in its contrast, relied on Mary's *alter ego* for its artist's model. It is as if the brunt of all masculine prejudice against women and their human sexuality was loaded on to images of this much-maligned creature. One of the most dreadful portrayals of Mary of Magdala, the sculpture by Donatello (*c.*1386–1466) entitled *La Maddalena*, turns her into a grotesque parody of womanhood, an emaciated hag whose sexual experience in the topsy-turvy world of Christian logic earned the reward of desolation and despair. Hers is the fate of the natural body that has tasted earthly fulfilment. The Madonna and the Maddalena! The provocative and haunting words of a Gnostic text from Nag Hammadi draw us back, inexorably, to the suspicion that each of these caricatured women is only half a personality without the other.

> *I am the abiding and I am the dissolution.*
> *I am the one below and they come up to me.*
> *I am the judgement and the acquittal.*
> *I am sinless and the root of sin derives from me.*
> *I am lust in appearance and self-control exists within me.*
> [*Thunder, Perfect Mind* vi.2.19, after Robinson, 1988]

Through the inspiration of Renaissance art, the one becomes the mutually exclusive mirror of the other in a world where good becomes synonymous with denial, and evil blends seamlessly with sexuality. Here are Ishtar and Ereshkigal, life and death, stripped of their original pagan identity.

Renaissance artists did not abandon other pagan elements in their representation of Mary. Byzantine art had linked the *three* Marys, bringing them together in an echo of the trio of pagan *Matres*, and this vogue continued. A finely executed fifteenth-century Crucifixion study, again from the studio of Quentin Massys, is typical. The Virgin, dressed in white and adorned by her famous blue sash, kneels in anguish at the foot of the Cross, accompanied by Mary of Bethany in blue and the red-haired Mary of Magdala in red with a green cloak. Some of the other women said to have attended Christ's death stand in the background.

Although there are arguments among scholars that Mary's imagery is closer to that of Kybele, who became the Roman *Magna mater*, it is the Egyptian goddess Isis who provides much of the inspiration. The Greeks and Romans, thoroughly besotted in their adoration of most things Egyptian, had identified Isis as the Star of the Sea and they believed her to make her nightly appearance in the heavens as the north star. *Stella maris* is a title loaded with meaning since the sea has always been regarded as a source of bounty and fertility. So it does not come wholly as a surprise to discover that, from about the ninth century, Mary was also enjoying the title of *Stella maris*. It forms, for example, the title of John of Garland's thirteenth-century book of miracles associated with Mary. This picturesque imagery will never be found in her biblical story but, ignoring any lack of serious credentials, Mary was soon being looked up to as the dependable lodestar guiding life's voyagers from her heavenly vantage point. The *Stella maris* theme has also attracted composers. The *Ave Maris Stella* became the subject of an unsurpassed hymn from Monteverdi's 1610 Vespers. Monteverdi managed to include most of her assumed qualities in one all-encompassing line: 'Hail, star of the sea, life-giving mother of God and perpetual virgin, happy gate of heaven' [Bartlett].

The coming of the sixteenth century brought with it one of the most turbulent upheavals in the history of the Christian movement, the Reformation. This was the rebellion against corruption in the Roman Catholic Church and what was seen as its abrogation of the Bible as the sole source of divine revelation in favour of the whimsy of the apostolic succession in the papacy. The voice of Protestantism was raised and much of its fury was directed against Mariolatry. In 1525 Martin Luther declared that the cult of Mary worship was nothing short of 'abominable idolatry'. Far from praising her it was, he said, 'slandering her in the extreme and making an idol of her'. Luther's fellow reformist Philip Melanchthon declared in Article XXI of the *Augsburg Confession* (1530), 'Christ is the only high priest, advocate and intercessor before God. He alone has promised to hear our prayers.'

All that Protestantism did in Roman Catholic spheres was to drive Marianists to even more fervent adoration. If Catholic argument was to be believed, Joachim took no part in the miracle of Anna's divine impregnation so Pius V suppressed his feast-day.

Over the issue of the presentation of Mary in the Temple, a

matter seriously lacking in credibility for anyone who cared to look beyond the bare outlines of the story, Pius went a stage further in his manipulation of the record. As we have established, a female child could not have been admitted to the Yahwist sanctuary to be raised by a male priesthood. Conscious of the delicate nature of the matter, Pius issued a directive that the Feast of the Presentation was also to be struck from the calendar. The text of the *Protevangelium* was to be suppressed and the dubious nature of the Temple visit disguised by appropriate borrowings from the canonical gospels. At first diplomatically retaining the word 'presentation', the Feast of the Presentation of *Mary* was pushed into the background in favour of the much safer Feast of the Presentation of *Christ* in the Temple, the date for which was set as 2 February. The word 'Presentation' was dropped altogether when the name became altered to the Purification of the Blessed Virgin Mary. The latter celebration was to mark the occasion, forty days after the birth of Jesus, when Mary complied with Jewish law by going to the Temple, equipped with a sacrifice, so that the priest might cleanse her from sin – a curious decision since Mary was allegedly untainted by sin! While Mary was being heaped with adulation and placed upon an ever more exclusive pedestal, the linking of ordinary women and sin became progressively more extreme, with Christians even being encouraged to believe that Satan was female, an argument which persisted for hundreds of years. In the sixteenth century St Ignatius of Loyola commented on the wiles of the devil.

'The enemy acts like a woman, in being weak against vigour and strong of will. Because, as it is the way of the woman when she is quarrelling with some man to lose heart, taking flight when the man shows her much courage: and on the contrary, if the man, losing heart, begins to fly, the wrath, revenge, and ferocity of the woman is very great, and so without bounds.'

[*Spiritual Exercises: for perceiving and knowing in some manner the different movements which are caused in the soul.* 12]

In the impassioned climate of the Counter-Reformation, which ran for about a hundred years from the middle of the sixteenth century and set out to combat the effects of Protestantism through reform of the Roman Catholic Church, a determined Franciscan, St Lawrence of Brindisi who died in 1619 CE, declared, 'Her kingdom and empire is no less than the kingdom of God and the Empire of Christ.' Not all the world agreed. Many still believed that Mary was born in original sin and were therefore opposed to the dogma of the Immaculate Conception. Such was the level of concern that by the 1700s the Austrian emperor, Charles VI (1711–1740) was imprisoning all who refused to accept the Immaculate Conception. Curiously, the Protestant Reformer, Martin Luther (1483–1546), was a staunch advocate of the idea that Mary was a virgin when she conceived. According to one anecdote, he offered to hand over one hundred florins to anyone who could prove that *almah* did not mean virgin, but young woman. Had he been alive today he would, of course, have had to part with his money!

During the Counter-Reformation visionary experiences, probably stimulated by the burgeoning romantic art of Mary, were in danger of running out of control. In the seventeenth century they were being reported throughout France on an almost daily basis and eventually cautionary voices began to be heard. Sightings of virginal apparitions multiplied after the French Revolution and, before his inauguration as Pope Benedict XIV in 1740, Prospero Lambertini was prompted to write a pamphlet entitled *De revelatione*. In this, he adopted the refreshingly common-sense view that approval by authority was no guarantee of an apparition having genuinely taken place.

As the bigotry and intolerance associated with Marianism became progressively more extreme, several developments occurred that stand in stark contrast to the liberalisation in art and the hysteria of visionaries. Pope Paul IV (reigned 1555–9) devoted his energies to reactivating the Roman Inquisition. Violently anti-Protestant, he accused Jews of abetting Protestantism, confining them in ghettos in Rome and forcing them to wear distinctive headgear. He also created, through the formal body of inquiry known as the Congregation of the Inquisition, a new form of censorship. In 1557 he authorised the Index of Forbidden Books, which was further revised in 1559. In terms of its unprecedented severity against freedom of literary expression, the Index far outstripped previous edicts and restrictions such as the *Decretum Gelasianum*.

In 1571 Pope Pius V (reigned 1566–72) consolidated the Index by setting up a new administrative apparatus to be known as the Congregation of the Index. So draconian were its powers that hundreds of Italian printers were forced to flee to Germany and Switzerland in order to escape arrest. Pius V's austerity and strong measures against dissenters from orthodoxy propped up the defences of the Roman Catholic Church during the Counter-Reformation and he used the machinery of the Inquisition to stamp out anything that he considered to smack of heresy. It was he who excommunicated Queen Elizabeth I of England. It is particularly disturbing, therefore, to discover that Pius V was also responsible for deliberate manipulation of the record. The Catholic breviary, the Roman Church's compendium of rules and regulations, had included an annual festival to honour St Joachim, claimed to be the father of Mary by the *Protevangelium of James* and several other apocryphal works. It was believed that Joachim and Anna, Mary's mother, moved from their original home in Galilee to Jerusalem where Mary was born and reared, and that both parents had died in Jerusalem. Some time in the fourth century a church had been built over the site of their house and their tombs had lain in its crypt, until the ninth century when the church was converted to a Moslem school. Celebration of Joachim's life did not, however, support the claim that Mary was the product of sex-free conception. If orthodox argument was to be believed Joachim took no part in the miracle of Anna's divine impregnation, so Pius suppressed his feast-day.

Over the issue of the Presentation of Mary in the Temple, the bizarre account of her being handed into the care of Temple priests from the age of three, Pius V went a stage further in his manipulation of the record. This is a matter that holds a serious lack of credibility for anyone who cares to look beyond the bare outlines of the story, since a female child could not have been admitted to the Jewish sanctuary to be raised by a male priesthood. Pius issued a directive that the Feast of the Presentation was also to be struck from the Church's calendar and that the text of the *Protevangelium* was to be banned. While retaining the key word 'Presentation', Mary's introduction to the Temple was pushed into the background in favour of the Feast of the Presentation of *Christ*.

Neither of Pius V's attempts at doctoring wholly succeeded. Joachim's feast-day was eventually restored by Gregory XV in 1622 and, just over a hundred years later in 1738, Clement XII fixed its annual celebration on the Sunday after the Assumption. The old Feast of the Presentation of Mary was also taken up again by Pope Sixtus V in 1585 but it was a half-hearted revival that never achieved the same broad recognition that the festival had enjoyed in past centuries.

Pius V's conduct does, however, bring into sharp focus the question of what can be believed of the papacy in terms of its guardianship of Christian history. Some thirty years after his reign, Paul V, who held office from 1605 to 1621, formed a collection of classified information, including banned books, the secret arch-ives. To this day the contents of the archive, both historical and doctrinal, defined arbitrarily by the Church as heretical, are largely unknown because the bulk of it is inaccessible other than for a privileged few among the Roman Catholic hierarchy.

FIFTEEN

To the Twentieth Century

In his book *Virgin Birth? The True Story of Mary and her Son Jesus*, one of the leading authorities on heresy, Gerd Ludemann, points out that the development of Marianism provides a good example of the way in which theological principles developed.

> Castles are built in the air, each more beautiful and inviting than the next, and the whole is then regarded as the firm citadel of revealed truth, a turn of phrase which means, in effect, that the word of God is delivered privately to certain selected beneficiaries whose integrity on the matter we are then asked to accept blindly as an act of faith. [Ludemann, 1998]

The Catholic Church has continued its distortion of the Marian record, has built its castles in the air and has managed to weld them into the very highest levels of Church doctrine as 'revealed truth' which the flock does indeed accept as a blind act of faith.

One of the clearest examples is what has happened to the tradition of the Immaculate Conception. Ignored or discounted by the canonical writers as a popular myth, it was destined to gain the status of official Catholic dogma. The ideology had been in circulation for hundreds of years, but the process of formal acceptance was begun in the reign of Pope Gregory XVI in 1831. He promoted the Immaculate Conception heavily although it was left to his successor Pius IX (reigned 1846–78) to ratify it as part of the official dogma of the Church in 1854.

Pius's action probably held political as well as doctrinal significance. The dogma is thought by some Church historians to have been picked out as a 'safe' populist idea, over which few would object, in order to set a precedent of 'papal infallibility'. In 1870 Pius IX summoned the First Vatican Council and, on 18 July, in a constitution known as *Pastor aeternus*, he declared that the definitions of the pope on faith and morals were infallible in their own right. The principle was thus enshrined in the Roman Catholic Church's statutes that whatever pronouncements the incumbent of the papacy chose to deliver amounted to messages from God, irrespective of whether or not they were reasonably sanguine. Papal infallibility was seen by some to be a measure of Vatican ostentation and short-sightedness but, against predictions, it turned a growing tide of disaffection among the faithful and, more than ever, placed Mary, not Christ, as the focus of Catholic faith.

The last two centuries of Roman Catholicism have been characterised by a newsworthy phenomenon associated with Mary, that of her appearances to visionaries. A wave of miraculous sightings, creating much romantic fervour, began in Paris in 1830. In that year of revolt, a nun named Catherine Labouré saw the heart of St Vincent, 'Father of the Poor', hovering in the mother house of the Sisters of Charity. She was subsequently alleged to have been visited by the Virgin who delivered warnings of the impending collapse of the French monarchy. Sixteen years later, when the region was braced for fresh revolt, two teenage girls at La Salette in the French Alps received a message from a weeping and luminous Virgin who showed them a sacred spring. By 1852 the foundations of a basilica had been laid and La Salette entered Roman Catholic history while triggering a plethora of shrine-building to the 'Virgin of the Alps.'

It was in February 1858, however, that Mary is alleged to have made one of her most celebrated appearances, in a natural grotto close by the Cave de Pau at a place called Lourdes in the French Pyrenees. The incident had the convenient effect of boosting credibility for the papal dogma of the Immaculate Conception, then just four years old. A small, innocuous village, Lourdes was transformed into a bustling centre of pilgrimage. It now has an airport and a station stop for the TGV express. Lourdes boasts the highest number of hotels in any one French town, barring Paris, and a plethora of religious monuments including a large cross on the top of a mountain reached conveniently by cable car.

All is attributable to the sickly fourteen-year-old child of a convicted father and a mother given to drink, Bernadette Soubirous. After witnessing eighteen visitations that contained various warnings and introduced her to a spring with curative properties, Bernadette was prompted to entertain the visiting crowds by telling her rosary, scampering up and down the hillside at astonishing speed, drinking the waters and eating grass on the command of her unseen mentor. When interviewed by a sceptical local bishop shortly after the first visitation, she had been asked to find out the name of the apparition, whom she described, with improbable eloquence given her uneducated background, as 'a young, wondrously beautiful lady, completely bathed in light'. During a second visitation Bernadette asked the name of her mysterious friend, upon which the lady introduced herself as 'The Immaculate Conception', confirming her identity on several subsequent occasions. This was accepted as credible, not only by Bernadette's bishop but by the entire Roman Catholic office. What might appear to be extreme gullibility makes better sense if one takes the view that the whole rash of phenomena, which saw no respite in the early part of the nineteenth century, was orchestrated by the Catholic Church. In the case of Bernadette Soubirous, the Church was in need of heavenly endorsement for its dogma of Immaculate Conception, still the subject of scepticism. A young girl at the impressionable and sometimes hysterical age of puberty, illiterate and from an impoverished home, emerged conveniently from nowhere, was primed with an appropriate question and thus was able to confirm the infallibility of the Pope's words.

In the twentieth century Spain and Portugal have tended to

take over from France as the main countries receiving Marian visits. Oddly, Italy has never been a real contender. In more recent times, the appearances have been related less to Catholic dogma than to political or strategic events, though with the desire for Catholic promotion never far away. A village called Fatima, north of Lisbon, shot to fame when, in 1915, at the height of the First World War, three children including Lucia, the illiterate eight-year-old daughter of an alcoholic herdsman, witnessed the Virgin floating in the air. Lucia was instructed to spread a message that the rosary should be recited daily so that the world, and Portugal fighting as an ally of the British, could return to peace. On 13 October 1917, after several more visitations and considerably more publicity, about 70,000 people gathered in Fatima and, it is said, witnessed Mary engineering the sun to 'spin in the sky like a Catherine wheel throwing off great arcs of fiery light'. In later years, when communism was emerging as the main threat to the Catholic Church and Lucia had become a Dorothean nun, she allegedly received a three-part message from Mary concerning the future role of Russia in world affairs. Lucia revealed two parts but the third remained undisclosed although she wrote it down in 1943 and it was deposited in the Vatican's secret archives. Pius XII (reigned 1939–58) is said to have recognised the importance of Fatima's experience in the furthering of Mariolatry and his successor, Pope John XXIII (reigned 1958–63), is said to have read the undisclosed part of the message in 1960. Its contents have never been made public.

Fascination with Marian relics has continued into the modern era and there has been a constant urge to discover new and miraculous phenomena associated with Mary's shrines. Amidst often hysterical excitement her statues have been reported to weep, nod their heads, bleed, walk, talk and glow in the dark. Most of this stands as pagan-derived magic. People have also become obsessed with finding tangible evidence of where Mary had lived. Details of a vision revealed to an Augustinian nun and mystic, Anne Catherine Emmerich, published in 1876, were greeted with immense interest. Emmerich had already gained acclaim as a stigmatic bearing the wounds of crucifixion in her hands, feet and side, so all of her utterances tended to be taken seriously by the ecclesiastical authorities. At a time when her Westphalian Catholic Church was under great strain, she claimed to have seen the house in Ephesus where Mary allegedly lived out her retirement under John's protection. A team of Catholic archaeologists was despatched to the site and uncovered the ruins of a tiny first-century building which was subsequently restored. Not only did the Westphalian Church receive a much needed boost but, to certain chagrin in Jerusalem which was also making similar housing claims, Ephesus became a centre of new Marian devotion.

Even the bodily relics of Mary's visionaries have taken on special powers. Many of the women who claimed these experiences were persuaded by the Church to spend the rest of their lives prudently closeted away from public eye and inquiry. In death, however, their lips sealed against the chance of revealing indiscreet details, they were returned to the public forum. Some of their physical remains have resisted decay and have become freakish attractions for voyeurs, tourists and disciples alike. Merely to stand in the proximity of these tired body parts, immured behind hermetically sealed glass, is said to be enough to benefit from their supernatural powers while cash donations towards the upkeep of their mausoleums are generally reckoned to provide added benefit.

Mary's association with war has been another strictly pagan feature of her fictitious biography. Practically all the mother goddesses, with the notable exception of Isis in Egypt, were also goddesses of battle. As we have seen, this had been an element of Mary's cult since imperial Roman times but it came particularly to the fore in Spain during the seventeenth century when Spanish power and influence was beginning to wane. Philip IV proclaimed Mary as 'Our Lady of Victories, Patroness of the Royal Arms' and ordered the celebration of her feast-days throughout the Spanish dominions. It had already been the norm that when the Spanish explorers and conquistadors entered the Americas and began to suppress the ethnic inhabitants, they did so as foot soldiers of Mary who could justify their catalogue of brutality in terms of righteously defending Catholicism against its enemies.

Closer to home, in the Thirty Years War between the Catholic armies of Ferdinand of Austria and the Protestant Reformers, an icon of the Madonna was thought to have been sufficiently instrumental in securing a crucial victory near Prague for a church in Rome, already heavily associated with visions of the Virgin, to be renamed S. Maria della Vittoria. As recently as the Crimean War, Mary's image was cast on medals which were then surreptitiously inserted into the bandages of the wounded.

In the Iberian peninsula during Franco's long term of office, when Catholicism stood firmly against communism, Protestantism and Freemasonry, aggressive Mariolatry sometimes verged on frenzy. At the end of the Spanish Civil War, the Portuguese bishops led half a million grateful devotees to the Fatima shrine to give thanks for protection against the 'Red menace'. The aftermath of hostilities also saw the rise of various quasi-militant, right-wing religious movements with Mary as their 'founder and patroness'. In Spain, there was a popular legend that Mary had been exiled in Aragon and, on arrival, had planted a stone pillar in thanks for her safe journey. She became known as the Virgin of Saragossa, the Nuestra Senora del Pilar, and, during the war, Saragossa had become a rallying point for the Nationalists. On 26 August 1936, the local press published an account of how a triumphant Falangist battalion had marched to her shrine yelling, 'Long Live Death! Long Live the Virgin of the Pillar' and, after the conflict, Franco conceded that, 'If the Virgin of the Pillar had not given us all energy, bravery, the spirit of sacrifice, living conscience of the past and blind faith in our future, all our armed guards would have kept vigil in vain.' Whether the Generalissimo pondered on the logic of these valedictory observations we will never know but Mary certainly became a patroness of the Spanish army. The military were fond of decorating her with honours, to the accompaniment of loud cannonades and rousing martial music.

From about the mid-nineteenth century a new kind of romantic militancy began to invade European Catholicism. In the face of the growth of modernism, communism and other sects not kindly disposed towards the Church, many quasi-religious right-wing movements came into being with Mary as their 'founder and figurehead'. Often they were given militaristic titles. Out of the experience of Fatima in 1917 there arose the Blue Army of Mary, although the organisation was not actually formed until thirty years later when a New Jersey priest, Harold Colgan, heard the Fatima message. Named after the colour of the sash that Mary traditionally wears around her waist, the national centre of the Blue Army was founded in Plainfield, New Jersey, and a local shrine for English-speaking pilgrims was established in Fatima. The organisation spread rapidly across the world and now claims membership in millions.

The largest apostolic organisation of lay people in the Catholic Church is the Legion of Mary with over three million active members worldwide. It was founded in Dublin in 1921 by a civil servant, Frank Duff, with the maxim, 'Glorification of God through the sanctification of members'. It has been approved by the last six popes and was officially endorsed by the Second Vatican Council which began in 1962.

During the 1920s and 30s in Poland a tuberculosis-ridden Franciscan friar named Maximilian Kolbe set about building another strongly right-wing Catholic organisation named the Militia Immaculatae, the Knights of the Immaculata. Kolbe claimed that the power of its evangelising members came from 'total consecration to the Blessed Virgin Mary'. By the outbreak of the Second World War he had seen the organisation expand to nearly one million members. He died in Auschwitz in August 1941 and was canonised in 1982. Similar organisations have come into being the world over. Founded in 1927 by Josemaria Escriva de Balaguer, a lecturer on religion from Aragon, Opus Dei was, and still is, undoubtedly one of the most powerful. Through Catholic Action, designed as a bulwark against political subversion, Catholic doctrine and devotion to the Immaculata was made compulsory in universities throughout Spain. Young people were dragooned into social work and conversion of workers to the cult of the Immaculata was a paramount objective. Catholic Action, however, was under the control of the secretive Opus Dei organisation, which owed its 'sponsorship and foundation' directly to Mary.

In America, the Knights of Columbus (advertised as 'the world's largest and strongest Catholic fraternal organisation') recruited its members with the lure of low-cost life insurance, amassed great wealth and wielded considerable influence under the guiding hand of the Immaculata. Mary was paraded as 'anti-communist' and some of the most alarming aspects of militant Mariolatry surfaced during the 1950s and 60s with the McCarthyite witch hunts, during the course of which the Knights were powerful allies of the Un-American Activities Committee. Mary led the charge against anyone even remotely left-of-centre. In Ireland, one finds a near namesake, the Knights of St Columbanus, whilst Australia is host to the Knights of the Southern Cross. All of these organisations professed a militant devotion to Mary. Her soldiers were encouraged to wear her blue sash as an overt and politically expedient badge of loyalty.

During the 1980s and 90s, Marian devotion may have taken us even closer to nuclear Armageddon than is generally appreciated. On 2 November 1984, an American journal entitled the *National Catholic Reporter* based in Kansas City, promoting itself as an independent voice within the Church, guided by commitments of justice, peace and a sustainable world, published an article suggesting that ex-President Reagan was a subscriber to an alarming view: in the seconds before the first missile of World War III struck, vaporising most of us instantly, Mary's righteous millions would be lifted into the air and saved. Some of the more aggressive posturing of the Reagan era is said to have stemmed from an implicit belief among born-again fundamentalists that détente was largely a waste of time because Mary had her hand over the nuclear button. Sanguine human intervention has left us ignorant of whether or not, and under what circumstances, she would have pressed it.

Another pagan aspect of Mariolatry which has survived from early in the Christian era is an association with sacred trees. From the time of Constantine the Great, the Sacred Tree – in Christian terminology the Tree of Life – became woven into the fabric of the Crucifixion. The Great Cross of Lateran, a magnificent work of art by an unknown hand, has been the model for many subsequent studies but, in some of these later works, the outline of the cross has become perfunctory. We can find a carving, made in Rennes during the 1830s, where the tree has a bird, now the dove of the Holy Spirit, perched in its branches while a snake, symbol of knowledge and evil, coils at its roots. Winged cherubim look on and the tree is ringed by rosettes. All of these symbols were included in the ancient Near Eastern imagery of the Sacred Tree when it stood for the presence of the pagan goddess Ishtar.

Today, little has changed. The proper Mass for the Feast of the Immaculate Conception includes words that raise a familiar, if non-Christian, echo:

> I was exalted like a cedar in Libanus, and as a cypress tree in Mount Sion. I was exalted like a palm tree in Cades, and as a rose plant in Jericho; as a fair olive tree in the plains and as a plane tree by the water. In the streets was I exalted. I gave a sweet perfume like cinnamon and aromatic balm. I yielded a sweet odour like the best myrrh.

Many folk traditions link Mary with trees. At Whitsun, churches used to be decorated with boughs of birch, a tree which Samuel Taylor Coleridge described as 'The Lady of the Woods'. In Russia, until very recently, the tradition has extended to dressing up a young birch tree in women's clothes and decorating it with ribbons. Although not directly linked with Marian tradition, the maypole possesses similar connotations. In days gone by, this took the form of a young fir or birch tree, freshly cut for May Day and carried into the village to be decked with ribbons and flowers. In Leadenhall Street in the City of London, incidentally, the church of St Andrew Undershaft owes its name to an enormous phallic pole which Chaucer referred to as the 'Great Shaft of Cornhill' and which stood on the site until it was demolished by the Cromwellian Puritans who found it distasteful.

Other pagan elements have proved impossible to dislodge, including the contentious title Queen of Heaven. The final antiphone of the Compline Mass includes a hymn of praise:

Hail, Queen of Heaven
Hail, Lady of the Angels.
Salutation to the root and portal,
Whence the light of the world has arisen.

Today the cult of Mary is arguably the greatest single obstacle blocking the way to Christian unity and it also creates some of the strongest passions not only between Catholic and Protestant but between the Roman and Greek Orthodox Churches. The Roman Catholic catechism demands of its parishioners faith in the four 'unalienable facts': Immaculate Conception, Divine Motherhood, Perpetual Virginity and Bodily Assumption. Yet these are biologically impossible and contain no more than shreds of biblical authenticity. Aside from the concept of the *Theotokos*, they are resented by the Greek Orthodox Church and they were not always universally supported even by the Church of Rome. As Benjamin Disraeli put it in the context of one of his novels, 'Pray, are you of those Christians who worship a Jewess, or of those who revile her, break her images and blaspheme her pictures?'

It is something of an irony, in view of moves towards Christian unity, that during the last half of the twentieth century as much was done in the name of Mary to offend the Protestant and Orthodox Churches as at any time in Christian history. The dogma of Carnal Assumption was ratified in Rome in 1950 by Pope Pius XII. He appeared on the balcony of St Peter's on 1 November and announced to a rapturous congregation of more than a million people that Mary had been carried bodily to heaven. The papal bull *Munificentissimus Deus* decreed, 'We proclaim, declare and define that it is a divinely revealed dogma that the immaculate Mother of God, the perpetual Virgin Mary, after she ended her earthly life, was taken up body and soul into heavenly glory.' Despite the initial euphoria, this piece of dogma incited considerable dissent. In particular, the Greek Orthodox Church believes that the ascent of a whole body – bones, flesh and blood – into the clouds is a privilege reserved strictly and uniquely for Christ. Four years later, on 11 October 1954, Pius XII devoted another papal decree – *Ad coeli reginam* – to assert that Mary reigns as Queen of Heaven.

Between 1962 and 1965, under Pope John XXIII and his successor, Paul VI, the Vatican held its second General Ecumenical Council (known as Vatican II). One of its main purposes was to produce a document defining the nature of the Church in the twentieth century; among the many suggestions of other topics for discussion, was the demand for a debate on the Mother of God. This aroused a mixed response. On the one hand there was concern that putting Mary on the agenda might result in another grand papal gesture of the kind made by Pius XII when he ratified the Carnal Assumption, which would further irritate the Protestant and Orthodox Churches. On the other hand, there were worries among a sizeable body of the delegate bishops that a plot was afoot to downgrade Mary. After an acrimonious vote, a debate about the Virgin was squeezed on to the agenda by a narrow majority and it resulted in Paul VI forcing through a new title for Mary, which added to that of 'Mother of God' by also proclaiming her to be the 'Mother of the Church'. Many members of Vatican II considered that Paul VI had overstepped the implicit wishes of the Council.

When the ultra-conservative John Paul II took the Vatican throne he was known to have a keen interest in the promotion of Mariolatry. The world did not have to wait long to discover that

John Paul was committed to the notion of intervention in earthly affairs by Our Lady and to the positive nature of her miraculous appearances. After the attempt on his life in St Peter's Square in 1981, he made the point that he was 'indebted to the Blessed Virgin' for sparing him. He felt 'extraordinary motherly protection that turned out to be stronger than the deadly bullet' and one of his wishes was to elevate Mary to the role of co-redemptrix. Jesus Christ had, of course, always been viewed by the Catholic faithful as the Redeemer but to make his mother a partner in this capacity, the *Redemptoris mater*, added a new and interesting dimension to the arguments already surrounding Mary.

As was mentioned in the Introduction, on 24 March 1984 John Paul II took advantage of the medium of television to reach a worldwide audience of millions when he knelt before the figure of Our Lady of Fatima in St Peter's Square and dedicated the entire planet to the Immaculate Heart of Mary. He confirmed that her motherly embrace encircles the world, irrespective of religions and division. It was a consecration which, he clamoured, 'lasts for all time and embraces all individuals, peoples and nations'. Among the claims made by the Blue Army of Mary is an argument that Russian communism was overthrown as a result of this act of global consecration.

In 1987, John Paul II announced a Marian Jubilee on the pretext that if the bi-millennium in 2000 was to celebrate the anniversary of Christ's Nativity, his mother's birth of thirteen years earlier should also be properly celebrated as a preparation, based on the theme of the Magnificat. During an astonishing, some even suggested quasi-miraculous, global television 'road show', eighteen satellites beamed simultaneous pictures from shrines around the world. At its opening, John Paul II lit a sacred flame for Mary and later claimed that she had been called upon to share in, and collaborate with, the 'dawn of redemption' in an exceptional and extraordinary way. He also made outspoken claims that Mary was to be regarded as an essential mediator. This was nothing new, but John Paul II went further in claiming that the role of mediatrix was her exclusive initiative and that the episode of the marriage at Cana was a biblical announcement of this role. She was, in placing herself between Christ and humanity, a kind of filter screen. John Paul II has been at pains to point out that the chief mediator is still Jesus Christ and that his mother is only a secondary 'maternal mediator' but, none the less, it is dangerous doctrine and theologically unsubstantiated. There is no hint in the biblical texts that the Mother of Christ is a mediator between Redeemer and Redeemed. John Paul II has also claimed that Mary is actually present at several of her shrines around the world, including Lourdes, Fatima and Guadeloupe in South America. The ideology moves, yet again, towards fundamentally pagan principles.

We have travelled down two millennia of Christian history and almost reached the end of our search for the truth about Mary. The real woman whom we have discovered through stripping off the layers of paint to reveal the original portrait is a very different person from the one represented in the modern Christian view. We have also discovered that the early cult of Mary was based on criteria and principles which are at odds with some of those we recognise today. If there is one great irony for a religious movement which parades her as a bastion of orthodoxy, it is that the principles arose not out of Judaism, nor Christianity, but largely out of paganism. In the early centuries, these principles were manipulated largely on political and sociological grounds but now the same is only partly true. The principles are, to a far greater extent, a tool to encourage faith. This involves no less of a manipulation.

Does it really matter whether faith in Mary is based on historical fact or an impossible fairy-tale? When all is said and done, what we choose to believe as a matter of faith is not necessarily reliant on proof positive, or scientific accuracy, or historical veracity. Faith cannot be put to the test or determined by formulae nor can it be influenced by intellectual argument. We either believe or we do not believe!

Yet faith also needs to involve some measure of morality beyond belief in a pure abstract principle. It needs to be built on trust and confidence, the fidelity of promises given honestly and openly, otherwise there is no point in having it. If faith is founded on lies, deceit and calculated manipulation, then it becomes impossible to justify and there is even a question mark against whether it can reasonably be called faith. Were we still the largely ignorant and superstitious flock in whom the Marian deception first took root and in whom it became twisted into an 'infallible truth', we might have an excuse for being taken in by it. But at the dawn of the twenty-first century, many of us can no longer claim to be ignorant or superstitious and our blinkered faith becomes open to more serious criticism. This is particularly true when we know that bigotry is involved and that our understanding of a fictitious Mary has been controlled by men with vested interests, determined to safeguard their own patriarchal social position in the name of religion.

Faith is not universally practised at the same level. Millions of Catholics, in South America for example, are largely uneducated and their faith in Mary remains almost a blind one. There are also ranks of highly educated men in the Church who know the extent of the manipulation and deceit and choose to perpetuate it. By inventing an artificial nature for Mary, the Catholic Church supports a piece of cruel nonsense, a link between female sexuality, a normal facet of a woman's biological nature, and death and physical decay. It has inflicted, and continues to inflict, on women the myth that the most fundamental and primeval of God-given desires and urges is sinful except for the procreation of children.

The conservative male hierarchy of Roman Catholicism clearly has reason to nurture the Marian myth and to support the *status quo* in her cult. The fable of humility, lowliness in the sight of God and lack of sexuality, allows a still deeply misogynistic Church organisation to demean and degrade on grounds of gender. The Roman Catholic Church remains firmly committed to the dogma of original sin foisted on the world by the first woman, and per-

petuated through 'the curse of Eve'. Through wholly unsubstantiated claims that Mary was free from original sin, the perfect
example, the shining light, the paradigm of virtue, the organisation
has disassociated her from ordinary 'sinful' womanhood. In the
same breath it has justified Mary's elevation to the role of a mother
goddess whose glory eclipses that of her divine son. The nearest
that any woman of less esteemed pedigree may come to absolving
herself from the eternal shame of being born female in the Roman
Catholic world of the twenty-first century is through renouncing
normal human desires and biological urges and retiring to a cloistered life of celibacy. Any radical change in this position could, of
course, have a profound effect on the Catholic Church's moral
teaching and its very bedrock of dogma. The present ultra-conservative incumbent of the papacy, John Paul II, has done nothing
to ameliorate this position and, if anything, has reinforced it.

If we reverse the process of revealing the true canvas, we can
see that in order to juggle two parallel but dogmatically conflicting
religious beliefs and incorporate them into the single mantle of
Christianity, the early ecclesiastical authorities created an image,
layer by layer, that was almost pure fantasy. They built an image
of a superwoman who could be all things to all people – those who
pursued the orthodox Christian ideology and those determined to
keep alive the pagan aspects of Mary's persona. Once the initial
level of untruth was laid down, the daubing of new colour on the
canvas accepted, it became progressively easier for the Church to
embellish historical reality, scant as it is, with lie upon lie.

If we gather all the evidence together, the true canvas presents
a clear picture. Whatever her real name, as distinct from her
professional job description, Jesus' mother was born in a region
of Palestine that was more pagan than Jewish in its leanings. She
was a child of parents who were probably from the priestly tribe
of Levi, many of whom were known to be corrupt and engaged in
pagan practice and devotion at the time of her birth. She was
raised, against all Yahwist norms and Jewish social conventions, in
a temple that was almost certainly staffed in part by priestesses. If

this was the case, it is highly likely that the activities of the temple included pagan worship of a mother goddess modelled immediately on the Phrygian Kybele, the *Magna Mater*, or on the Egyptian Isis, and indirectly on the *divas* of Mesopotamia.

The Immaculate Conception and the Annunciation are pretty pieces of romantic fiction, rooted in ancient Near Eastern traditions, including those of Palestine, from the time of the Patriarchs, and probably based on even earlier camp-fire stories which travellers had brought out of Mesopotamia. Traditional tales of angelic visitations followed by miraculous pregnancies found their way into Christian texts many years after the time of the Nativity but, in any event, the myth of the virgin birth of the *messiah* is based on misinterpretation of a single word from an Old Testament prophecy. Isaiah never anticipated virginity in the case of either Anna or Mary and, even if he had done so, the term 'virgin' meant something quite different in the ancient world from the meaning it has acquired through Christian teachings. It did not define a woman with an intact hymen but one of feisty and independent disposition. There was indeed Jewish belief in virgin birth, in the sense of parthenogenesis, but it was vastly older than Christianity. The tradition held good throughout the ancient Near East each time it was necessary that a demigod, a sacred king, a *messiah*, a *christos*, be born to a human, earthbound mother.

Unless we really believe that the angel Gabriel visited Mary in Bethlehem to announce her impending celestial insemination, then, whatever the circumstances of Jesus' conception, it can only have resulted from normal biological intercourse. Since it is highly improbable that Mary left the Temple where she had been trained as a virgin priestess and committed casual adultery with a passing Roman soldier or some other stranger, the conception must have been a more planned ceremonial event. If she took the traditional part of the *maryam*, the counterpart of the Mesopotamian *entum* priestess, she became one in a long line of venerated women, a member of an élite band who, in the past, had gone under a variety of names. Like her predecessors, she will have engaged in a joyous rite of sex and impregnation in order to conceive an anointed king, a *messiah*. Had Joseph not been an aged and probably impotent member of the house of David, he might have been directly involved but, more realistically, Mary's partner in the Sacred Marriage was a temple High Priest who acted as proxy to the king.

Jesus' attitude to Mary provides some of the real clues to her position. During his lifetime he more or less distanced himself from her and, on the odd occasions when they met, came close to insulting her. For him, she was the anonymous priestess who had done her sacred duty. He did not, on his own admission, regard Mary as his real mother, his heavenly goddess, only as the temporary vehicle for his incarnation. Yet this may not be the whole story because we have found evidence for the existence of an apocryphal work, the *Genna Marias*, indicating that Jesus committed incest, on at least one occasion, with his mother.

Orthodox Jews, opposed to the *maryam* priestesses and the fertility cult, ostracised Mary in life and abused her in death. The writers of the gospels and the Acts, either because they knew her to be of no consequence or because they recognised her paganism and its potential for trouble, prudently ignored Mary, as did Paul in his various correspondence.

The writer Geoffrey Ashe made the succinct observation in *The Virgin* (first published in 1976) that, 'If Christ himself existed, Christ's mother did, but a sceptic who questioned whether we know any more would have a case.' Ashe's proposal may be accurate in the pure sense because the biblical evidence is indeed slim, but it is also unreasonably narrow. While we may not know very much with scientific certainty, we have actually been in a position to discern a great deal from direct literary sources and circumstantial evidence. We can also draw the reasonable conclusion that, were it not for the Christian association of sex with the decay of our earthly parts and naïve fantasies of the ultra-pure being transported bodily into the heavens after death, we might well have been handed down a truer picture of Mary. We might see her as a normal, highly esteemed woman who once took part in a springtime rite in order to bear a sacred king intended to redeem his people in a time of great national need. As it is, we have to make sense of a curiously hybrid creature whose human personality seems only to become complete when we blend Christian Immaculata with pagan whore by merging the two extreme characters of Mary the Virgin and Mary of Magdala. None of these conclusions are intended to suggest that our faith in the icon of 'Mary the Virgin' is improper. They merely show, through deliberate fabrication, that the Roman Catholic Church has made a grotesque travesty of the icon and that it has done so in order to sustain its own power base. In this respect I believe that, historically, the Orthodox Church of the East has taken a more morally acceptable line in largely limiting the portrayal of Mary to that of the *Theotokos*.

I have decided to end this book as I began it, by wandering through the myriad of art works for which Mary has been the subject. I do so with good reason because, among the masterpieces of the medieval period and the Counter-Reformation, there are works that sum up far better than I can ever hope to achieve in words the perplexing, beguiling experience that is Mary, her relationship with God and with her son. It is a relationship that flaunts the rules which should be dictums of Christianity, and yet somehow survives free from taint in the hearts of millions of devotees. Some of the most striking and fervent images of Mary emerge from the troubled period when Catholicism was recovering from the Protestant onslaught and these, more than others, reveal the full breadth of her multi-faceted personality. That Mary remained an integral part of the godhead for many of the great painters of Catholic Christian Europe during the seventeenth century is beyond argument, but they also pursued a strong desire to emphasise her humanity. Velásquez' unequalled study of the *Immaculate Conception* is one in which, to my mind, both of these aspects, apotheosis and childlike humanity, become blended into a complete and breathtaking whole that stirs our deepest emotions.

In some ways, art has brought Mariolatry full circle. Reminiscent of Byzantine imagery, Velásquez also chose to restore Mary more emphatically to the status of a goddess queen. A scarcely less memorable portrait, his *Coronation of the Virgin*, hangs in the Marnel Collection of the Museo del Prado, Madrid. Here Velásquez has captured a *diva* far removed from the mortal and sorrowful mother of Michelangelo's *Pietà* or the sweetly approachable *Madonna della Rondine*. Assumed bodily to the supreme heights, she is poised to take the title *Maria Regina Coeli* and the impression of the *Theotokos* is paramount. She sits awaiting her accolade while Christ and the Ancient of Days hold over her head the crown of triumph. The Holy Spirit represented by the dove, wings outstretched, hovers above her head within a sunburst which reminds one of the winged disc that protected sacred kings and mother goddesses of earlier eras.

It is, however, in a seventeenth-century portrait by a different Spanish master that I find the most complete expression of the paradoxical creature that is Mary. In Bartholomé Murillo's huge and spellbinding *Two Trinities* God rests at the apex of the picture and beneath him, in a vertical column, one finds the dove of the Holy Spirit and then the Christ child. Mary holds Jesus' right hand and Joseph his left. The figure of God is in soft focus and Joseph is only partially lit. He seems redundant, looking out of the picture. Mary looks to Christ who in turn looks upward as God returns his gaze. Of the four faces, the light falls more or less evenly on to Christ and his mother, yet the eye of the watcher is drawn hypnotically to the face of Mary. Here, surely, is one of the most exquisitely beautiful and timeless faces ever painted. The remote goddess queen has gone but what has replaced her is, truly, an enigmatic and fascinating mix of pagan, Jewish and Christian. Mary is the eternal, gentle mother, the beautiful lover, the serene intercessor, the compassionate, innocent, knowing, sexually desirable friend and confidante that so many of our human hearts cling to so tightly and dearly.

In the fullness of time, I believe that the image of Mary, the mother of Christ, will grow dim. Her portrait has been carried down to us on the wings of an enduring myth but even the best of myths tend to fade with the passage of time. Mary, the most outstanding of the *maryams*, will become part of the catalogue of humankind's past creeds, an academic memory to be explored in libraries of the future, much as today we blow away the dust to discover Inana and Ishtar, Isis and Kybele. Like them, she may be able to claim some element of historical truth but she is mostly a fable, a gross deception. In part, it has been perpetrated to suit the self-seeking demands of the few. But it also responds to our innate human need for a motherly hand, an *Ewigweib* steering the affairs of men. For this reason I am no less convinced that in her passing some new Madonna, a fresh Queen of Heaven as yet unheralded, will take her place to stand as the next embodiment of that timeless womb of life and death. Meaningless terms like pagan and Christian, orthodox and heretical, will either become redundant or will continue to provide us with an essential source of irritation. Mary will re-emerge by another name. The goddess of the earth and the stars will still carry us through the struggle of our birth, stand resolutely yet serenely beside us as we experience the joys and the ordeals of life, cradle us to her comforting breast as we come to die and, sure-footed, guide us on whatever mysterious pathway lies beyond.

✦

JEWISH AND
CHRISTIAN PRIMARY TEXTS

(a) GENERAL

The Holy Bible, King James Version, Oxford

The Interpreters Bible, ed. G. A. Buttrick, New York, 1956

The New Testament Apocrypha (NTA) ed. E. W. Schneemelcher, Louisville, KY

The Apocryphal New Testament (ANT), J. K. Elliott (trans. based on M. R. James) Oxford, 1993

The Apocryphal Old Testament (AOT), ed. H. F. D. Sparks, Oxford, 1984

The Old Testament Pseudepigrapha (OTA), ed. J. H. Charlesworth, New York, 1983

The Nag Hammadi Library (NHL), J. L. Robinson, Leiden, 1988

The Mishnah, trans. Jacob Neusner, Newhaven, CT, 1988

The Complete Dead Sea Scrolls in English, Geza Vermes, London, 1997

(b) SELECTED WORKS

Apocalypse of Adam	*The Nag Hammadi Library*, J. M. Robinson
Apocalypse of Daniel	*The Old Testament Pseudepigrapha*, ed. J. H. Charlesworth
Apocalypse of the Holy Mother	*The Ante-Nicene Fathers*, vol. 9, trans. M. R. James, Peabody, MA, 1995
Apocalypse of Paul	*The Apocryphal New Testament*, J. K. Elliott
Assumption of the Virgin	*The Apocryphal New Testament*, J. K. Elliott
Book of Enoch	*The Old Testament Pseudepigrapha*, ed. J. H. Charlesworth
Book of Jubilees	*The Old Testament Pseudepigrapha*, ed. J. H. Charlesworth
Discourse of Theodosius	*The Apocryphal New Testament*, J. K. Elliott

First Book of Pistis Sophia	*The New Testament Apocrypha*, ed. E. W. Schneemelcher; *Gnostic Society Library* (electronic), 1999
Gospel of the Birth of Mary	*The Apocryphal New Testament*, J. K. Elliott
Gospel of Mary	*The Nag Hammadi Library*, J. M. Robinson
Gospel of Peter	*The Ante-Nicene Fathers*, vol. 9, trans. J. A. Robinson, Peabody, MA, 1995
Gospel of Philip	*The Nag Hammadi Library*, J. M. Robinson
Gospel of Pseudo-Melito	*The New Testament Apocrypha*, ed. E. W. Schneemelcher
Gospel of Thomas	*The Nag Hammadi Library*, J. M. Robinson
History of Joseph the Carpenter	*The Apocryphal New Testament*, M. R. James
Jeremy	Source mislaid
Gospel of Pseudo-Matthew (Liber de Infantia)	*The Apocryphal Gospels and other Documents relating to the History of Christ*, B. H. Cowper, Edinburgh and London, 186X
Maccabees	*The New Testament Apocrypha*, ed. E. W. Schneemelcher
Odes and Psalms of Solomon	Trans. from the Syriac by J. Rendel Harris, Cambridge, 1909
Protevangelium of James	*The Apocryphal New Testament*, J. K. Elliott
Psalms of Solomon	*The Old Testament Pseudepigrapha*, ed. J. H. Charlesworth
Susanna	*The Holy Bible*, Revised Standard Version, (electronic), University of Pennsylvania Center for Computer Analysis of Texts
Testament of Adam	*The Old Testament Pseudepigrapha*, ed. J. H. Charlesworth
Testament of Isaac	Source mislaid; *The Apocryphal Old Testament*, ed. H. F. D. Sparks
Vision of Isaiah	*The New Testament Apocrypha*, ed. E. W. Schneemelcher
The Wisdom of Ben Sira	Trans. P. W. Skehan, Anchor Bible Series, New York, 1987

EARLY CHRISTIAN
WRITINGS

AFRICANUS No extant material; quoted in Eusebius, *History of the Church*

AMBROSE *De Virginibus*; *In Lucam*; *Letters*: C. C. Richardson, *Early Christian Fathers*, London, 1953

ARNOBIUS *Adversus nationes*: Richardson, *Early Christian Fathers*

ATHANASIUS *Deposition of Arius*; *Epistula de decretis Nicaenae synod*: New Advent Library (electronic) *The Fathers of the Church*, 1999

AUGUSTINE OF HIPPO *On the Trinity*; *Sermons*: Richardson: *Early Christian Fathers*

CLEMENT OF ALEXANDRIA *Miscellanies*: Richardson, *Early Christian Fathers*

CYRIL OF JERUSALEM *Catechetical Lectures*; *Twentieth Discourse*: new Advent Library (electronic) *The Fathers of the Church*, 1999

THE DIDACHE *Ancient Christian Writers*, 6, ed. J. Quasten and J. C. Plumpe (trans. James A. Kleist), New York, 1948

EPIPHANIUS *Panarion*, trans. Frank Williams, 2 vols., Leiden, 1994

EUSEBIUS *The History of the Church from Christ to Constantine*, trans. G. A. Williamson, Harmondsworth, 1965
Life of Constantine, New Advent Library (electronic) *The Fathers of the Church*

FIRMICUS MATERNUS *De errore profanarum religionum*, ed. J. A. Wower, 1999

'GELASIUS' *Decretum Gelasianum*: B. M. Metzger, *The Canon of the New Testament: Its Origin, Development and Significance*, Oxford, 1987

HEGESIPPUS No extant material; quoted in Eusebius, *History of the Church*

IGNATIUS OF LOYOLA *Spiritual Exercises* (p. 247), Christian Classics Ethereal Library (electronic), trans. Fr Elder Mullan, 1999

IRANAEUS *Libros Quinque Adversus Haereses*, trans. A. Roberts, Ante-Nicene Christian Library, 1867

JEROME *Ad Paulinum* in J. P. Migne, *Patrologiae Cursus Completus*, 1862
Contra Helvidius: The Fathers of the Church, trans. J. H. Hritzu,
Washington, DC, 1965
Letters, New Advent Library (electronic) *The Fathers of the Church*,
1999

JOSEPHUS *History of the Jewish War (Bello Judaica)*: trans. H. St J.
Thackeray, Loeb Classical Library, Cambridge, MA, 1997
Jewish Antiquities, trans. L. H. Feldman, R. Marcus, A. Wikgren and
H. St J. Thackeray, Loeb Classical Library, Cambridge, MA, 1965
The Life: trans. H. St J. Thackeray, Loeb Classical Library, Cambridge,
MA, 1997

ORIGEN *Commentary on John*: New Advent Library (electronic) *The
Fathers of the Church*, 1999
Contra Celsum: The Ante-Nicene Fathers, ed. A. Roberts and J.
Donaldson, Grand Rapids, MI

PHILO *De specialibus legibus*; *Rewards and Punishments: The Works of Philo*,
trans. C. D. Yonge, Peabody, MA, 1993

STRABO *Geography*, trans. H. L. Jones, Loeb Classical Library,
Cambridge, MA, 1997

TACITUS *Annals*, trans. J. Jackson, Loeb Classical Library, Cambridge,
MA, 1937
The Histories, trans. C. H. Moore, Loeb Classical Library, Cambridge,
MA, 1925

TERTULLIAN *Apology: The Ante-Nicene Fathers*, ed. A. Roberts and J.
Donaldson, Grand Rapids, MI
De praescriptione Haereticorum, trans. J. Betty, Oxford, 1722
On Idolatry, New Advent Library (electronic) *The Fathers of the Church*,
1999
On the Apparel of Women: Fathers of the Church, Washington, DC, 1950
To His Wife, New Advent Library (electronic) *The Fathers of the Church*,
1999

THEODORET *Graec. affect. curat.: Acta Conciliorum oecumenicorum*, ed. E.
Schwartz, Strasbourg, 1914

VIRGIL *Eclogue*, trans. H. R. Fairclough, Loeb Classical Library, 1997

ZOSIMUS *Historia nova*, trans. J. J. Buchanan and H. T. Davis, San
Antonio, FL, 1967

BIBLIOGRAPHY

AHARONI, Y., *Archaeology of the Land of Israel* (trans. A. F. Rainey), London, 1982

AISTLEITNER, J., *Worterbuch der ugaritischen Sprache*, Berlin, 1963 (3rd edn 1967)

ALBRIGHT, W. F., *Yahweh and the Gods of Canaan*, New York, 1952
Archaeology and the Religion of Israel (3rd edn) Baltimore, 1953
The High Place in Ancient Palestine, suppl. to *Vetus Testamentum* IV, 1957

ALEXANDER, P. S., 'The Rabbinic Lists of Forbidden Targumim', *J. of Jewish Studies* no. 27, 1976

APPLETON, ROBERT (ED.), *The Catholic Encyclopaedia*, New York, 1911

ARI-YONAH, M., *The Jews under Roman and Byzantine Rule*, Jerusalem, 1984

ARMSTRONG, T. A., BUSBY, D.L. AND CARR, C. F., *A Reader's Hebrew–English Lexicon of the Old Testament*, Grand Rapids, MI, 1989

ASHE, GEOFFREY, *The Virgin*, London and New York, 1976

BALSDON, J., *Roman Women, Their History and Habits*, London, 1962

BARBER, M., *The Trial of the Templars*, Cambridge, 1978

BARTH, KARL, *Die christliche Dogmatik im Entwurf. Erster Band. Die Lehre vom Worte Gottes*, 1927

BAUER, WALTER, *Orthodoxy and Heresy in Earliest Christianity* (trans. by a team from the Philadelphia Seminar on Christian Origins), ed. A. Kraft and G. Krodel, London, 1972

BAUER, H. AND LEANDER, P., *Historische Grammatik der hebraischen Sprache*, Halle, 1992 (repr. 1969)

BECKWITH, J., *Early Christian and Byzantine Art*, Harmondsworth, 1970

BEEK, M. A., *Atlas of Mesopotamia*, London, 1962

BENKO, STEPHEN, *The Virgin Goddess: Studies in the Pagan and Christian Roots of Mariology*, Leiden, 1993

BEN-SASSON, H. H., *A History of the Jewish People*, 1969 (Eng. trans. Weidenfeld & Nicolson, 1976)

BERNHARDT, K. A., 'Asherah in Ugarit und im Alten Testament', *MIO 13*, 1967

BERRY, G. R., *The Interlinear KJV Parallel New Testament in Greek and Latin*, Grand Rapids, MI,

BEUGNOT, A. A., *Histoire de la destruction du paganisme en Occident*, 2 vols., Paris, 1835

BICKERMAN, E. J., *Chronology of the Ancient World* (rev. edn), London, 1980

BLACK, J. A., 'The New Year Ceremonies in Ancient Babylon', *Religion*, 11, 1981

BLOCH, H., 'The Pagan Revival in the West at the End of the 4th Century', in *The Conflict between Paganism and Christianity in the 4th Century*, ed. A. Momigliano, Oxford, 1963

BRECKENRIDGE, J. D., 'The Reception of Art in the early Church. Atti del IX congresso int. di archeologia cristiana', *Studi di antichità cristiana*, 32, Rome, 1978

BRIFFAULT, R., *The Mothers* (3 vols), London, 1927

BRIGHT, J., *A History of Israel*, London, 1984

BROOKS, E. W., 'John of Ephesus, lives of the Eastern Saints', *Patrologia orientalis*, 17, Paris, 1924

BROWN, F., DRIVER, S. R., AND BRIGGS, C., *A Hebrew and English Lexicon of the Old Testament*, Oxford, 1906

BUDGE, E. A. WALLIS, *One hundred and ten Miracles of Our Lady*, trans. from Ethiopic manuscripts, London, 1923
History of the Blessed Virgin Mary and the History of the Likeness of Christ, London, 1899 (repr. New York, 1976)
Babylonian Life and History, New York, 1993

BULTMANN, R., *The History of the Synoptic Tradition* (trans. John Marsh), Oxford and New York, 1963

BUTTRICK, G. A. (GEN. ED.), *The Interpreter's Dictionary of the Bible*, New York, 1962

CAMPBELL, J., *The Masks of God – Occidental Mythology*, Harmondsworth, 1976

CARROLL, M. P., *The Cult of the Virgin Mary*, Princeton, NJ, 1986

CHADWICK, H., *The Early Church* (Pelican History of the Church, vol. 1), Harmondsworth, 1967

CHRISTIE-MURRAY, D., *A History of Heresy*, Oxford, 1989

CHUVIN, P. A., *A Chronicle of the Last Pagans* (trans. B. A. Archer), Cambridge, MA, 1990

CLARK, R. T., *Myth and Symbol in Ancient Egypt*, New York, 1960

COLLON, D., *Western Asiatic Seals*, London, 1982

CONSTANTELOS, D. J., 'Paganism and the State in the Age of Justinian', *Catholic Historical Review*, 50, 1964

COURCELLE, P., 'Anti-Christian arguments and Christian Platonism from Arnobius to St Ambrose', in *The Conflict between Paganism and Christianity in the 4th Century*, ed. A. Momigliano, Oxford, 1963

COWPER, B. H., *The Apocryphal Gospels and Other Documents relating to the History of Christ*, Edinburgh and London, 186X

CUMONT, F., *Les religions orientales dans le paganisme romain* (4th edn), Paris, 1929

DAHOOD, M., *Ancient Semitic Divinities in Syria and Palestine*, ed. S. Moscati, Rome, 1958

DANIÉLOU, J. AND MARROU, H. I., *The Christian Centuries, I: The First Six Hundred Years* (Eng. trans. Vincent Cronin), London, 1964

DEIMEL, A., *Codex Hammurabi* (3rd edn), 1953

DODDS, E. R., *Pagan and Christian in an Age of Anxiety*, Cambridge, 1965

DRIJVERS, H. J. W., 'The persistence of pagan cults and practices in Christian Syria', in *East of Byzantium: Syria and Armenia in the Formative Period*, ed. N. Garsoian *et al.*, Washington, DC, 1982

DRIVER, G. R., *Canaanite Myths and Legends*, Edinburgh, 1956 (rev. J. C. L. Gibson, 1978)

DRIVER, G. R. AND J. C. MILES, *The Babylonian Laws*, Oxford, 1952

EHRMAN, BART D., *The Orthodox Corruption of Scripture*, Oxford, 1993

EISENMAN, R., *James the Brother of Jesus: Recovering the True History of Early Christianity*, London, 1997

EISSFELDT, O., 'El and Yahweh', *J. of Semitic Studies*, I, 1956

FABER, FELIX, *Evagatorium in Terrae Sanctae Arabiae et Egypti Peregrinationem*, Stuttgart, 1843

FARNELL, LEWIS, *The Cults of the Greek States*, Oxford, 1907

FERGUSON, J., *The Religions of the Roman Empire*, London, 1970

FISHER, E., 'Cultic Prostitution in the Ancient Near East', *Biblical Theology Bulletin*, vol. 6, nos. 2–3, 1976

FOWLER, H. T., *A History of the Literature of Ancient Israel*, London, 1912

FRANKFORT, H., *Cylinder Seals*, London, 1939
Ancient Egyptian Religion, New York, 1948

FRAZER, SIR J. G., *The Golden Bough*, London, 1922

FREEDMAN, D. N. (GEN. ED.), *Anchor Bible Dictionary*, New York, 1992

FREUD, S., *The Interpretation of Dreams*, London, 1953

FREYNE, S., *Galilee from Alexander the Great to Hadrian*, Wilmington, DE, 1980

GARNETT, K. S., 'Late Corinthian Lamps from the Fountain of the Lamps', *Hesperia*, 44, 1975

GARNSEY, P., 'Religious toleration in Classical antiquity', in *Persecution and Toleration*, ed. W. J. Sheils, Padstow, 1984

GEBARA, I. AND BINGEMER, M. C., *Mary: Mother of God, Mother of the Poor*, New York, 1987

GIBBON, E., *Decline and Fall of the Roman Empire* (6 vols.), New York, 1910

GORDON, CYRUS H., *Ugaritic Literature*, Rome, 1949
Ugaritic Textbook, Rome, 1965
'Ugarit and its significance', *ARTS* (journal of the Sydney University Arts Association), vol. 9, 1974

GRABAR, ANDRÉ, *L'Iconoclasme Byzantine*, Paris, 1957
Christian Iconography. A Study of its Origins, London, 1969

GRANDMAISON, A. MILLIN DE, *Voyage dans les départments du Midi de la France*, Paris, 1807–11

GRAY, J., *The Canaanites*, London, 1964

GREGORY, T. E., 'The Survival of Paganism in Christian Greece', *AJP*, 107, 1986

HAILE, WILFRIED, *Dogmatik*, 1995

HAMILTON, B., *Religion in the Medieval West*, London, 1986

HAMILTON, M., 'The pagan elements in the names of saints', *BSA*, 13, 1906/7

HAMINGTON, M., *Hail Mary? The Struggle for Ultimate Womanhood in Catholicism*, New York and London, 1995

HARNACK, ADOLPH VON, *History of Dogma*, trans. Buchanan, N. (7 vols.), London, 1894–9

HART, GEORGE, *A Dictionary of Egyptian Gods and Goddesses*, London and New York, 1986

HARVEY, A. E., *Jesus and the Constraints of History*, London and Philadelphia, 1982

HELM-PIRGO, M., *Virgin Mary, Queen of Poland*, New York, 1957

HERMET, G., *Les Catholiques dans l'Espagne Franquiste*, Paris, 1980

HEYOB, S. K., *The Cult of Isis among Women in the Greco-Roman World*, Leiden, 1975

HOOKE, S. H., *Babylonian and Assyrian Religion*, London, 1953
Myth, Ritual and Kingship, Oxford, 1958

HUILLIER, ARCHBISHOP PETER LE, *The Church of the Ancient Councils*, New York, 1996

JACOBSEN, THORKILD, 'Sumerian King List', *Journal of Assyriological Studies*, 11, Chicago, 1939
'Towards the Image of Tammuz', *History of Religion*, I, New Haven, CT, 1962
The Treasures of Darkness, New Haven, CT, 1976

JAGERSONA, H., *The History of Israel*, London, 1985

JAMES, E. O., *The Cult of the Mother Goddess*, New York, 1959

JOACHIM, JEREMIAS, *Jerusalem in the Time of Jesus* (trans. F. H. and C. H. Cave), London, 1969

JONES, A. H. M., 'The social background of the struggle between paganism and Christianity', in *The Conflict between Paganism and Christianity in the Fourth Century*, ed. A. Momigliano, Oxford, 1963
The Later Roman Empire, London, 1964

JORDAN, M., *Gods of the Earth*, New York, 1988
The Encyclopedia of Gods, London, 1992
Myths of the World, London, 1993

JUNG, CARL G., *Four Archetypes: Mother, Rebirth, Spirit, Trickster*, Princeton, NJ, 1970
The Structure and Dynamics of the Psyche (1927) from *The Collected Works* (ed. G. Adler, M. Fordham and H. Read), London and New York, 1960

KELLY, J. N. D., *Early Christian Creeds* (3rd edn), London, 1972
Oxford Dictionary of Popes, Oxford, 1986

KING, LEONARD W., *The Letters and Inscriptions of Hammurabi*, London, 1898–1900
Chronicles Concerning Early Babylonian Kings, London, 1907

KITZINGER, ERNST, *The Cult of Images before Iconoclasm*, Dumbarton Oaks Papers 8, Cambridge, MA, 1954

KLINGER, F., 'Vom Geistesleben im Rom des ausgehenden Altertums' (1941), *Romische Geisteswelt* (3rd edn), Munich, 1956

KOEHLER, L. AND BAUMGARTNER, W., *Hebrew and Aramaic Lexicon of the New Testament* (trans. M. E. J. Richardson), Leiden, 1955

KRAMER, S. N., *Sumerian Mythology*, Philadelphia, 1944
'Inanna's Descent to the Netherworld', *J. of Cuneiform Studies*, 5, 1951
From the Tablets of Sumer, Indian Hills, KY, 1956
The Sacred Marriage Rite, Bloomington, IN, 1969
The Sumerians, Chicago, 1976

LANE FOX, R., *Pagans and Christians*, Harmondsworth, 1986

LANGDON, S., *Sumerian and Babylonian Psalms*, Paris, 1909
Tammuz and Ishtar, Oxford, 1914
'A Babylonian Wisdom Text', *Proc. Soc. Bibl. Arch.*, vol. xxxviii, pp. 105ff., 1916
Sumerian Law Code (SC), *J. Royal Asiatic Society of Great Britain and Ireland*, London, 1920
Semitic Mythology, 1931

LAURENTIN, R., *The Life of Catherine Labouré*, London, 1983

LEA, H., *An Historical Sketch of Sacerdotal Celibacy in the Christian Church*, Philadelphia, 1867

LEACH, E. AND AYCOCK, D. A., *Structuralist Interpretations of Biblical Myth*, Cambridge, 1983

LIEBESCHÜTZ, W., 'Pagan mythology in the Christian empire', *Int. J. of the Classical Tradition*, 2, 1995

LIGUORI, ALPHONSO MARIA DE, *The Glories of Mary* (trans. R. A. Coffin), London, 1868

LINDSEY, H., *The Countdown to Armageddon*, New York, 1981

LOOFS, F., *Nestorius and his Place in the History of Christian Doctrine*, Cambridge, 1914.

LOUW, J. P. AND NIDA, E. A., *Greek–English Lexicon of the New Testament* (2 vols), New York, 1988

LUDEMANN, GERD, *Heretics* (Eng. trans. John Bowden), London, 1996
Virgin Birth? The True Story of Mary and her Son Jesus, London, 1998

MACMULLEN, RAMSAY, *Paganism in the Roman Empire*, New Haven, CT, 1981
Christianity and Paganism in the Fourth to Eighth Centuries, New Haven, CT, and London, 1997

MALE, EMILE, *L'Art Religieux du Douzième Siècle en France*, Paris, 1966

MALLOWAN, M. E. L., *Nimrud and its Remains* (3 vols), London, 1966

MARTINDALE, C. C., *Bernadette of Lourdes*, London (undated)

MCEWAN, J. G. P., *Priest and Temple in Hellenistic Babylonia*, Wiesbaden, 1981

MCKENZIE, J. L., *The World of the Judges*, New Jersey, 1966

MEEK, T. J., *Hebrew Origins*, New York, 1950

METZGER, B. M., *The Canon of the New Testament: its Origin, Development and Significance*, Oxford, 1987

MEYER, E., *Der Papyrusfund von Elephantine*, Leipzig, 1912

MILLAR, FERGUS, *The Roman Near East*, Cambridge, MA, 1993

MOMIGLIANO, A., 'Christianity and the Decline of the Roman Empire', in *The Conflict between Paganism and Christianity in the 4th Century*, ed. A. Momigliano, Oxford, 1963

MONTGOMERY, J. A. AND HARRIS, Z. S., *The Ras Shamra Mythological Texts*, Philadelphia, 1935

MULLEN, P., *Shrines of Our Lady*, London, 1998

MYERS, ALLEN C. (ED.), *The Eerdmans' Bible Dictionary*, Grand Rapids, MI, 1987

NEUFELD, E., *Ancient Hebrew Marriage Laws*, London, 1944

NICKLESBURG, G. W. E., *Jewish Literature between the Bible and the Mishnah*, Philadelphia and London, 1981

NIDITCH, S., 'The Wronged Woman Righted', *Harvard Theological Review*, vol. 72, nos. 1–2, 1979

NILSSON, M. P., 'Pagan divine service in late paganism', *Harvard Theological Review*, 38, 1945

NORTHBROOKE, JOHN, *A Treatise against Dicing, Dancing, Plays and Interludes, with other Idle Pastimes*, 1577 (repr. London, 1843)

NOTH, M., *Horizons in Biblical Theology*, Pittsburgh, *The History of Israel*, London, 1958 (repr. 1960)

OSTROGORSKY, G., *A History of the Byzantine State* (Eng. trans. J. Hussey), Oxford, 1986

OVERBECK, J. A., *Atlas der griechischen Mythologie*, Leipzig, 1872 *Griechische Kunstmythologie*, Leipzig, 1871–89

PAGELS, ELAINE, *The Gnostic Gospels*, New York, 1979, and London, 1980

PALLIS, S. A., *The Babylonian Akitu Festival*, Copenhagen, 1926

PALMER, L. R., *The Interpretation of Mycenaean Greek Texts*, Oxford, 1963

PATAI, RAPHAEL, 'The Goddess Asherah', *J. of Near Eastern Studies*, 24, 1965 *The Hebrew Goddess*, New York, 1967

PELIKAN, JAROSLAV, *Mary through the Centuries*, New Haven, CT, 1996

PERRY N. AND ECHEVERRIA, L., *Under the Heel of Mary*, London, 1988

POLLACK, R., *The Body of the Goddess*, Shaftesbury, 1997

POMEROY, S. A., *Goddesses, Whores, Wives and Slaves*, New York, 1975

POSTGATE, J. N., *Early Mesopotamia – Society and Economy at the Dawn of History*, London, 1994

PREMUDA, LORIS, *Storia dell' Iconografia Anatomica*, Milan, 1956

PRENNER, A., *Hestia-Vesta*, Tübingen, 1864

PRICE, R. M., 'Pluralism and religious tolerance in the empire of the fourth century', Papers presented at the 11th Conference in Patristic Studies, 1991, *Studia Patristica*, 24, 1993

PRITCHARD, J. B., *Ancient Near Eastern Texts relating to the Old Testament*, Princeton, NJ, 1950

REISMAN, D., 'Iddin-Dagan's sacred marriage hymn', *J. of the Cuneiform Society*, 25, 1971

RICCI, CARLA, *Mary Magdalene and Many Others* (trans. Paul Burns), Tunbridge Wells, 1994

RICHARDSON, C. C. (ED.), *Early Christian Fathers*, London, 1953

RICHARDSON, M. E. J. (TRANS.), *Hebrew and Aramaic Lexicon of the Old Testament*, Leiden, 1955

RICHTER, I. A. (ED.), *The Notebooks of Leonardo da Vinci*, Oxford, 1980

ROBINSON, J. M., *The Nag Hammadi Library* (NHL), Leiden, 1988

ROMER, W. H. P., *Sumerische Königshymnen der Isin-zeit*, Leiden, 1965

ROWLEY, H. H. AND BLACK, M. (EDS), *Peake's Commentary on the Bible*, London, 1962

RUNCIMAN, S., *The Eastern Schism. A Study of the Papacy and the Eastern Churches in the XI and XII Centuries*, Oxford, 1955

SANDERS, E. P., *Paul and Palestinian Judaism*, London and Philadelphia, 1977
Paul, the Law and the Jewish People, Philadelphia, 1983
Jesus and Judaism, London, 1985
Judaism – Practice and Belief 63 BCE–66 CE, Philadelphia, 1992

SANDERS, E. P. AND DAVIES, MARGARET, *Studying the Synoptic Gospels*, London, 1989

SCHAFFER, AARON, *Sumerian Sources of Tablet 12 – Epic of Gilgamesh*, Philadelphia, 1963

SCHERMAN, N. AND ZLOTOWITZ, M., *History of the Jewish People*, Mesorah, 1982

SCHMOGER, C. E., *The Life of Anne Emmerich*, 1870

SEGAL, J. B., *Edessa and Harran An Inaugural Lecture ... 1962*, London, 1953

SHERES, ITA AND KOHN BLAU, ANNE, *The Truth about the Virgin*, New York, 1995

SHINNERS, J., 'The Cult of Mary and Popular Belief', in *Mary, Woman of Nazareth*, New York, 1989

SJOBERG, A. AND BERGMANN, E., *Texts from Cuneiform Sources*, Locust Valley, NY, 1969

SLADEK, W. R., *Inanna's Descent and the Death of Dumuzi* (PhD thesis paper), Baltimore, 1974

SMITH, JODY B., *The Image of Guadalupe*, Macon, GA, 1994

SODEN, W. VON, *Akkadisches Handworterbuch*, Wiesbaden, 1965

SOUTHERN, R. W., *Western Society and the Church in the Middle Ages* (Pelican History of the Church, 2), London, 1970

STARK, J. K., *Personal Names in Palmyrene Inscriptions*, Oxford, 1971

STARK, R., *The Rise of Christianity. A Sociologist Reconsiders History*, Princeton, NJ, 1996

STEELE, F. R., 'The Code of Lipit-Ishtar', *American Journal of Archaeology*, 52, 1948

STEVENS, E. P., 'Marianismo: the other face of Machismo in Latin America', in *Female and Male in Latin America: Essays*, ed. Ann Pescatello, Pittsburgh, 1973

STEVENSON, J. (ED.), *A New Eusebius* (rev. edn), Cambridge, 1987

STEWART MCKAY, *A History of Ancient Gynaecology*, London, 1961

STONE, E. C., 'The Social role of the naditu women in Old Babylonian Nippur', *J. Economic and Social History of the Orient*, 25, 1982

STREETER, B. H., *The Four Gospels: A Study of Origins*, London, 1927

TAVARD, GEORGE C., *The Thousand Faces of the Virgin Mary*, Collegeville, MN, 1996

THUREAU-DANGIN, F., *Rituels Accadiens*, Paris, 1921

TROMBLEY, F. R., *Hellenic Religion and Christianization c. 370–529* (2 vols), Leiden, 1993/4

VAN GEMEREN, W. A. (GEN. ED.), *New International Dictionary of Old Testament Theology and Exegests*, Carlisle, 1966

VAUX, ROLAND DE, *Ancient Israel – Its Life and Institutions* (Eng. trans. John McHugh), London, 1961

VEGA, C. DE, *Theologia Mariana* (fols. 38, 255), Lugduni, 1655

VERMASEREN, M. J., *Cybele and Attis* (trans. A. H. H. Lemmers), London, 1977

WAND, J. W. C., *A History of the Early Church to AD 500*, London, 1937

WARD, W. H., *The Seal Cylinders of Western Asia*, Washington, DC, 1910

WARNER, MARINA, *Alone of all her Sex*, London, 1976

WEADOCK, P. N., 'The giparu at Ur', *Iraq*, 37, 1975

WEHR, H., *Arabisches Worterbuch fur die Schriftsprache der Gegenwort*, Leipzig, 1952 (suppl. Wiesbaden, 1957)

WHITBY, M., 'John of Ephesus and the pagans: Pagan survivals in the sixth century', in *Paganism in the Later Roman Empire and in Byzantium*, ed. M. Salamon, Cracow, 1991

WIGRAM, G. V., *The Englishman's Hebrew Concordance of the Old Testament*, London, 1843 (1997 edn)

WILSON, R. R., 'Genealogy and History in the Biblical World', *Yale Near Eastern Researches*, 7, New Haven, CT

WISEMAN, J., 'The Fountain of the Lamps', *Archaeology*, 23, 1970

WOLKSTEIN, D. AND KRAMER, S. N., *Inanna, Queen of Heaven and Earth*, London, 1984

WORKMAN, H. B., *Persecution in the Early Church*, London, 1960

WRIGHT, W., *Contributions to the Apocryphal Literature of the New Testament*, London, 1865

WYNN, R. M. AND JOLLIE, W. P., *Biology of the Uterus*, New York, 1989

ZIMMERN, H., *Sumerische-babylonische Tamuzlieder*, Leipzig, 1907

INDEX

Louis XI, King of France, 282
Lourdes, 292–3, 303
Ludemann, Gerd, 291
Lugalbanda, king of Sumer, 68
Luke, St, 4, 5, 122–3, 248–9
Luke, Gospel of: sources, 95–6, 110;
genealogy, 124–6; references to Mary
in, 101–2, 108, 128, 269; on Joseph's
lineage, 118; Nativity story, 110, 111–
13, 161, 179–80, 221; presentation of
Jesus in the Temple, 114; Mary of
Magdala in, 148, 151; anointing of
Jesus, 150, 151; Jesus' attitude to
Mary, 163; Crucifixion, 116
Luther, Martin, 14, 275, 286, 288

Maccabean revolt, 77, 131
Maccabees, Books of, 75–6, 77, 78
McCarthyism, 298
MacMullen, Ramsay, 13, 176, 203
Magdala, 147
Magnificat, 269
Mahlon, husband of Ruth, 127
Mallowan, M.E.L., 139
Mambre, 85
Manasseh, tribe of, 20, 29
Manasseh, King of Judah, 51–2, 55, 56, 57
Mani, 12
Manichaeans, 12, 192, 227
Manoah, father of Samson, 186
Marcion, 11
Marcionites, 227
Marcosians, 195, 262
Marcus, 201–2
Mariamne, wife of Herod, 156–7
Mark, Gospel of, 5, 95–6, 107, 114, 115,
116, 148, 150, 151, 152
marriage: intermarriage with foreigners,
48–9, 119–20; early Christian atti-
tudes to, 210–11, 213–14
Martha, sister of Mary of Bethany, 149
Martin I, Pope, 227
Martin de Tours, St, 265
Marx, Karl, 70
Mary (first wife of Joseph), 154
Mary (mother of John Mark), 155

Mary (wife of Clopas), 154
Mary (wife of Zebedee), 154–5
Mary of Bethany, 147, 149, 150–2, 154, 285
Mary of Egypt, 158
Mary of Magdala (Mary Magdalene),
236, 308; biblical references to, 148;
relationship with Jesus, 147–8, 164–
8, 174; as prostitute, 148–9, 152, 159;
anointing of Jesus, 151, 152, 154;
intelligence, 165–8; at the Crucifixion, 115, 147, 148; and the Resurrection, 147; representations of,
148–9, 284–5
Mary the Virgin: authenticity, 3, 4;
prophesies of *messiah*, 92, 93; biblical
accounts of, 4–6, 95, 99, 110–16;
lineage, 110–11, 118–19, 128; conception and birth, 211, 232, 253–4;
name, 143, 146–7, 159; early life, 15,
17–18, 20, 99, 101–6; upbringing in
Temple, 5, 103–6, 266–7, 286–7, 289–
90; marriage to Joseph, 105, 106–8,
184, 199; Annunciation, 264, 266,
277, 306; virgin birth, 2–3, 5, 7, 102,
108–14, 128–9, 178, 179–85, 189,
264, 265, 277, 288, 291–2, 293, 306;
Nativity story, 5–6, 160–1, 272–3,
281; permanent celibacy, 196, 198–
200, 202, 215, 226–7, 228, 232–3, 251,
254, 310–11; as Jesus's mother, 114,
160–4, 307; at the Crucifixion, 115–
16, 148, 283–4; hatred of, 132–3, 157;
death and Assumption of, 9, 116–17,
132–3, 238–40, 266, 273, 300–1;
development of cult of, x–xi, 6–9, 12–
16, 206–7, 210–16, 220–5, 226–52; in
apocryphal texts, 97–9, 102–9, 112,
116–17, 120–1, 207; as sacred prostitute, 128–9, 132–3, 142, 174–6; as
antithesis of Eve, 174, 196–7, 198,
232; *Theotokos* dogma ('Mother of
God'), 202, 220–5, 226, 227, 228, 243,
251–2, 253; lack of early literature
about, 205–6; representations of, 1–
2, 230–2, 241–2, 243–4, 247, 248–9,
250–1, 270, 272, 277–86, 308–9; as

Nicaea, Seventh Council of (787 CE), 279
'Nicene Creed', 219–20
Nicholas I, Pope, 240
Nicolaitan sect, 191
Nicomedia, 242, 243
Nineveh, 37, 54, 184–5
Ninmetabarri, priestess (Mesopotamian), 61
Noah, 197
Norbert, St, 259
North Africa, 209
Notre-Dame, Paris, 282
nuclear weapons, 298–9
Numbers, Book of, 48, 66, 109, 121–2, 143
nuns, 258–62

Obed, grandfather of David, 127, 131
Obsequies of the Holy Virgin, 238–9
Old Testament: evidence of apostasy, 20, 22–3, 24–5; condemnation of pagan sexuality, 34–53; as exercise in political jingoism, 70; Song of Solomon, 133–6, 138–9
Olympias, 156
omega symbol, 231–2
Omri, King of Israel, 133
Onan, second son of Judah, 43
Opus Dei, 297–8
Order of St John, 258
Origen, 11, 129, 139, 148, 176, 181–2, 193, 201, 207, 215, 218–19, 224, 228, 230, 237
Origenists, 195, 262
Origin of the World, 207
Osiris, god (Egyptian), 93, 187
Ossaeans, 195, 262
Othniel, Israel's first judge, 130

Pachomius, St, 257
paganism, 19, 100; and early Christianity, 9–12, 209–10; apostasy, 20, 22–5; Baal cult, 28–32, 33, 34–5; Solomon and, 32–3; *asherah* symbol, 34–8, 39–40, 41, 45; *massebah* symbol, 38–9, 41; ritual sex, 40–2; in Judah,

55–8; in Israel, 57, 70–2, 74–6; in Judaea, 58–9, 82–3; allegations of Jewish interest in, 87–90; Sacred Marriage, 62–9, 133, 138–40, 141, 163, 169–70, 171–3, 174–5, 191, 195, 233, 251; Romans prohibit, 177; virginity, 186–7, 212
Palestine, 17–18, 19; *see also* Israel; Judaea; Judah
Palestrina, Giovanni Pierluigi da, 284
Pallas Athene, goddess (Greek), 212
Panagia Angeloktistos, Cyprus, 244
Panarion, 155, 173, 191–2
Panium, Battle of (200 BCE), 77
Pantherus, 129
Papias, 222
Paris, 292
Parthians, 81
Patriarchs, 18, 19–20, 26–7, 38–9, 48–9, 70, 181
Paul, St, 4, 120, 196, 218; message of, 101; reference to Mary, 102, 123, 161–2, 180, 228; condemns fornication, 168–9, 170, 171, 189–91; on marriage, 235; martyrdom, 208; Acts of the Apostles, 189–90; letter to the Corinthians, 168, 170, 190–1; letter to the Ephesians, 235; letter to the Galatians, 102, 123, 161–2, 180; Epistle to the Romans, 116, 216–17; letter to the Thessalonians, 191
Paul II, Pope, 264
Paul III, Pope, 255
Paul IV, Pope, 288–9
Paul V, Pope, 290
Paul VI, Pope, 301
Paul of Samosata, Bishop of Antioch, 216
Pentateuch, 39, 47, 57, 121
Pentecost, 155
Persians, 58, 73
Peter, St, 165–6, 167, 208
Phares, ancestor of David, 126, 131
Pharisees, 81, 84, 89, 94
Philip IV, King of Spain, 295
Philistines, 2, 19
Philo, 42, 120, 137–8, 172

sugetum (priestess), 62
Sumer, 59–60, 62–3
Susanna, 137
Switzerland, 289
Synoptic gospels, 95–6, 115
Syria, 81, 113, 171, 283

Tacitus, 3–4
Talmud, 87
Tamar, Canaanite prostitute, 43–4, 45,
 126, 128, 131, 132, 136, 184
Tammuz, demi-god (Akkadian), 35, 67,
 93, 153, 160–1, 171, 273
Tavard, George H., 17, 18
Telepinu, god (Hittite), 40
Templars, 256, 258, 261
Tertullian, Bishop of Carthage, 11, 170,
 176, 198, 200–1, 203, 209, 214–15,
 276–7
Testament of Moses, 84–5
Thebaid, 211
Theodora, Empress, 247, 260, 279–80
Theodore, Abbot of St John of Stoudios,
 279
Theodore of Mopsuestia, 237
Theodore Anagnostes, 248
Theodoret, 226, 227
Theodosius, Archbishop of Alexandria,
 117, 132
Theodosius I, Emperor, 10, 176–7, 210
Theodosius II, Emperor, 223–5, 226,
 228, 248
Theophilus, Patriarch of Alexandria, 10
Theotokos dogma ('Mother of God'), 202,
 220–5, 226, 227, 228, 243, 251–2, 253
Thessalonia, 191
Thirty Years War, 296
Thomas, Didymos Judas, 162
Thrace, 194
Thunder, Perfect Mind, 207
Tiglathpileser III, King of Assyria, 21,
 39
Tigris, River, 62
Tirzah, Canaanite royal city, 133
Tobiads, 75, 77
Torah, 81, 89, 93
Trajan, Emperor, 4, 9

Transitus, 240
trees: *asherah* symbol, 34–8, 39–40, 87–
 8; sacred trees, 299–300
Trinity, 219
'Triumph of the Virgin', 282

Ugarit, Canaanite royal city, 26, 28, 29,
 139–40, 231
Un-American Activities Committee,
 298
United States of America, 8, 298
Ur, 60–1, 63, 64, 69
Ur Nammu, 69
Uriah the Hittite, 128
Uruk, 63, 64
Uzziah, King of Judah, 57

Valentinians, 129, 191
Valentinus of Rome, 11, 217
Valerian, Emperor, 265
Valesians, 192, 262
Vatican archives, 177, 290, 294
Vatican Council, First (1870), 292
Vatican Council, Second (1962–65),
 297, 301
veils, 135–8
Velásquez, Diego, 1–2, 8, 16, 308–9
Vesta, goddess (Roman), 212
Vestal Virgins, 212
Vincent, St, 292
Virgil, 100–1
virginity: virgin birth, 2–3, 5, 7, 68–9,
 102, 108–14, 128–9, 178, 179–89,
 201, 264, 265, 277, 288, 291–2, 293,
 306; Israelites, 43; in pagan religions,
 212; *see also* celibacy
Vision of Isaiah, 184
visionaries, 264–6, 288, 292–4
Vulgate Bible, 67

Waldenses, 261
Waldo, Peter, 261
Walsingham, 266
Western Christianity, 243
Westphalia, 295
Whitsun, 299
William II, King of Sicily, 281